HOW TO READ MAYA HIEROGLYPHS

JOHN MONTGOMERY

HIPPOCRENE BOOKS, INC.
New York

For information, address:
Hippocrene Books, Inc.
171 Madison Avenue
New York, NY 10016

Library of Congress Cataloging-in-Publication Data

Montgomery, John, 1951–
    How to read Maya hieroglyphs / John Montgomery.
        p.   cm.
    Includes bibliographical references and index.
    ISBN 0-7818-0861-8
    1. Mayan languages—Writing.   I. Title.

F1435.3.W75M662001
497'.415211—dc21

2001039649
CIP

Printed in the United States of America.

In memory of
Linda Schele

Table of Contents

Acknowledgments

The information presented in the following chapters draws on the work of many individuals. First and foremost, Linda Schele inspired an entire generation of epigraphers, and certainly I would never have pursued my professional degrees but for her influence. Linda was the first to employ my services as a professional draftsman, commissioning drawings for a majority of her book-length publications. Second, Dr. Flora Clancy launched my academic odyssey through her series of Precolumbian classes and seminars at the University of New Mexico, Albuquerque. Others whose work contributed significantly, whether directly or indirectly, include Peter Mathews, always ready with encouragement; Nikolai Grube and David Stuart, well-known for their openness to aspiring epigraphers; Kathryn Josserand and Nicholas Hopkins for their long-term support; Simon Martin for his invaluable and uncanny ability to read damaged texts and his personal help on individual projects; Barbara MacLeod and Robert Wald, both of whom spent time and effort discussing with me the intricacies of verbal inflection; Tom and Carolyn Jones who inspired me to pursue seriously the study of Maya glyphs; and John Carlson for allowing me to reproduce several of the drawings he commissioned. Marc Zender conducted an extensive email correspondence with me, patiently answering dozens of questions and generously offering his many invaluable and often unpublished insights into the nature of the Maya script. Much of the content of this book benefited tremendously from Marc's careful and methodical analyses.

I owe a special debt to Justin Kerr for making available his superb archive of roll-out vases and other photographs, a tremendous source of hieroglyphic material. Similarly, I would like to thank George Stuart of the National Geographic Society for supplying a large array of photographic materials to complete the Piedras Negras drawings, many of which serve as illustrations for the present book.

Others whose insights have proven invaluable include the late Floyd Lounsbury, as well as David Kelley, Dorie Reents-Budet, Stanley Guenter, Eric Boot, Anne Kaula, Nicholas Hellmuth, Weldon Lamb, Ben Leaf, Peter Keeler, John Harris, Linda Quist, and the numerous participants of the

Advanced Hieroglyphic Seminar of the Maya Meetings at Texas. Still others have contributed in countless additional ways.

I thank also Mark Van Stone for making available his hundreds of photographs of individual hieroglyphs from Palenque. Equally I owe a debt of gratitude to Donald Hales for providing access to his vast and extraordinary archive of photographs, and for help with adding T-numbers and locating numerous individual glyphs. My good friend Phil Wanyerka made available his fine transcripts of the Maya Meetings at Texas, as well as photographs from his archive of monuments from southern Belize. Phil also played a key role in my decisions about simplifying the orthography used in this book and the presentation of Maya grammar, helping me to focus on teaching the Maya script rather than trying to prove or disprove a scholarly point of view. In addition, I would like to thank the Foundation for the Advancement of Mesoamerican Studies, Inc. (FAMSI) and in particular Sandra Noble for allowing me to reproduce the drawing of the Tablet of the 96 Glyphs from the archives of Linda Schele.

Lastly, I wish to thank my wife Mary for her support and patience, and my daughter and son, Helen and Robin. Of course, any errors or omissions or misrepresentations of data remain my own.

Introduction

Only five times in world history have civilizations invented original, fully functional systems of writing. Evidence suggests that all other major written forms of language evolved from or were inspired by these five scripts.[1]

In Mesopotamia, the "land between the two rivers," in the area of modern-day Iraq, some enterprising intellectual developed cuneiform ("wedge-shaped") script. Impressed in clay tablets or carved on stone monuments, cuneiform was widely used to record both economic transactions and stories, including the legendary tale of Gilgamesh, history's earliest known narrative literature. Although the stages behind its development remain controversial, cuneiform was in use by the end of the fourth millennium B.C.

By about 3100 B.C. in ancient Egypt, and present on its earliest monuments, another system called "hieroglyphs" found its way into the courts and institutions of the pharaohs and into documents of public affairs. Meaning "sacred writing,"[2] hieroglyphs were carved or painted on temple and tomb walls, or drawn on paper manufactured from papyrus reeds. Both Egyptian hieroglyphs and Mesopotamian cuneiform eventually inspired alphabetic scripts, and a few signs from each can be traced to modern letters used to write English and other European languages.

Half a world away in Asia, the Chinese had invented a form of writing by approximately 1,500 B.C. This script, which subsequently was adopted by the Japanese, remains essentially unchanged in modern times. A fourth writing system was developed circa 2,500 B.C. in Harappan civilization, with its origins in the Indus River Valley of today's Pakistan and northwest India (and may have been inspired by Mesopotamian cuneiform, although the systems are different).

A fifth system, probably the world's most visually graphic script, forms the subject of this book—the misnamed "hieroglyphic" writing of the ancient Maya. Likely derived from less-functional non-Maya scripts developed in late Olmec or Epi-Olmec times (the Middle Preclassic Period, or 900 to 500 B.C.), long before the Maya carved their monuments, Maya hieroglyphic writing served as the basis for a rich linguistic tradition capable of reflecting the full breadth of the Mayan language.[3]

Map of the Maya world with major archaeological sites.

Like other original scripts, Maya hieroglyphs extol political propaganda and the noble exploits of great rulers—their genealogies, their battles, their civic accomplishments. So far, no records have been discovered that contain inventories of tribute, economic transactions, or other mundane subjects, although references to tribute do in fact appear in late inscriptions. Maya scribes painted texts on multicolored pottery vessels and murals, and carved them on stone monuments and portable artifacts of jade and other materials. Occasionally texts were modeled in stucco and emblazoned across architectural facades or carved into the facade itself. And like Egyptian and other scribes the Maya wrote in books, made of accordion-folded sheaves of barkpaper coated in stucco to create a writing surface.

❋ ❋ ❋ ❋ ❋

Likely originating as primitive hunter-gatherer bands, the ancient Maya inhabited an area that today encompasses the Central American republics of Guatemala, Belize, and western Honduras and El Salvador, and the Mexican states of Chiapas, Tabasco, Campeche, Quintana Roo, and Yucatán. Today some eight to ten million Maya still live there, assimilated into European economic and political traditions but retaining traces of their ancient culture.

Maya civilization thrived in the larger cultural context of Mesoamerica, a geographically diverse region corresponding to those areas of Central America and Mexico that saw the rise of great civilizations, including the Olmec (ca. 1200–600 B.C.), Teotihuacan (ca. A.D. 1–700), the Toltec (ca. A.D. 900–1200), and the Mexíca or Aztec Empire, which was centered in the area of present-day Mexico City (ca. A.D. 1350–1521). The Maya region consists of lowland and highland zones and ranges from high pine-clad granitic and volcanic mountains to vast tracts of tropical rain forest. A narrow piedmont separates the highlands from the Pacific Ocean in the south, while lush verdant forests north of the mountain massif give way to an extremely dry country, and ultimately to thorny scrub brush at the tip of Yucatán. Underlying the whole vast system of northern forests, the huge, nearly flat limestone shelf of the Yucatán Peninsula lacks significant rivers or lakes but instead includes numerous sink-holes called *senotes* and vast underground caverns. Through the southern lowland zones, however, broad sluggish rivers such as the Usumacinta and Pasíon wind their way west and north, while farther west the jungles give way to the low mountains of Chiapas.

But the Maya hardly developed uniformly in this country. Village life slowly evolved during the period called the **Preclassic** (ca. 1500 B.C.–A.D. 250), which in turn incorporated sub-phases called the **Early Preclassic** (1500–900 B.C.), the **Middle Preclassic** (900–300 B.C.), and the **Late Preclassic** (300 B.C.–A.D. 250).[4] Monumental architecture and the beginnings of true cities appeared by Middle Preclassic times, and early settlements at El Mirador and Nakbé burgeoned into spectacular urban centers boasting some of ancient America's largest constructions.

Hieroglyphic inscriptions with fully decipherable dates mark the inception of the **Classic Period** (ca. A.D. 250–900). Although Late Preclassic settlements along the Pacific piedmont and in the highlands of Guatemala, among them Abaj Takalik and Kaminaljuyu, used a kind of "proto-Maya" script, these settlements were fully eclipsed during the Classic Period by those of the northern rain forest districts. The Classic Period incorporates three sub-phases—the **Early Classic** (ca. A.D. 250–460), when the great civilization as we know it established itself; the **Middle Classic** (ca. 460–700), a kind of static, intermediate period; and the **Late Classic** (ca. 700–900), when Maya civilization reached its apogee.

It was during the Classic Period that Maya civilization created most of its still visible remains, when the spectacular ancient cities and works of art reached a peak in terms of number, monumentality, and sophistication. Of the many achievements, the most renowned include knowledge of astronomy, sophisticated calendrical and mathematical systems, masterpieces of intaglio and bas-relief sculpture, books made from barkpaper, polychrome mural and ceramic paintings, monumental and private architecture, and the hieroglyphic script. Among the many Maya cultural centers, Copán, Tikal, Yaxchilán, Palenque, Uxmal, and Chichén Itzá represent the most impressive, crowded in their downtown precincts with huge terraced pyramids, intricate palaces, and plazas capable of holding thousands of spectators, all crisscrossed with elevated paved causeways or processional boulevards.

The archaeological parameters of the Classic Period rest largely on the span of so-called **Long Count** dates recorded in Maya inscriptions. The earliest inscription with a securely dated Long Count comes from Tikal and corresponds to A.D. 292, while the latest inscriptions come from Toniná and Tzibanche and correspond to A.D. 904, around the time of the Maya collapse.[5]

Maya civilization ended in the southern lowland jungles and western Honduras not long after the last Long Count dates, although the collapse and abandonment of Maya cities had been underway since the late eighth century A.D. Sometimes called the **Terminal Classic Period**, this last fitful gasp spanned a period of military bellicosity, possible invasions, and severe economic and environmental degradation.

Although Classic Period civilization ceased, the Maya continued their tradition of written histories at the sites of Chichén Itzá and Uxmal in northern Yucatán, incorporating a dating technique called the **Short Count** that was used until about A.D. 1100. Hieroglyphic books were written as late as the **Spanish Colonial Period** (beginning around 1540 in the Maya area), at which time a large number of hieroglyphic manuscripts were burned by overzealous missionaries trying to break the spirit of native "superstition." Four such books survive—the Dresden, Paris, Madrid, and Grolier Codices—while one of these, the Madrid Codex, was written perhaps as late as the seventeenth century.

European culture eventually succeeded in stamping out Maya hieroglyphic writing. By the end of the eighteenth and the beginning of the nineteenth centuries there were no longer any native peoples who could read the script. In fact, no one in the world could—Maya or otherwise. The meaning of the glyphs, once written and read by thousands, had been lost entirely.

It would take nearly two hundred years, roughly from 1827 until about 1990, to unravel the hieroglyphic mystery and restore the written script to its legitimate bearers—the Maya themselves. Only prolonged effort and collaboration on the part of dozens of specialists achieved that goal. The result of their effort, and how it was accomplished, comprises the subject of this book.

* * * * *

I first learned of the Maya when I was twelve, and I never really shook the image of buried and ruined cities lost to the rain forest. In 1974 my introduction to their world, like the experience of so many others, began when I first visited Palenque, perhaps the most beautiful and elegant of any Maya ruin. But Palenque hardly dampened my curiosity, and I soon forged onward to Bonampak and Yaxchilán, deep within the barely inhabited jungles of Chiapas. I then crossed the Usumacinta River and entered Guatemala, visiting Tikal and other ruins along the way.

Part of my restlessness originated from the state of the ruins themselves. Then, as now, few guidebooks existed. Academic studies were difficult to find in Central America and expensive. Worse, local tourist guides favored "alien theories" or other outrageous accounts of Precolumbian civilization.

So the questions persisted: What did the ruins *mean*? Who built the cities? What were they used for? Of course, I knew the *Maya* were responsible. But like anyone approaching a lost culture I instinctively knew that *individuals* were involved. Yet who were they? What were their names? At the time, no one had answers. Or at least so I thought.

Unknown to me, a group of scholars would meet at Palenque not long after I passed through, asking the same questions and attempting real answers. Meanwhile, I stumbled along as best I could, trying to familiarize myself with individual signs, with how the calendars worked, with the basics of what seemed an overwhelming and bewildering task—to try and understand or "crack" the hieroglyphs without any prior knowledge, instruction, or help. Needless to say, I made very little progress. More than ten years passed, without coming much closer to my goal.

It was on a rainy day in 1986 when everything suddenly changed. Having read from some misplaced flyer about an exhibition in Fort Worth, being hailed as the most important exhibition of Maya art and inscriptions of the twentieth century, I immediately set out to attend. Soon I found myself standing face to face with the Cleveland Panel, an exquisite little limestone carving in nearly pristine condition, mounted in the gallery of the Kimbell Art Museum. Much to my astonishment, a pair of singular creatures—I later found out they were called "glyphers"—walked right up and began reading every hieroglyph written there as if the most natural thing in the world. What left me thunderstruck was how these show-offs were reading the glyphs not in English, but in *Mayan*. Somehow, somewhere, despite years of familiarity with the subject, I had missed something.[6]

The Blood of Kings exhibit and its accompanying catalog were the true turning point for me. Not only did I realize for the first time that the Maya script had been cracked, that there were students who could even read it phonetically, but soon afterwards I heard a booming, stentorian voice lecturing Kimbell docents in an alcove off the gallery, a voice that would change my life in ways I hardly believed possible. Obstreperous, confident, full of cuss-words, it produced instant recognition in my mind—I knew who it belonged to, though I had never met her in person or even seen her photograph.

This, of course, was Linda Schele.

The following year I attended Linda's annual Maya Meetings at Texas and Advanced Hieroglyphic Seminar, perhaps the world's largest meeting on the Maya script. At that time no formal instruction book (or even informal one) attempted to teach beginners systematically what the script required. It took years to patiently work through every past notebook, every article, every volume ever written about the script. Even now no instruction book exists on a purely academic level, although plenty of spiral-bound notebooks have come forward. Unlike Egyptian hieroglyphs, which biannually sprout new how-to-read series, epigraphers—those who decipher inscriptions—have only slowly informed others in the academic world who study the Maya. A knowledge-hungry public has been even less informed.

The present book tries to remedy this situation, presenting straightforward instruction on how to learn Maya hieroglyphs for individuals, classrooms, or seminars. Based on years of participation in workshops around the country, and discussions with leading experts in the field concerning how to teach the writing system, it offers a rounded, balanced view of the state of Maya epigraphy.

Prefaced by a narrative history of Maya glyph decipherment, from the earliest attempts to a summary of the current state of the art, the text introduces the script's basic components and familiarizes the student with the more common glyphs (Chapters 1 and 2). The many complex calendars and how they function are the focus of the following chapters (3–6). Phonetic content, grammatical structure, and how to "spell" words using the various glyphic elements, are presented as the next essential steps to learning the script (7 and 8) and to recognizing and interpreting the subject matter of Maya inscriptions, the major events, personal names, titles, relationships between named individuals, objects, physical locations, gods, and supernaturals (9–13). The following chapter explains the differences between painted and carved inscriptions on pottery vessels, and presents the formulaic **Primary Standard Sequence** (14). The concluding chapters discuss advanced features of the script and techniques of decipherment (15 and 16). Appendices provide sample practice texts and information on Maya calendar programs available for computers. The reference section offers detailed information on further resources, particularly sources of inscriptions, with special emphasis on sites found on the Internet. Illustrations and diagrams throughout the text permit the learner to readily recognize and identify each glyph or phrase under discussion.

NOTES

1. Jones (1984).
2. From Greek *hiero* "sacred" and *glyph* "writing." Greek writers used the term *hieroglyph* to identify Egyptian writing because it occurred so frequently on temple walls.
3. In current general practice the word "Maya" refers to the Maya culture or people, or Maya civilization, while "Mayan" refers to the language. Thus, "the Maya built a great civilization," while the people "speak the Mayan language."
4. Alternatively, scholars call the Preclassic the **Formative Period**, with concomitant **Early Formative**, **Middle Formative**, and **Late Formative** periods.
5. Other types of dates, primarily the **Calendar Round**, occur both earlier and later than the Classic Period and can be roughly dated on stylistic grounds, but because of the Calendar Round's repetitive nature and other interpretive problems their exact dates remain uncertain.
6. To this day I could swear that one of the pair was Donald Hales, co-author of *The Maya Book of the Dead*.

Pronunciation

Mayan, the language represented by the hieroglyphic writing system, offers some challenges to speakers of European languages.[1] Certain sounds approximate English ones but others have no English equivalent. There are also a few English sounds that have no counterpart in Mayan.

Glottal Stops

Mayan incorporates a distinctive sound that linguists call the "glottal stop" and that functions as an important element both in the many different dialects of Mayan and in the hieroglyphic writing system. When transcribing hieroglyphs or their Mayan equivalent, (') represents the glottal stop, which sounds similar to the stoppage of air in English *uh-oh* or in *button* when spoken rapidly. Pronounced simultaneously with the vowel or consonant that it accompanies, the glottal stop gives the word a characteristic "pop."

Glottal stops would pose little problem if they carried no meaning. Yet consider the difference between the Mayan word *kab'* "bee" and *k'ab'* "manual labor"—not unlike the difference between *sweet* and *sweat* in English. The glottal stop makes a significant difference to the meaning of the word.

Vowels and consonants are affected differently by the presence of a glottal stop in the writing of a word. Theoretically, a glottal stop precedes every vowel that begins a word or stands alone. Here the glottal stop has no impact on meaning, and many writers of Mayan therefore omit the glottal stop in these contexts altogether. For purposes of this book, the signs used in the writing system to represent the five Mayan "vowels" should be understood as having an initial glottal stop (which technically makes them syllables, not vowels), although I include (') only when its presence makes a difference in meaning. Thus, in the word *une* "tail," I omit the initial glottal (*une* instead of *'une*) but in a glyphic spelling such as **mo-o** "macaw," the extra **o** indicates the glottal stop and the result becomes *mo'*. (*Mo* without the glottal stop means "freight" or "cargo.")

Mayan languages also include five glottalized consonants, whose glottal stops do affect meaning:

> ch'
> k'
> p'
> t'
> tz'

Thus, in the hieroglyphs, **k'a** cannot be used to spell **ka**, and Mayan dictionaries list words beginning with *k'* separately from those beginning with *k*. Other consonants may take glottal stops, for example *b'*, but in these cases the glottal stop can be included or omitted at the discretion of the writer without difference in meaning. Out of the set of consonants where the glottal stop does not affect meaning, the present book follows the currently widespread practice of adding the glottal only to *b'* (thus *b'* instead of *b*) and leaves all other consonants without the glottal stop.

Vowels

Written transcriptions of both Maya hieroglyphs and the Mayan language use the same vowels as Spanish, but distinguish between long and short vowels. Lengthening the vowel can change the meaning. The present book *doubles* long vowels, as in the theoretical example *ka'* "two" versus *kaa'* "again."

The following pronunciation should be used for short vowels, and long vowel sounds are simply a prolongation of these:

A	The sound of *a* in "father"
E	The sound of *a* in "fate"
I	The sound of *ee* in "feet"
O	The sound of *o* in "go"
U	The sound of *o* in "who"

Consonants

The hieroglyphs and the language employ nineteen consonants,[2] all but six pronounced like their Spanish equivalents. Note that Mayan lacks *d, f,* or *v*, while making substitutions for *c*, *g*, *j*, *q*, or *z*. For the most part *r* in Mayan remains exceptionally rare.

B'	The sound of *b* in "bed" but with the breath-stream stopped
CH	The sound of *ch* in "church"
CH'	The sound of *ch* in "church" but with the breath-stream stopped
J	Sounds like English *h* in "house"; but unlike English it can occur before other consonants, as in *jmen* "shaman"
K	Sounds like English hard *c* in "caught" or "cat"
K'	Sounds like English hard *c* but with the breath-stream stopped
L	Like Spanish or English *l*
M	Like Spanish or English *m*
N	Like Spanish or English *n*
P	Like Spanish or English *p*
P'	Like Spanish or English *p* but with the breath-stream stopped; as of this writing, no sure signs beginning with p' have been found in the hieroglyphic script
S	Like Spanish or English *s*
T	Like Spanish or English *t*
T'	Like Spanish or English *t* but with the breath-stream stopped; as of this writing, no sure signs beginning with t' have been found in the hieroglyphic script
TZ	Sounds like *ts* in English "let's" or "toots"
TZ'	Like *ts* in English "let's" but with the breath-stream stopped
X	Sounds like English *sh* in "shoe"
W	Like Spanish or English *w*
Y	Sounds like English *y* in "yes"

NOTES

1. Some thirty-one dialects of Mayan have been identified, including obscure and extinct ones.
2. Depending on the orthographic system used. See "Orthography."

Orthography

Perhaps the most vexing question facing decipherers of the Maya script concerns the spelling of words in our modern alphabet. Few epigraphers agree when to use hard and soft *h*, or whether vowels should include an initial glottal stop, which can have significant impact on certain words while having no effect on others. To complicate matters, epigraphers rarely apply orthographic conventions uniformly. For instance, an inspection of recent transcripts from the Maya Meetings at Texas reveals numerous examples of *'u* as the initial element of a word, together with plain *u* in the same context and on the same page. Nor do epigraphers generally explain their spelling preferences.

The present book adopts the conventions agreed upon by the Academia de las Lenguas Mayas de Guatemala, to bring order to a chaotic situation but also in deference to the Maya themselves. Native speakers of Mayan deserve to control the use of their language and its spelling conventions and should take precedence over the desires of linguists and other non-Maya investigators. With this in mind, the present book makes no distinction between hard and soft *h*, as in the difference between *ja* in *jasaw* "banner" and *ha'* "water." Current research has indicated that the distinction between hard and soft *h* began to be lost by Late Classic times, and to avoid inconsistency in the discussions that follow I have chosen to use *j* for both consonants. Thus, *jun* "book" is the spelling used rather than *hun*. Readers should remember that *j* is pronounced like Spanish *j*.

Conventions for
Transcribing Maya Glyphs

I have followed the conventions for transcribing hieroglyphic phonetic values established by George Stuart for the *Research Reports* published by the Center for Maya Studies.[1] Consequently, the following conventions apply.

Signs Written in Boldface

BOLD UPPERCASE: Used to distinguish the phonetic value of hieroglyphs that stand for logograms or complete words.

bold lowercase: Used to distinguish glyphs that function purely as phonetic syllables to spell words and that have no meaning by themselves.

Example 1: **CHAAN-na**

CHAAN is given in bold uppercase because it denotes the logogram for "sky," whereas **-na** functions as a phonetic complement to clue the reader to the ending sound (and possibly to mark the vowel in **CHAAN** as "complex").

Example 2: **AJ pi-tzi-la-ja**

In this case **AJ** occurs in bold upper case because it serves as the male agentive prefix meaning "he" or "he of." The remainder is given in bold lowercase because these elements function to spell phonetically the word *pitzlaj* "the youthful."

Words in *Italics*

Words given in *italics* correspond to words in the Mayan language, regardless of the specific dialect. In order to avoid controversy concerning vowel complexity and disharmony (see Chapter 7: Phoneticism in the Maya Script), transcriptions of Mayan given in this book distinguish long and short vowels by doubling the vowel. Thus the spelling used is *chaan* "sky," not *chan* and not *cha:n*. Often the *italicized* Mayan word, generally from the Yucatec or Ch'olan versions of the language, follows the **bold** transcription.

Elements Given in (), {}, and []

In rendering glyph transcriptions, elements in () represent unpronounced sounds. Thus in **mu-t(a)** the **()** indicates that the final **a** remains silent. {} indicates that an element was intentionally left out by the Maya but was meant to be pronounced, as for example **AJ k'u-{JUN}-(na)**, where {JUN} is a deleted but pronounced logogram. [] indicates an element infixed inside a glyph or within a word. This element is pronounced or left unpronounced depending on context. Thus **CHUM-[mu]** indicates a logogram with infixed **-mu**, the latter functioning as an unpronounced phonetic complement infixed inside the main sign **CHUM**, rather than attached as a postfix.

NOTE

1. The same principles were outlined somewhat less systematically in James Fox and John Justeson's appendix to *Phoneticism in Mayan Hieroglyphic Writing*.

T-Numbers

Discussions throughout this book make use of a series of numbers preceded by a capital T, the so-called "T-numbers." T-numbers correspond to glyphs identified in the catalog published in 1962 by J. Eric S. Thompson, which inventories all glyphs according to whether they function as main signs or affixes. In Thompson's system, a colon immediately after any number indicates that the glyph corresponding to that number lies physically *above* the following sign. Glyphs following a period lie to the *right* of the previous sign. For example, in T126:533.130, a compound which can be transcribed as **ya-AJAW-(wa)**, the colon indicates that affix 126 lies above or on top of sign 533, while postfix 130 lies on the right. In addition, the T-number sequence makes use of abbreviations (all of which can be found in the "Abbreviations" section) to identify types of glyphs, and Roman numerals to transcribe numbers. Thus the sequence TIV:501hv represents the Tzolk'in day position "4 Imix," with Imix rendered in its personified version as a head variant. T-numbers also include lowercase letters that proceed a, b, c, d, and so on, and that indicate variations of the same or similar glyphs. Although not perfect (Thompson inevitably miscataloged or omitted a number of items), the system serves as the standard reference for unequivocally identifying specific glyphs. Thompson's catalog remains in print through the University of Oklahoma Press as an essential tool that every epigrapher should own.

Abbreviations

affix	af*
Calendar Round	CR
Distance Number	DN
Distance Number Introducing Glyph	DNIG
Emblem Glyph	EG
full figure	ff*
head variant	hv*
Initial Series	IS
Initial Series Introducing Glyph	ISIG
Long Count	LC
main sign	ms*
no number	nn*
Period Ending	PE
plural	pl.
Primary Standard Sequence	PSS
singular	sing.
variant	v*

*Used in "T-numbers" only.

CHAPTER 1

●

History of Decipherment

One thing I believe, that its history is engraven on its monuments . . . Who shall read them?

John Lloyd Stephens
*Incidents of Travel in Central America,
Chiapas, and Yucatan,* 1840

The hieroglyphs were an enigma, a riddle without solution, one that surely held the key to a great civilization. John Lloyd Stephens, nineteenth-century explorer, diplomat, and travel writer, along with his artist-companion Frederick Catherwood, stood among the fallen ramparts of a fabulous lost city, straining to make sense of strange symbols, oval cartouches, little portraits that he was certain were some form of hieroglyphic script. Nothing that day offered clues for translation.[1]

On October 3, 1839, Stephens and Catherwood had set sail from New York for the English territory of Belize, then continued by steamship down the Caribbean coast to Guatemala and Lago Isabel. Piqued by accounts of the eccentric Frenchman Jean-Frédérick Waldeck, who had lived among some ruins near a town called Palenque a few years previously, as well as by reports from the German naturalist Alexander von Humboldt, Stephens was determined to substantiate or discount the claims of lost cities. Writers were inclined to lump ruins from that part of the world under the catch-all term "Mexican," without making a distinction between them. Others were outright skeptical: Indians, widely regarded by Europeans as ignorant, primitive, and savage, could hardly have founded the sort of "world-class" civilization implied by the rumors. It then followed that any Central American ruins were the work of Atlanteans, the lost tribes of Israel, Phoenicians, or even Egyptians, but *never* the work of those who actually lived there, a people called the Maya.

21

Nevertheless, Stephens had armed himself with at least three names that he suspected were significant ruins: Copán, Palenque, and Uxmal. As he stood at Copán entering, as he later wrote, "upon new ground," all rumors were swept aside. Stephens instantly recognized that here indeed were remnants of great art, vestiges of a highly developed culture. "America, say historians, was peopled by savages; but savages never reared these structures, savages never carved these stones. . . ."

One thing seemed certain as Stephens pondered the carved trachyte monuments: the signs written on them held the key. And as he lingered before the half-toppled, half-eroded sculptures, unable to answer his most pressing question, he continued to wonder: Who will read the hieroglyphs?

More than a century would pass before answers came forward. And it would be even longer before scholars accepted those answers. The secret of the Maya would remain buried with those who once could read and write this highly inventive script.

Discovery Phase: Early Attempts

The story of how scholars "cracked" the Maya hieroglyphs[2] reflects one of the more exciting intellectual triumphs of modern research. Yet for years, impeded by academic and international politics, by false leads and dead ends, scholars thought the hieroglyphs impossible to understand.

Unknown to Stephens and Catherwood, individuals were already taking first steps towards a solution of this complex riddle. Essential to the decipherment of any unread script are examples of the writing itself. A sufficiently wide range of contexts must be found to test a proposed value as thoroughly as possible. In addition, phonetically deciphered glyphs can produce words that may not survive in existing grammars. A comprehensive sample may turn up additional words which *do* survive, thus proving the phonetic value of the sign being "tested."

It was therefore a remarkable feat when Constantine Rafinesque, an autodidactic, self-made naturalist, managed his initial contribution from just one short set of badly drawn glyphs. Working from reproductions of the Dresden Codex, one of the only four surviving Maya hieroglyphic books, Rafinesque successfully identified the basic bar and dot system as mathematical signs. In 1827 his results appeared in an open letter to the editor of the *Saturday Evening Post*,[3] but his work remained forgotten until the late 1980s, when it was rediscovered by George Stuart of the National Geographic Society.

Not long after Rafinesque, two important discoveries of enormous impact on the future of decipherment were made by Brasseur de Bourbourg, an *abbé* from northern France. In the mid-nineteenth century while living in Guatemala, de Bourbourg discovered the *Popol Vuh*, the sacred "Book of Council" of the Quiché Maya. Considered the single greatest work of Native American literature, the *Popol Vuh* recounts the Quiché Maya creation and migration myths, episodes with counterparts in the hieroglyphic inscriptions.

But it was Brasseur's other find, made in the Royal Academy in Madrid, which offered the first real "key." This was the manuscript of Diego de Landa, a sixteenth-century Franciscan priest who had made systematic observations of the Maya. Landa, later to become Bishop of Yucatan, was determined to stamp out idolatry and other pagan practices. Towards that end, sometime around 1560, he collected all of the hieroglyphic manuscripts he could find and burned them in the town square at Mani. Recalled to Spain for his excessive zeal, Landa wrote an account of the Maya, their land, and their culture, partially as a defense against his trial. Although scholars initially failed to appreciate its value, *Relación de las Cosas de Yucatán* ("Account of the Things of Yucatan") ironically led to the final solution of the writing system that Landa had tried so hard to eradicate.

Landa's manuscript, among other things, describes the calendars of the so-called 52-Year Cycle, a device to track the days and months. Landa also included a curious hieroglyphic chart, identified as an "a, b, c"—a diagram of signs with phonetic values, shown in the form of an alphabet. The problem, scholars quickly realized, was the more than 700 additional signs not included by Landa—far too many for an alphabetical system (and too few for a purely logographic or word-sign script such as Chinese). Although Landa clearly stated that the script was much too cumbersome for him to provide more than general details, scholars persisted in assuming that he misunderstood how the script functioned, and that he erred in presenting his examples as an alphabet. Thus, most everyone interested in the script at the time assumed that Landa's description would help up to a point, but no farther.

Brasseur de Bourbourg, armed with Landa's material and copies of the Dresden and Paris Codices, was able to read right away the days and months of the calendar, then repeated Rafinesque's discovery of the bar and dot notation. Unfortunately, the good *abbé* turned to Landa's "alphabet" to generate glyphic "readings"—all hopelessly and obviously inaccurate, and in some cases translated backwards. Alphabetical use of the glyphs as "letters" generated only garbled results.

Initial Decipherments

On de Bourbourg's heels came several modest victories. Assuming on the basis of Landa's description that Maya hieroglyphs were phonetic, the Frenchman Leon de Rosny productively read various signs whose values scholars still use, identifying in particular the glyph-groups for cardinal directions (east, west, north, and south). Interpreting signs largely from Maya manuscripts, he also identified the glyphs for "earth" and "turkey."

By the end of the century, others had joined de Rosny's phonetic approach, among them the American Cyrus Thomas who was responsible for identifying **OTOCH** "house" and the **ku-** variant that initiates the signs for "turkey" (*kuts*) and "vulture" (*kuch*). Thomas's truly great contribution was the discovery that glyphs were to be read primarily from left to right in pairs of columns from top to bottom. Structurally, glyph sequences made sense only if read this way. Thomas emphasized how parallel passages—the identification of repetitive structure—could indicate the function of inscriptions even without knowledge of their actual meaning.

It seems curious that so many early investigators achieved such excellent results, only to stumble over general principles. Thomas, his critics pointed out, had blundered in attempting to establish a "phonetic key" and by approaching the decipherment as though the glyphs functioned on the principle of an alphabet. Use of Landa's work would prove more deleterious after all.

Perhaps the most outspoken critic of Thomas was Eduard Seler, one of the great Precolumbian scholars of his time who taught classes on both the Mayan and Nahuatl languages. Born in Germany in 1849, Seler was well-traveled in Mesoamerica and thoroughly familiar with every extant codex, or hieroglyphic book, then known. Seler pointed out that Thomas had worked uncritically, misidentifying all sorts of objects with his proposed readings. Thomas had relied on Landa's "alphabet," which Seler pronounced a "fabrication" introduced by the Spanish friars. While perhaps the Maya wrote in some such fashion initially, according to Seler it was only at the instigation of the missionaries that the system became fully developed.

Against Seler's withering criticism Thomas produced even more farfetched phonetic readings, doggedly clinging to his idea of a "phonetic key" and disregarding his original, solid decipherments. In the end, Thomas simply capitulated. As he finally announced in 1903, the Maya hieroglyphs contained "little, if anything, related to the history of the tribes by whom they were made." Phoneticism, he wrote, was "doubtful." It was a dark day for Maya studies. But the lowest point was yet to come.

Of curious interest during this early period and little noted at the time or even later, Charles Bowditch, a Bostonian authority on Maya chronological inscriptions, made an astute observation that might have easily established the script's basic historical content. Bowditch focused his attention on a monument from Piedras Negras, Guatemala, an upright stone shaft or *stela* designated Stela 3. Bowditch speculated that its initial date represented the birth date of the person portrayed, the second date an "initiation" at age twelve, the third date his choice as "chieftain" at age 33, and the fourth the person's death date.[4] Although Bowditch never lived to learn the truth, he had come remarkably close.

* * * * *

Long moldering in the Royal Library at Dresden, one of only four surviving Maya books offered the next major clues. Made from barkpaper folded screen-fashion, and coated in stucco to form the writing surface, the Dresden Codex was the kind described by Landa as containing the Maya's knowledge, including accounts of wars, epidemics, hurricanes, and other historical events, as well as computations of the days, months, and years. While the manuscript at Dresden has proven much more restricted in subject matter, it definitively expanded the range of possibilities then available.

By studying the book, Ernst Forstemann, the Royal Librarian at Dresden in the late 1800s, discovered that the Maya counted in base twenty, that is *vegisimally* (just as Arabic numerals are calculated in base ten, or *decimally*). The Dresden Codex provided other information as well: Forstemann identified a series of specialized calculations as a "Venus Table"—a record of Venusian phases—and identified the glyphs for "star" and "zero." The latter was a discovery of enormous importance, as only the Hindus were known to have invented the mathematical concept of "nothing." Forstemann then turned to monument inscriptions and quickly established the Initial Series and Lunar Cycle, using recently published photographs from the Peabody Museum of Harvard.

Still other important discoveries were made at this time. While a "German school" of decipherment, loosely focused around Ernest Forstemann, Paul Schellhas, and Eduard Seler, had made exceptional progress in calendrics, mathematics, and astronomy, an "American school" was beginning to take shape.[5] Working with exceptionally clear and detailed photographs by the explorer Alfred P. Maudslay, newspaperman J. T. Goodman—who some years earlier had given Mark Twain his start on the Virginia City *Enterprise*—identified head-variant numerals, or portraits of deities that stood for numbers. More importantly, Goodman offered a correlation between the Maya dating system and our own Gregorian calendar, working from correlations of dates given in historical documents and calculating back in time to dates recorded in the ancient texts. Successively amended by J. Martínez Hernández and J. Eric S. Thompson, the solution proposed by Goodman has come into acceptance as the Goodman-Martínez-Thompson correlation, or GMT, and continues to be used as the standard among the majority of scholars today.

Turn-of-the-century explorers like Maudslay and Teobert Maler tried to make permanent photographic records of their discoveries in often appalling forest conditions. Using large-format bellows cameras and glass-plate negatives coated in a collodion chemical wash, they had to transport their equipment on the backs of mules or in canoes, often for several hundreds of miles along muddy root-concealed trails or past seething rapids. In many cases their very clear, well-exposed negatives, often shot at night with gunpowder flashes, represent the only surviving record of masterpiece sculptures, the originals having since crumbled away or eroded beyond recognition. As the result of their work, more and more hieroglyphic texts were at last becoming available.

The reader will recall how, as the single most critical element of decipherment, an adequate number of examples must be found. Maudslay and Maler laid the groundwork for a "corpus" of inscriptions, and from their publications many important gains were quickly realized. Herbert J. Spinden, on examining Maler's photograph of Piedras Negras Stela 12, suggested that the small texts carved on the front of the monument might identify the several portraits of individuals depicted there, and that these small texts served as name captions. More uncanny, he suggested that those that began with "bat heads" read something like "here follows a name." He would be proved correct decades later by David Stuart.

By the first decades of the twentieth century, the stage was set for decoding the Maya glyphs. Landa's manuscript suggested a phonetic-based system. A wealth of texts was available. Several calendars could be read and matched with their equivalent in our own calendar. Mathematical signs, the reading order, and even the possibility of historical content had been established. So what happened? Remarkably, the next decades saw progress decline, and the frustration of every possible solution.

The Age of Thompson

Europe lay devastated before the Allied advance, Berlin was in Soviet hands, and amidst the expiring Third Reich, Germany's National Library burned out of control. Flames leapt at its combustible collection, destroying the treasure trove of books. From this chaos a young Red Army artillery spotter snatched a single volume, a facsimile, he later discovered, of what was the Dresden Codex of the ancient Maya. Although he did not know it at the time, in many ways this single act would lead to one of the great achievements of modern research: as Michael D. Coe eloquently put it, "breaking the Maya code."[6]

Although the nineteenth century had seen breakthroughs in the Maya calendars, the reading order, and the complex mathematical system, by the time of the second World War scholars were generally agreed that Maya inscriptions contained only calendrical, astronomical, and divinatory formulas. The intellectual straightjacket of Western academics proclaimed that "reading" the script in terms of language was an impossibility in all but the most limited sense.

Key to this position was the English scholar Sir J. Eric S. Thompson, at the time the foremost expert on Maya writing. Thompson was a product of an Edwardian background, hailing from upper middle-class conservative parents of Anglo-Argentinian descent. Convinced that the glyphs contained only calendrical-ritual information, Thompson refused to believe that the lofty inscriptions included anything about lowly human lives, or that they contained historical information. Dominating research for most of the first half of the twentieth century, Thompson ardently attacked any challenge to his theories.

Few dared contradict Thompson, even if privately they disagreed. Those who did often faced impossible criticism in the scholarly arena. Sylvanus G. Morley accepted Thompson's ideas, although initially he held broader views of what the glyphs contained. So, too, did Herbert J. Spinden—the man who identified the Piedras Negras caption texts. If one or two dared to offer alternatives, as did Benjamin Worf with his phonetic approach, they were summarily dismissed by Thompson.

So when a Soviet scholar, the very same artillery spotter who had rescued the Dresden Codex during World War II, announced in 1946 that he had finally deciphered the Maya inscriptions, Thompson went to work. He assumed that Yuri Knorosov—the Soviet upstart—was a Stalinist, and that here was another of the Soviets' bloated claims at superseding capitalism. Thompson quickly demonstrated that Knorosov had erred repeatedly in the numerous examples he used to illustrate his theory (which in fact he did, misidentifying several animals when he translated their glyphic names).

Yuri Knorosov had originally studied Egyptology at Moscow University, but had gone on to explore Japanese literature, the Arabic language, and ancient Chinese and Indian writing. Thoroughly grounded in writing systems of early states, Knorosov pointed out that Maya hieroglyphs typically conformed to a "mixed script" wherein signs for complete words intermingled with phonetic components. The "alphabet" reproduced in Landa's *Relación de Yucatán* was in fact "genuine," but only in the sense that it gave hieroglyphic equivalents for the Spanish alphabet, elicited by Landa from his informant. This did not mean, however, that Maya glyphs were themselves alphabetical.

Knorosov proposed stringing individual glyphs together *logo-syllabically*, that is, putting the glyphs together as essentially a system of words and syllables in the manner of Egyptian and other early scripts. He offered decipherments of passages from the Dresden Codex and other Maya books as demonstrations.

If Knorosov had managed to survive the ravages of World War II, he was to succumb, at least intellectually, to Thompson's scorn. Few took Knorosov seriously, and once again any possibility of progress faded away. After his few publications—hard to find and published in Russian—Knorosov's ideas disappeared.

Or so Thompson thought.

The Historical Phase of Decipherment

Piedras Negras lies along the banks of the Usumacinta River, the remote jungle-shrouded border between Mexico and Guatemala. Now in ruins and overgrown, the site once served as a major settlement, dominated by pyramids, palaces, and ball courts, and prominent during the Classic Period (A.D. 300–900). Already the source of lively interest, including Bowditch's identification of a historical framework and Spinden's suggestion of name glyphs, the site would attain new significance under the archaeologist's spade and the careful eye of an epigrapher.

When Tatiana Proskouriakoff, a Russian-born immigrant to the United States, first visited the crumbling walls and monuments, she did so as staff member of an archaeological project carried out by the University of Pennsylvania in the 1930s. Her relationship with Piedras Negras was to continue far beyond these initial field seasons, for it was Proskouriakoff who introduced an entirely new approach to Maya scholarship.

Already cracks had formed in the theories put forth by Thompson and the "German school." Flying in the face of common belief that the script contained only calendrical or ritualistic information, the German Heinrich Berlin had published during the 1950s a series of papers identifying "emblem glyphs," signs that seemed to refer to specific Maya cities (although he hesitated to call these place-names). In addition, Berlin identified glyphs that he thought represented the names of individuals.

Proskouriakoff never intended to "crack" the script when she turned to examine the Piedras Negras monuments not long after Berlin's work. Because Maya sculpture sometimes shows scenes of sacrificial victims, she hoped to find in the many long texts a hieroglyphic reference that visually represented this act. What she found instead began a whole new train of thought.[7]

Epigraphers—those who study inscriptions—have long known that the Maya at Piedras Negras erected carved stone shafts called stelae in regular and discrete groups. From the hieroglyphic dates recorded in each set, Proskouriakoff realized that no span of contemporary dates in any group exceeded a reasonable length for a human lifetime.

This was the first clue.

Each group of contemporary dates, Proskouriakoff found, began with a specific glyph—nicknamed for descriptive purposes the "upended frog" sign. This in turn was followed by another date and another specific glyph—this time the "toothache" glyph—that was subsequently referred to in later texts in the context of an "anniversary." While Bowditch had identified the same pattern of dates on Piedras Negras Stela 3 as early as 1901, Proskouriakoff's chief accomplishment was to extend this approach to encompass as many of the monuments at Piedras Negras as were legible—nearly fifty in all.

Here was clue number two.

Proskouriakoff noted how glyphs that followed both the "upended frog" and "toothache" were always the same within any given group of monuments and set of dates, but that they always varied from one group to the next. As Bowditch had put it, if one set matches another, even a dunce could figure out that both referred to the same individual—unless the two individuals were twins. Finding similar patterns throughout Piedras Negras and beyond, Proskouriakoff dispelled this possibility at once.

This was clue number three.

What this pattern suggested to Proskouriakoff (and Bowditch before her) was simple (although she was cautious enough to note that other possibilities might fit the pattern). The initial "upended frog" date referred to the birth (or some other early event such as a name-giving ceremony) of an individual whose name then followed. The subsequent "toothache" date referred to an event when the individual had reached maturity—possibly the date of his accession as ruler over the city.

Taking her ideas to their logical conclusion, Proskouriakoff analyzed inscriptions from Yaxchilán just upriver from Piedras Negras. There she identified a series of rulers she called, based on components of their name glyphs, Shield Jaguar and Bird Jaguar. In addition, she identified glyphs for the rulers' age and death. She felt fairly sure, as well, that Bird Jaguar was Shield Jaguar's son.

Here was the open door that scholars had waited for. Together with Heinrich Berlin's discoveries of names and Emblem Glyphs, the groundwork was finally prepared for understanding the Maya's own account of themselves. By 1964, when Proskouriakoff published the last of her work on Yaxchilán, few scholars investigating the Maya script doubted that she was right, and even Thompson, in the end, accepted her conclusions.

Yet one problem remained. Scholars now knew the glyphs contained historical information—accounts of kings and their accomplishments. But what did they actually say? How were they to be read? After more than one hundred years, John Lloyd Stephens' question remained: Who would read the glyphs?

Although few realized it, that riddle had already been solved.

Phonetic Decipherment

On a clear day you can see forever, or at least as far as the Gulf of Mexico. From a limestone shelf built into the Sierra del Chiapas, the Maya ruins of Palenque command a view across the broad, level expanse of the Tabasco plains, a low region of swamps and river deltas—a view which, before modern smog and industrial air pollution, extended as far as the coast, about ninety miles away. Enveloped by lush, wild rain forest and bisected by the cool, clear Otolum River, a wonderful respite during the hot season, Palenque clings like a brilliant jewel in its hillside setting. This was the ideal location to bring together scholars from around the world and hold a conference.

On a hot, humid day in 1973, as Linda Schele later recalled,[8] she was visiting Palenque, waiting for the conference to start, when she saw a singular sight approaching her. Linda had begun a career as an artist, a draftsperson, and an art teacher, but had wandered south of the border and into the Maya area with her husband, David, and her more dedicated art students. Now she was back at Palenque for yet another season, invited by Merle Greene-Robertson to work as her lighting assistant in documenting the stucco reliefs at the site.

Those in charge of organizing the Palenque conference had invited David Kelley, a rather rotund-faced Irish nonconformist, noted for his interest in transoceanic contact and other anomalies. A graduate of Harvard under Alfred Tozzer (the chief English translator of Landa), Kelley had made his mark on Maya decipherment shortly after Proskouriakoff by working out the dynastic sequence of Quirigua, Guatemala, using Proskouriakoff's methodology. It was Kelley who had championed the phonetic decipherments of Knorosov after hearing him lecture in Europe. In the wake of a Russian-to-English translation of Knorosov's work that was published by Michael and Sophie Coe, few had bothered to take the Soviet scholar seriously. However, the Coes and Kelley were steadfastly promoting his ideas.

Kelley, on sabbatical from his position at the University of Calgary, could not attend the Palenque conference that year. He sent instead his graduate student, a bearded expatriate from Australia who carried with him a suitcase stuffed with notes on every date ever recorded at Palenque.

It was this fellow whom Linda Schele saw approach on that December day just before the conference began.

✳ ✳ ✳ ✳ ✳

Peter Mathews was one of those young students dismayed by the political climate of the sixties, who abhorred war. A most open, likable, and generous epigrapher, he and Linda Schele took to each other immediately. Their work together launched an unprecedented era, one that continues to change the face of Precolumbian research.

As the conference got underway, officially christened the First Palenque Mesa Redonda, Schele and Mathews investigated the Palenque dynasty, working out in a matter of hours an almost complete king list (subsequently revised many times over the years). The highlight of their work was an investigation into a ruler identified by the so-called "propeller" glyph. A number of Maya artistic motifs made clear that the main sign in reality represented a shield, as seen on the several figures in military uniform. This glyph, originally suggested to be a ruler's name by George Kubler,[9] alternated with another sequence that merely *substituted* for this first one—a collocation that spelled **pa-ka-la** according to the methods of Knorosov. In this second sequence, the value **pa-** derived from Landa's prefix on the month Pax, where it served as a "phonetic complement." The value **ka-** derived from Landa's "alphabet," and **la-** was identified by Knorosov through his "auditioning" of various combinations of sounds—the "trial" of a value in all known environments to see if it works.

Now, **pa-ka-la**, or *pakal*, means "shield" in Yucatec and other Mayan languages, precisely the object depicted by the "propeller" glyph. Here, then, was strong *independent* confirmation of Knorosov's approach.

The Mesa Redonda played an instrumental role in generating a collaborative effort among scholars who would ultimately decipher the script. In the subsequent Mesa Redondas many new readings were proposed, inspiring an entire generation of scholars and opening new avenues of research. Other leading conferences proved equally important, in particular the Maya Meetings at Texas begun in 1976 by Linda Schele and often involving the participation of collaborating scholars in the fields of linguistics, archaeology, archaeoastronomy, and ethnohistory. Just as important were the twin exhibitions *Maya: Treasures of an Ancient Civilization* (1985–1986) and *The Blood of Kings* (1986), the latter also the work of Linda Schele (in collaboration with Mary Ellen Miller).

A new generation of scholars has challenged how we analyze Maya glyphs, and the true "golden age" of decipherment seems underway. As early as 1975, taking up Proskouriakoff's "historical" (and essentially non-phonetic) approach, Clemency Coggins completed a groundbreaking dissertation on the dynastic art of Tikal, combining epigraphy, archaeology, and the stylistic analysis of artistic forms. Shortly after, Joyce Marcus drew on Berlin's Emblem Glyphs to "map out" a political geography of the Maya lowlands based on epigraphic relationships between Emblem-bearing sites (although her results have been largely superseded by newer studies). In 1977, the next great breakthrough in decipherment identified "parentage statements" that named the ruler's parents. This was the work of Christopher Jones of the University of Pennsylvania and a key achievement, enabling scholars to trace descent and genealogy.

Yet the cutting edge of epigraphy lies in the hands of a scholar whom many consider the Champollion of Maya inscriptions. Born to an archaeologist who worked with the National Geographic Society, David Stuart made his initial forays into Mexico and Guatemala at the age of three on his parents' archaeological projects. Stuart was only nine when Merle Greene-Robertson held the first Palenque Round Table. By 1978, at the tender age of thirteen, he had joined the ranks of participants and presented his first paper.

Contemporary scholars universally recognize Stuart as the world's leading authority on Maya glyphs. Not far behind, Nikolai Grube has made major strides in the decipherment of the Primary Standard Sequence (see Chapter 14), the many and diverse dedication phrases, and the acclaimed **AK'OT** or "dance" glyph. Stephen D. Houston, an archaeologist-epigrapher who excavated at Dos Pilas and more recently Piedras Negras, and Simon Martin, an English scholar in collaboration with Grube, represent a bold new wave of epigraphy. Others include Barbara MacLeod, Robert Wald, Kathryn Josserand, and Nicholas Hopkins. Also investigating in a traditional historic-phonetic vein are Victoria Bricker of Tulane University, the German Dieter Dütting, Michael P. Closs, and Tom and Carolyn Jones, all semi-independents with somewhat different approaches.

Lately there has appeared on the scene a group of epigrapher-art historians, including Mary Ellen Miller of Yale, Dorie Reents-Budet, Carolyn Tate, and Karl Taube. Archaeologists particularly interested in applying epigraphic strategies to their methodology, though not trained in epigraphy, include the husband-and-wife teams of Diane and Arlen Chase and Barbara and William Fash, the Guatemalan Juan Pedro Laporte, and the Honduran Ricardo Agurcia Fasquelle. Actively involved in decipherment, Federico Fahsen of Guatemala has made significant contributions, as has the Mexican epigrapher Alfonso Lacadena.

These, and others, have all helped to "crack" the system of Maya hieroglyphic writing, so that decipherment of non-calendrical inscriptions has become indispensable to Mesoamerican studies. Sadly, several cutting-edge epigraphers have recently passed away, including the most well-known and loved Linda Schele, the amateur Ben Leaf, and the quiet and unassuming Floyd Lounsbury. Also gone is Yuri Knorosov, the Russian scholar who began the "phonetic revolution" in the 1950s (but who also repudiated the newer "historical-phonetic" approach).[10] The legacy of these scholars will ensure many rich and exciting decipherments long into the future. As Linda Schele certainly would agree, the best is yet to come.

NOTES

1. For this account of Stephens and Catherwood I drew on Stephens (1841), and von Hagen (1948 and 1973).
2. My version of the history of decipherment of the Maya script is based on Coe (1992), Kelley (1962), Miller (1989), information recounted by Linda Schele during the Maya Meetings at Texas, and conversations between the author and other epigraphers.
3. G. Stuart (1989).
4. Bowditch (1901), Coe (1992): 174, and Kelley (1976): 213–14.
5. Miller (1989).
6. Coe (1992).
7. Proskouriakoff (1961b).
8. Account given at the Maya Meetings at Texas, Austin. In addition to information provided by Linda Schele and Peter Mathews (personal communications), I have drawn for this portion largely from Coe (1992).
9. Schele and Mathews 1974; Kubler 1969. In his article Kubler also figured out the ruler's correct birth and death dates, although the latter was anticipated by Ruz in 1954 (p. 94).
10. All four died during the years 1998–1999.

CHAPTER 2

• •

The Basics

Examining an inscription of Maya hieroglyphs for the first time, the beginner faces what appears to be an overwhelming task. Symbolic and representative signs stare back indifferently. Cartouches, columns, and unfamiliar signs compress together in apparently random sequence. Even reading order seems hopelessly confused.

Cheer up. The Maya writing system incorporates a well-organized, quite logical scheme very quickly grasped with a little patience.

Organization

COLUMNS

Beginners should first learn the general layout the Maya used to organize what they had to say in an inscription. The script employs a system of vertical **double columns**, or vertical columns *read in pairs*, together with multiple horizontal rows. The result is a grid of squares or **glyph blocks**. Generally epigraphers label each column consecutively, beginning with A, while each horizontal row is numbered 1, 2, 3, et cetera. The reader starts with glyph A1, then B1, then A2, then B2 and so on, in left to right fashion until the bottom of the first two columns has been reached. From there the reader proceeds to the top of column C to read C1, then D1, then C2, then

D2, continuing from left to right in this manner until all of the columns have been read. If the inscription extends as far as column Z, the lettering starts over as A prime (A′) and continues with B′, C′, and so on.

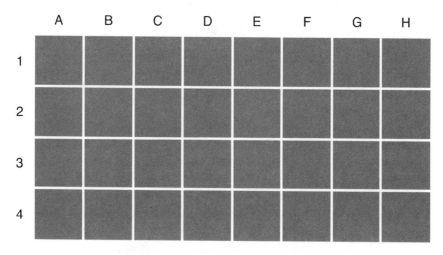

Fig. 2-1   Standard grid pattern of paired columns and rows.

To take a simple, beginning example, we can see how this organization works when we examine the basal text from the front side of Yaxchilán Stela 11. (See page 308 also.) Part of a larger monument with sculpture on both faces, and located along the bottom of the front face, the main Stela 11 inscription will serve as our primary example throughout this book. We will return to it repeatedly, working our way from beginning to end.

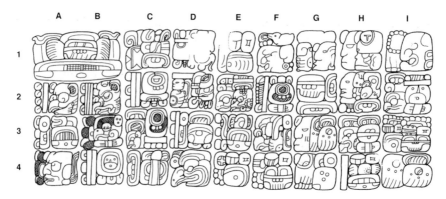

Fig. 2-2   Yaxchilán Stela 11, front, lower glyph panel.

The Stela 11 text incorporates nine columns, beginning with an initial pair labeled A and B. These should be read in their entirety before proceeding to the next two columns, C and D. After the first four pairs (or columns G and H) you read the last or ninth column (column I) by itself.

So much for *theory*. In actual practice, numerous exceptions to the "double column" arise. As our Yaxchilán example shows, inscriptions can incorporate odd numbers of columns, with the last column read by itself. Rarely—*exceptionally* rarely—rows can read backwards (see figure 2-7). Other patterns consist of single horizontal lines of glyphs, read one glyph at a time, and single columns that stand alone. There are also L-shaped configurations that proceed by single glyph blocks until the vertical column is reached, after which the column is read in its entirety. If, after the column is read, the single horizontal row continues, usually the reader jumps from the column's last glyph back to the single horizontal row.

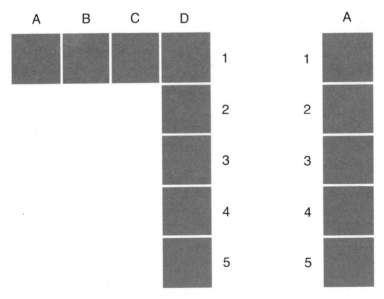

Fig. 2-3 Reading order: upside-down
         L-shape text.

Fig. 2-4 Reading order:
         single column text.

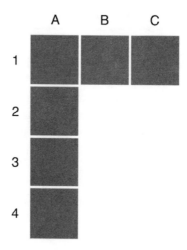

Fig. 2-5   Reading order: upside-down backwards L-shape text.

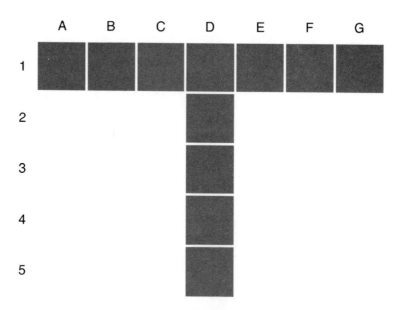

Fig. 2-6   Reading order: T-shape text.

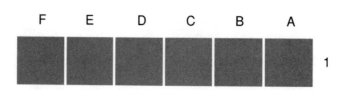

Fig. 2-7   Reading order: backwards single line text.

Several other anomalous configurations exist, notably on ceramics. Here even professional epigraphers can find themselves stumped. In order to follow the sequence of glyphs in problematic contexts, the reader usually has to rely on a knowledge of writing conventions and discourse structure (see Chapter 15), adapting what they know to the given circumstance.

GLYPH BLOCKS

The designation of vertical columns by letters and horizontal rows by numbers offers a convenient way to indicate precisely an individual square of the overall grid. In the text of Yaxchilán Stela 11, position A1 designates the extreme upper left-hand square or **glyph block**. (Note, however, that in this particular inscription the elements at A1 spill over to fill position B1 as well; in this case, the hieroglyphs fill two squares of the grid, or A1–B1.)

Glyph blocks form the main aggregate in Maya writing. Usually composed of two or more **signs**, they serve as the fundamental building blocks, easily taken in at one glance not unlike words that form a sentence. However, it would be a mistake to think of glyph blocks as words or of their components as representing letters in an alphabet-type system, as we will see in the chapter on phoneticism (Chapter 7). In addition, as far as scholars can tell, units in glyph blocks form no consistent parts of speech that correspond to the size or shape of the units themselves or their position within the glyph block. Rather, grammatical use depends on context; the same words can be formed with a given set of signs in one context but with other types of signs elsewhere. This will be explained in greater detail in Chapter 7.

Fig. 2-8   Example of a glyph block.

The columns in inscriptions generally proceed in pairs from left to right and top to bottom as previously stated, and so do the glyph blocks and their various internal elements. Very rarely, however, glyph blocks, and the order of the columns that contain them, will read backwards—that is, from right to left.

The key to reading order lies in *the direction that the glyphs face*. Since in addition to other types of signs most inscriptions incorporate human or animal forms, these will face *opposite* the direction in which the reader proceeds. If the glyph faces left, the reader proceeds from left to right. If the glyph faces right, the reader proceeds from right to left.

Another important clue is which side of the glyph block any bar-dot numerals occupy, if present. When reading order proceeds from left to right, numerals lie along the glyph block's *left side*. When reading order proceeds from right to left, the numerals lie along the *right*.

In our example from Yaxchilán Stela 11, the human and animal head variants face left, and the bars and dots lie along the left side of the glyph blocks, rather than the right. Thus the reading order of this inscription proceeds from left to right.

The reading order of elements *within* glyph blocks, which can become quite complicated, will be discussed in Chapter 7.

Types of Glyphs: Carved Versus Painted Forms

The second step in learning the Maya writing system is to familiarize yourself with the basic *kinds* of signs, of which the Maya employed several types. To begin, it helps to learn the basic categories of signs in terms of their graphic or visual appearance. A good place to start is to explore how glyphs differ according to the material on which they were written. For instance, glyphs carved on monuments (Plates 1, 2, and 3) look somewhat different than painted ones (Plates 7 and 8), simply due to the technique of carving versus that of painting. When carving stone, the Maya created predominantly bas-relief sculpture where they cut away the background surface, leaving carved surfaces raised *in relief*. This was almost always the preferred approach when working in stone, although the Maya occasionally employed an intaglio technique where they cut lines *into* the stone. Stone monuments were diverse and often very large, and included stelae (plural; stela, singular) or upright stone shafts (from the Greek word *stele* of the same meaning) (Plate 1), door and window lintels (Plate 2), wall plaques, and thrones (Plate 3). Other carved features include architectural facade sculpture and monumental hieroglyphic stairways (the latter sculpted along either the stairway risers or treads, or both), as well as items of wood (Plate 5), bone, shell (Plate 6), and jade (Plate 4).

Painted glyphs were shaped with brushes in calligraphic style where the lines flare and narrow according to the brush's shape and the way the

Fig. 2-9 Examples of carved and painted
hieroglyphs: a) carved; b) painted.

artist turned his hand when drawing. Most prominently, painted inscriptions occur on polychrome ceramic vases (Plate 7), plates, and figurines, in temple and palatial murals, in hieroglyphic books or codices (Plate 8), and on architectural capstones, especially those used in burial vaults.

Types of Glyphs: Functional Forms

Another basic step involves learning to distinguish glyphs by *size* and *position*. The Maya generally employed two sizes or categories of *functional forms*, each placed in relatively restricted positions within the glyph block.

MAIN SIGNS

Main signs, of which more than 700 have been identified, comprise the most extensive sign group. As their name implies, main signs were rendered by the scribe as physically larger than other glyphs. Main signs often function as **logograms**, or whole or complete words (as opposed to signs that represent essentially syllables used to "spell" a word phonetically). In some cases, however, phonetic "syllables" become main signs, and vice versa. Also, the size and complexity of glyphs within individual glyph blocks sometimes makes it difficult to distinguish a main sign, or gives the appearance of more than one main sign. Fortunately, the reader's ability to

Fig. 2-10 Example of a main sign.

distinguish main signs makes no difference in interpretation. The convention of rendering glyphs as distinctive in size seems to be largely a matter of aesthetic convention and visual appeal.

Two main signs can sometimes **overlap** so that one emerges from behind the other (generally towards the opposite direction from the reading order). Not infrequently main signs **conflate** or fuse with each other or with other signs to become one glyph. In addition, main signs may be reduced and **infixed** one inside the other.

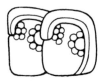

Fig. 2-11   Main signs: overlapping.

Fig. 2-12   Main signs: conflation.

Fig. 2-13   Main signs: infixation.

AFFIXES

The other important category of signs distinguished by size consists of the several hundred affixes, physically the smaller form of signs. Scribes usually rendered affixes *attached* to main signs, positioned around their sides either as **prefixes** (along the left margin of the main sign), **superfixes** (above the main sign), **postfixes** (along the right margin of the main sign), and **subfixes** (underneath the main sign). Functionally, affixes serve to modify the main sign's value, either by spelling a word in conjunction with the main sign or by **complementing** the main sign, and can have grammatical functions ranging from third-person possessive pronouns to numerical classifiers. Main signs, however, can sometimes serve the same purpose, indicating that size alone does not determine the sign's function.

Fig. 2-14　Example of an affix.

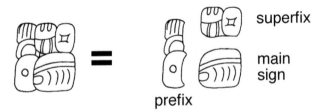

Fig. 2-15　Affixation: prefix, superfix, main sign.

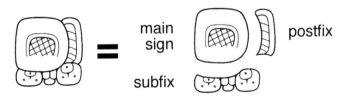

Fig. 2-16　Affixation: main sign, postfix, subfix.

As phonetic entities, affixes can function as **syllabic elements** that essentially represent "syllables" that spell out given words, and as **phonetic complements** that clue the reader as to how to begin or end a word's pronunciation. **Semantic determinatives** distinguish between two or more possible values as in the case of homonyms (words pronounced identically or similarly but that have different meanings, such as the English words "steel" and "steal").

Affixes can also function as main signs, and rarely, two affixes can function together where you would normally find the main sign. Again, the choice seems one of aesthetics on the part of the scribe, irrespective of meaning.

T188

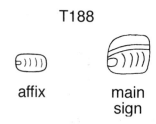

affix   main
sign

Fig. 2-17   Affix as main sign.

— T168 **AJAW**

— T130 **-wa**

Fig. 2-18   2 affixes as main sign.

✳ ✳ ✳ ✳ ✳

Main signs and affixes, arranged within the column-row grid plan, comprise the main ingredients of Maya inscriptions, the primary organizing features of the script in terms of the internal physical arrangement of glyph blocks. In contrast, columns and rows serve the same purpose as blocks of text and sequential lines on the printed page of an English book.

Reading order within individual glyph blocks, however, can pose considerable difficulties. While the reading order of columns and separate blocks remains clear, at least for the most part, the order in which to read affixes and main signs can baffle even the keenest epigrapher. As a rule, prefixes should be read first, followed by any superfixes, main signs, postfixes, and subfixes—in that order. In practice, however, considerable variation complicates reading order. For example, affixes that together will spell one word can *bracket* logographic main signs, as in the well-known Emblem Glyph combination T168:EG:130 or **AJAW-Emblem Glyph-(wa)**, where the subfix **(wa)** as a phonetic complement signals the final *w* sound of the superfix **AJAW** "ruler."

Fig. 2-19   Affixes bracketing main sign.

Types of Glyphs: Iconographic Forms

In theory, any given sign has at least three separate *graphic* or **iconographic** forms, again apparently determined by aesthetic choice. While one style might be used exclusively in an individual inscription, not infrequently the scribe mixed two or all three forms together in the same text. Hence certain inscriptions might begin with **full-figure** glyphs then switch to **symbolic** forms. Most often, texts combine symbolic and **head variant** signs. In this manner, the Maya scribe had at his disposal one of the most artistically rich and graphically spectacular scripts ever invented.

Symbolic or Geometric Variants

The most common of all iconographic signs, **symbolic variants**, also called **geometric variants**, tend to dominate other types of signs in an inscription. All glyphs are thought to have a symbolic form that usually incorporates some type of geometric or abstract arrangement with little visible connection to an identifiable object. Epigraphers have concluded that symbolic variants can function as any grammatical form—logogram, phonetic complement, or semantic determinative—depending on the scribe's intention.

Fig. 2-20   Symbolic or geometric sign:
crossed bands.

HEAD VARIANTS

Each glyph, again in theory, has a **personified** or **head variant** in addition to its symbolic form. Head variants in most cases represent humans or humanlike gods, animals, and supernatural creatures, almost always depicted as the figure's portrait turned in profile or, very rarely, in full frontal view. While personified forms are known for a wide range of signs, for many glyphs no head variants have yet been identified.

Fig. 2-21   Head variants.

An excellent and easily grasped example of personified head variants is the substitutions for the numbers 1 through 12, each represented as a god with unique attributes, instead of the more common bars and dots. (See Chapter 3: Introduction to the Calendars.) Attributes include differences in sex, age, and other physiognomic traits, as well as items of apparel.

FULL-FIGURE VARIANTS

Rarest of all, **full-figure variants** portray the god or creature's entire body, including head, legs, arms, and torso, again distinguished by the figure's personal attributes. Usually delightfully rendered, full-figure glyphs represent the most ornate writing in the Maya system. Scribes used the full form to create visual puns, miniature portraits of creatures offering inventive gestures sometimes related to their intended meaning. As complex, visual feasts they often present some challenge to novice and professional alike, especially in the case of newly discovered glyphs that epigraphers have not yet studied. Their attributes provide important clues to the meaning and origin of other types of signs, and new full-figure texts generally cause great excitement for their potential to resolve problems in decipherment. In essence, symbolic and head variants represent the fragmented details of a larger image, whereas the full-figure glyphs provide the entire picture.

Fig. 2-22 Full-figure glyphs.

Types of Glyphs: Grammatical Forms

While no specific *forms* of glyphs correspond to grammatical parts of speech—neither affixes, main signs, symbolic variants, or personified glyphs denote grammatical elements in and of themselves—several *categories* of glyphs do serve grammatical functions, and the beginner will find it useful to first learn these before exploring the script.

LOGOGRAMS

Certain signs, and in many cases combinations of main signs and affixes that at first appear to be separate, individual elements, serve to denote whole words, or **logograms** (from Greek *logo* "word" and *gram* "writing" or "word-writing"). For example, T561 represents the complete word **CHAAN** "sky," although the sign has no identifiable relationship to the physical qualities of the sky. Other logograms can visually represent the object that they signify, as in the sign **PAKAL** "shield" (T624v), which is depicted as a round object with crosshatching around the rim and often carried by armed warriors in Maya artistic scenes. Identifiable objects used as hieroglyphs represent a **pictographic** convention, a widespread method of writing in Mesoamerica. Logograms bear an assigned phonetic value corresponding to an entire word, and were meant to be read in the overall structure of a hieroglyphic sentence.

a   b

Fig. 2-23   Logograms: a) T561 **CHAAN** "sky"; b) T624v **PAKAL** "shield."

Many signs function in one context as logograms while in others as **phonetic signs**, a quality known as polyvalence. (See below, Polyvalent Signs.) For example, an image of an upturned frog's head (T740) or the animal's complete body (T740ff) can represent the word *sij* (transcribed as **SIJ**), meaning "birth," or it can function as a syllabic sign with the value **ju** that has no meaning in and of itself.

Fig. 2-24   "Upended frog."

PHONETIC SIGNS

Another grammatical category of signs includes those glyphs that have *syllabic* properties. **Syllabic** or **phonetic signs** generally take the form of consonant-vowel or of a vowel by itself, and combine to form whole words as in **pa-ka-la** or *pakal* "shield." Usually, the vowels in each syllable must match and the last vowel is almost always dropped. (See Chapter 7: Phoneticism in the Maya Script.) In actual practice, the final vowel may not in fact match the previous vowels, an anomaly that may depend on the vowel complexity in the root word being spelled. Cases where vowels match are called **synharmony**, whereas cases of non-matched vowels are called **disharmony**.

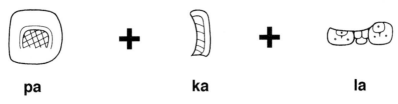

pa   **ka**   **la**

Fig. 2-25   Phonetic spelling of *pakal*.

As mentioned earlier, individual signs can function either as phonetic signs without meaning in and of themselves, or as complete words (logograms). As a rule, phonetic spellings of words are much more frequent in Late Classic texts. Early Classic inscriptions tend to include a higher percentage of logograms.

PHONETIC COMPLEMENTS

Glyphs attached or affixed to a main sign can sometimes indicate which value a main sign takes. (See Polyvalent Signs, below.) **Phonetic complements** act as "highway signs" to cue a reader to a logogram's phonetic value, essentially as pronunciation guides. For example, the word *chaan*, introduced above and usually represented as logographic T561 "sky," frequently takes the subfix T23 **-na** as a phonetic complement to supply the final *n* sound in the Mayan word *chaan*.

Phonetic complements occur much more frequently in Late Classic texts than in Early Classic ones.

CHAAN

-na

Fig. 2-26   Phonetic complement on *chaan*.

SEMANTIC DETERMINATIVES

A class of signs called **semantic determinatives** helps to distinguish one possible reading from another, as in the case of homonyms or words of different meaning that have equivalent or nearly equivalent pronunciation. Semantic determinatives prove useful in rebus-style writing, where pictures of objects stand for their homonyms. Imagine, to use an English example, that you drew an image of an automobile tire to represent the verb "tire" as in the sentence "I tire easily," but were worried that your reader might mistake the word for the tire of the automobile itself. To avoid conflict in meaning, you cleverly add an image of someone lying down, as if to rest, hoping that the reader will make the connection between someone resting and being tired.

Linda Schele publicly remarked more than once during the Maya Meetings at Texas that the only true semantic determinatives in Maya hieroglyphic writing were the oval or nearly round cartouches that surround day signs. Since the graphic images that represent day signs frequently serve as phonetic signs with completely different phonetic values than their day sign names, Linda argued that the cartouche served as a semantic determinative meaning "day sign." In this way Maya scribes unambiguously showed, through graphic conventions, a complete and major shift in meaning for individual signs.

Linda's ideas notwithstanding, the day sign both with and without its cartouche can function as a title rather than the day (usually in the form **AJAW-(wa)**), arguing against the cartouche as a true semantic determinative.

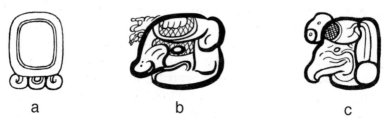

a   b   c

Fig. 2-27   Semantic determinatives: a) day sign cartouche; b) rodent with Jester God headband; c) vulture with **AJAW** (T533) headband.

Another example of the word *ajaw* where a semantic determinative may be involved is the "rodent" sign that wears on its head the Jester God, signaling a reading of **AJAW**. Similarly, a vulture's head can wear symbolic **AJAW** (T533) over its brow (T747) as part of the headband, to distinguish the vulture as **AJAW** from its more usual value of **ti/TI**.

Polyvalent Signs

One of the most difficult aspects of Maya hieroglyphic writing for beginners to grasp is the fact that certain signs have more than one value or meaning. In actuality, few, if any, of *exactly* the same signs carry different values, and close study will reveal some major or otherwise significant difference between the glyphs involved. For example, T528 commonly functions as the day sign **KAWAK**, surrounded by its cartouche and often supported on characteristic day sign brackets like a stand or tripod. Outside of its calendrical context, however, T528 functions syllabically as the phonetic sign **ku**. To complicate matters, T528 sometimes takes the phonetic complement T116 **-ni**, in which case T528 becomes a logogram or complete word that reads **TUN**, with **-ni** supplying the final *n* sound of the Mayan word *tun* "stone." Finally, T528 becomes logographic **JA'AB'**, meaning the 365-day year in non-day sign calendrical contexts and, when doubled and overlapping another T528, or when attached to an arch-like extension, it serves as syllabic **pi** (T177). Indeed, T528 in its various manifestations is one of the most versatile (and common) signs currently known.

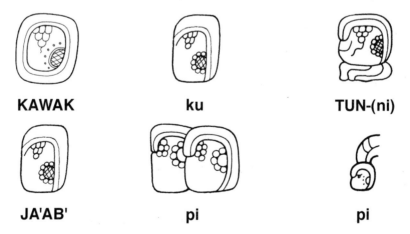

| KAWAK | ku | TUN-(ni) |
| JA'AB' | pi | pi |

Fig. 2-28   Examples of polyvalence.

The apparent polyvalence of signs has led more than one critic to question whether scholars have truly cracked the Maya script. Some argue that epigraphers add values to signs willy-nilly, according to whatever value they need when they find themselves in a pinch. The beginner should rest assured that every major script bears a certain degree of polyvalence. (Egyptian hieroglyphs incorporate quite a high ratio.) As an example from English, consider the sound in the letter combination *ch*. Readers will recognize instantly that not only does *ch* sound soft in such words as "chew," and can sound hard in names like Cocheran, but that the English words themselves offer no clues to pronunciation for the average modern reader (although a little knowledge of etymology helps to solve such problems).

While polyvalence poses certain difficulties, relatively few signs have more than one value, and those that do often change value when functioning as logograms or phonetic signs. Beginners can quickly learn the handful of more common polyvalent glyphs.

Selected Common Signs

Before going on to take a closer look at the Maya script, it will help to familiarize yourself with some of the most basic and frequent signs, many of which help to illuminate the overall writing system. The best way to learn the more common signs is to study them one by one, memorizing what they look like and how they function.

T1: The third-person possessive pronoun **U**. Also simply functions as the vowel **u**.

T12: The male agentive **AJ**, meaning "he of." Also used to indicate an association with a physical location.

T23: A stand-like postfix that functions as a phonetic sign with the value **na**.

T59: Functions as the phonetic sign **ti** and as a locative, or an "indicator of locations," with the value **TI**.

T116: Resembling a tail, its phonetic value of **ni** may derive from the word for tail, or *ne*.

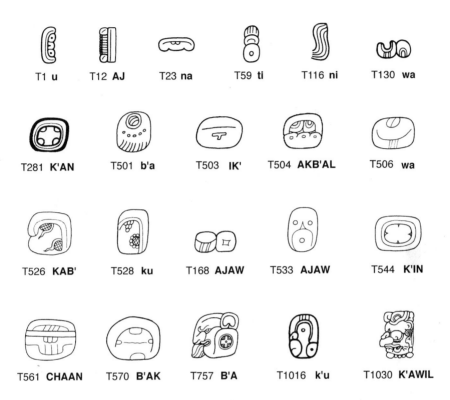

Fig. 2-29   Selected common signs.

T130: One of the most common verbal postfixes, the T130 combination resembles a sort of stand to support another glyph. Unequivocally functions in "positional" inflections on verbs and reads **wa**.

T281: A four-lobed cross associated with the value **K'AN** with the primary meaning of "yellow" and the secondary meaning of "precious."

T501: Represents in highly abstract form the blossom of a water lily with the value of **IMIX** in day sign contexts. Otherwise, as a phonetic sign the glyph reads **b'a** and as a logogram **B'A/B'AJ** "first," "image." However, when infixed with T533, which in other contexts reads **AJAW**, the value of T501 changes to **ma**, and when incorporating crosshatching, or sets of crossed parallel lines, it reads logographically **JA'** "water."

T503: Consists of a capital T-like shape superimposed over a blank field. Identified as a symbol for "wind" and given the logographic value **IK'**.

T504: Thought to represent the belly-scales (lower undulating marks) and markings (upper crosshatched semicircles) of a serpent. In day sign contexts it represents **AKB'AL**, the third day of the Tzolk'in calendar (see Chapter 4: The Calendar Round), with the additional meaning of "darkness."

T506: Consists of a sort of lower saddle shape with an oval lozenge above it. The sign relates to corn and, outside of calendrical contexts where it reads **K'AN**, it regularly has the values **wa/WA/WAJ**, the latter meaning "maize bread" or "tortilla." The sign itself often serves to depict individual "loaves" of bread in Maya artistic scenes. The sign T506 also has the logographic value **OL** "heart," and is therefore *polyvalent*.

T526: Consists of crosshatched upper and right-hand semicircular zones, the former framed by a device resembling a question mark. In day sign contexts the sign reads **KAB'AN** but otherwise has the value **KAB'**, "land, earth."

T528: Composed of elements that resemble bunched grapes along the top with a semi-circular shape that impinges from the right and has dots surrounding it. A few scholars have suggested the "bunched grapes" motif depicts massed rain clouds. Read **KAWAK** when used as day sign, T528 acquires other values depending on context and affixation: **TUN** when coupled with the subfix T116 **-ni**, **JA'AB'** in calendrical but non-day sign contexts, and phonetic **pi** when doubled or with an elbow-like bracket, as in the affix T177 **pi** (see figure 2-28).

T168, T533: The first represents a composite sign derived from two separate glyphs that are always meant to be read together as a logogram with the value **AJAW**, meaning "lord." The second is thought to represent in abstract form the face of a monkey, an unequivocal reference to the Sun God that has the same value **AJAW** "lord." However, when shown upside down, or upside down and doubled, the sign takes the value **la**.

T544: An image of a four-petaled flower blossom with a circle in the middle, possibly a plumeria flower. This well-known sign signifies the sun and the concept of "day," and stands as one of the chief emblems of the Sun God. Unequivocally a logogram that reads **K'IN**.

T561: Incorporates a bisected squared oval containing in its upper zone parallel bands, and in its lower zone three circles and short parallel lines superimposed over a tab. Unequivocally a logogram that reads **CHAAN** (Ch'olan) or **KAAN** (Yucatec).

T570: Depicts a bone, presumably human, and has the logographic value **B'AK** meaning "bone," although the sign can be used rebus-style to represent other words with the same sound.

T757: Identified as a rodent, possibly a gopher, with an infixed **K'AN** cross (T281) at the base of the neck below the ear. Has the phonetic value **b'a**, and the logographic value **B'A/B'AJ** meaning, among other things, "head," "image," and "first."

T1016: Known to portray the deity designated by the epigrapher Paul Schellhas as "God C," the sign carries the value **k'u** or **K'U** and represents a highly stylized face in profile. As a logogram this sign has the meaning "god."

T1030a-h: One of many portraits of gods in the Maya script, this sign represents a god's face with a mirror over the forehead from which emerges an ax, torch, or cigar that often is shown with smoke at its tip. Phonetic spellings of his name indicate that he was called K'awil, and so the sign itself has been assigned the logographic value **K'AWIL**.

CHAPTER 3

● ● ●

Introduction to the Calendars: Numbers, Initial Series, and Long Count

Of the many Maya accomplishments, none surpass the invention of the Maya calendars and mathematical system. The Maya concept of time was based on a highly sophisticated and complex positional notation system that allowed the scribe or priest to add, to subtract, and to calculate multiples of any given sequence. The cumbrous system of Roman numerals, which involves ever larger sequences of letters strung together, pales beside the ease and sophistication of the Maya **Long Count** and so-called **Distance Numbers**.

Numbers

The Maya's conception of time draws upon a discovery made only once before in human history—the concept of zero. The Hindus were the only people in the Old World to originate a symbol for "nothingness," the absence of anything, for use as a mathematical tool. It was through the Hindus that the concept passed into the Arab world and subsequently into Western culture.

But the Maya too invented the concept of zero. The brilliance of Maya mathematicians allowed them to understand, completely independent of Old World tradition, the economy and precision of zero in handling larger units. Zero "holds" a place in a positional arrangement, allowing the mathematician to "step up" to higher numerical orders: in our own

57

system, tens (10), hundreds (100), thousands (1000), and so on. For their own purposes, the Maya chose a base of twenty, or a vegisimal count, stacking their "places" vertically so that each higher-placed order represented a multiple of twenty of the place below it. Similarly, our own system reads across a horizontal line from right to left in groups of tens, or decimally.

SYMBOLIC NUMBERS

Scribes represented numbers with a very limited set of signs. The simplest forms are the symbolic variants: bars stand for "five," dots for "one." A bar and one dot equal "six," and a bar and four dots "nine." Two bars and one dot equal "eleven," while two bars plus four dots equal "fourteen." In several instances the depiction of a thumb represents the number one (T329), as though part of a formal count of hands and toes.[1] Another sign with the value "one" assumes the form of a bifurcated vegetable motif that resembles scrolling leaves (T117 and variants of T86).

At least two separate symbolic signs have the value "zero": a kind of football-shaped shell, and a crosshatched trifoliate sign reminiscent of part of a German Cross.

If we turn to our example introduced in the previous chapter—Yaxchilán Stela 11—we can see that glyphs A2–B4 contain several examples of bars and dots, with notations of 9, 16, 1, and 13. Other glyphs in this sequence include the crosshatched trifoliate sign denoting "zero" (B3 and A4). Other positions hold numbers as well—D1a, C2, D2, C3, D3, E3, and finally H4. Learn to distinguish these simple bar-dot combinations from the non-numerical bars located at E2b, F2, and I2, which look similar but form part of a different image.

HEAD-VARIANT AND FULL-FIGURE NUMBERS

The Maya imagined numbers as much more than abstract symbols. Rather, numbers represented actual gods, living and breathing entities that assumed human and animal forms. These "personified" numbers literally carried periods of time, by groups of twenty years, 400 years, and so on, either in their arms or with the use of tumplines in backpack fashion. They relayed time from zero or the "beginning" virtually into infinity, handing off from one god to the next in an unbroken, endless chain. In inscriptions,

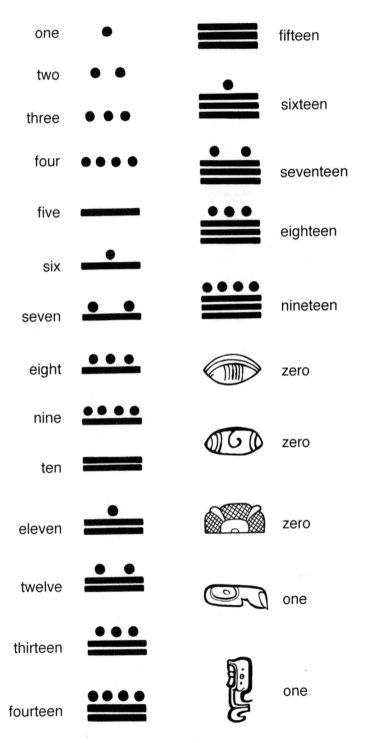

Fig. 3-1   Numbers: symbolic variants.

portraits of numerical gods shown in profile substitute for the more geometric bar-and-dot numbers and are given distinctive facial features, costume paraphernalia, and attributes of gender and age. Occasionally the
entire god was portrayed—head, body, extremities—in exceptionally rare
"full-figure" inscriptions. The gods were the true essence of the calendars,
the physical agents of the cosmos and the movers of time.

One (JUN): (T1000) Represented by a young female deity, possibly the Moon
Goddess. A single lock of hair serves as her chief characteristic, flanking the
back of her face before her ear and curling forward along her jawline.

Two (KA/CHA): (T1086) Represented by the head of a man of indefinite
age with a hand on top of his head.

Three (OX/UX): (T1082) A young man with distinctive headdress that
sometimes includes a disk at the front. The headband often resembles the
glyphic sign for a "thatched roof," and the god can also take an infix of the
IK' "wind" sign (T503) on his cheek or within his ear ornament.

Four (KAN/CHAN): (T1010[544]) The Sun God, or Jun Ajaw (also called
K'inich Ajaw), identified by a squared loop under the eye, a square pupil,
and sometimes a **K'IN** "flower" sign (T544) infixed within the brow or at
the back of the head. The figure generally includes a tau, or T-shaped, front
tooth and a barbel at the corner of the mouth. The barbel may refer to the
Hero Twins as recounted in the *Popol Vuh*, where the Twins were reborn as
catfish after their demise at the hands of the death gods.

Five (JO): (TV) An "old god" who wears the **TUN** (T524) "year" sign on
top of his head.

Six (WAK): (TVIhv) Identified by a loop under his eye and an ax infixed
where the pupil ought to be. Sometimes includes a multi-banded loop or curl
in front of his forehead and a tau-shaped, front tooth.

Seven (WUK): (TVIIhv) The anthropomorphic form of the Jaguar God of
the underworld, Number Seven has a loop under its eye that sometimes
curls over the bridge of the nose to form a "cruller." He can also have a
hook within the eye and the tau-shaped front tooth.

Eight (WAXAK): (T1006) Universally recognized as the Corn God, the
archetypal young lord, Number Eight has a curl in front of his forehead

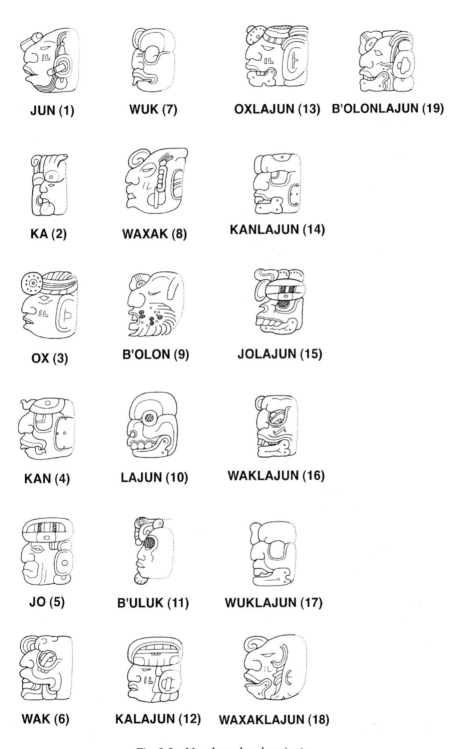

Fig. 3-2 Numbers: head variants.

that represents a new sprout of corn. Sometimes the back of his head morphs into foliate elements, or foliage decorates the cheek.

Nine (B'OLON): (T1003) Represents a man with heavy beard, unusual among Native Americans. Often has jaguar spots on the cheek and the symbol **YAX**, meaning "first," "blue," or "blue-green," in front of the forehead.

Ten (LAJUN): (T1040) The skull of the Death God, often with prominent fleshless jawbone.

Fig. 3-3   Full-figure number: ten (**LAJUN**).

Eleven (B'ULUK): (TXIhv) Represents the head of the Earth Goddess with the sign for **KAB'AN** (T526), a crosshatched area with a curl beside it that resembles a question mark, infixed beside the forehead.

Twelve (KALAJUN): (TXIIhv) A young god who wears the "sky" (T561) symbol (**CHAAN** or **KAAN**) on top of his head or across his cheek.

Thirteen through Nineteen (OXLAJUN through B'OLONLAJUN): All numbers thirteen or higher combine the profiled heads of lower-order numbers, three through nine, with the jawbone of the Death God skull of Number Ten (3+10=13, 4+10=14, and so on).

Completion (CHAM?): (T1033) Because the Maya numerical system proceeds vegisimally, or by groups of twenty, the number after nineteen was "completion," specifically the "completion of a group of twenty." Thus the Maya system conceived of zero as functionally equivalent to "nothing" but ideologically quite different. The sign, a god-head with a "death eye" in front of the forehead and a human hand over the lower jaw, represents "death" or "expiration," with possible associations to a ritual where sacrificial victims had their lower jaw ripped off.

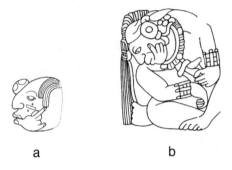

a   b

Fig. 3-4   Personified examples of "zero" or "completion" (**CHAM?**): a) head variant; b) full figure.

OTHER SIGNS FOR "ZERO"

Seating (CHUM): (T644) While "completion" serves the same function as zero in the decimal system and represents the "place-holder" for the twenty-based calendrical system, "seating" has the same capacity but in the sense of "beginning" or "start," rather than "end." The **Seating Glyph** therefore comes before the number "one," when sequences run "0 through 19," rather than "1 through completion." The concept of seating occurs in documents written by the Maya in European script at the time of the Spanish conquest, where "seating" reads *chum*. Its function extends to the well-known Seating Glyph that denotes accession.

Fig. 3-5   "Seating": **CHUM-[mu]**.

End of (k'a-ab'): A final way to write "zero" is with T548 **AB'** prefixed with T128 **k'a**, or **k'a-ab'** *k'ab'*. The **k'a-ab'** compound occurs only in the number position in the **Ja'ab'** month count of the Calendar Round or 52-Year Cycle. (See Chapter 4: The Calendar Round.)

8 Manik   "end of"   Kej

Fig. 3-6   "End of": **k'a-ab'**.

Systems of Time

Tikal, Palenque, Copán, and other Classic Period centers combined properties of the mathematical system with three main sets of calendars to keep track of time. The **Calendar Round**, a time cycle used throughout Mesoamerica from Preclassic to Colonial times, functioned in a manner more or less similar to our day and month calendar. With the **Long Count**, scribes recorded the larger overall cycles of the solar year, set within a framework of "centuries" and "millennia." The Calendar Round and Long Count together form the **Initial Series**, an interlocking set of cycles that usually provides a beginning date for an inscription.

To further embellish time, the Classic Maya recorded a nine-day "week" referred to as the **Lords Of The Night**, a **Lunar Series** that provided the age of the moon, and an esoteric **819-Day Count** that relates to divisions of time according to color-coded directional quadrants. The Maya also calculated back and forth in time through simple addition and subtraction with a series called **Distance Numbers**.

Initial Series

The **Initial Series** functions to a certain degree like the combined sequence of our own Gregorian calendar, as in January 1, 2001. In the Maya system, our day number and month correspond to the **Calendar Round**, with the year 2001 corresponding to the **Long Count**. In hieroglyphic texts, the Initial Series serves as the "anchor" date from which later dates are derived. This record typically begins an inscription, and is located either above the head of the text or positioned in the upper left corner. (Note that exceptions abound in Maya hieroglyphic writing and that, on rare occasions,

Initial Series occur within the actual body of the text.) Generally, an Initial Series stands out from the text like a prominent advertisement, and starts with an oversized **Introductory Glyph** as a visual clue for the reader.

Initial Series Introductory Glyph: As a sort of prologue to the date, the Initial Series Introductory Glyph (or ISIG for short) "announces" that the Long Count and Calendar Round will follow. In this capacity it generally spans at least two glyph columns and occupies the space of two glyph blocks and more usually four (although as always the reader will find exceptions). The ISIG consists of three constant signs and a central variable. The constant elements consist of the **TUN** sign (T548, the same sign worn on the head of the god of numbers "five" and "fifteen") that functions in essence as the main sign and has the value **AB'**, along with a superfix of scrolls that reads **tsi-** or **tso-** (T124), and two comb-like elements (T25:25) that flank the variable sign, each with the value **ka**. Combined, the ISIG reads *tzik ab'*, or "count of years." The variable element indicates the month in which the Calendar Round occurs and offers a sort of "preview" of the date that will follow in the Long Count. In our example from Yaxchilán Stela 11, the ISIG opens the text at A1–B1.

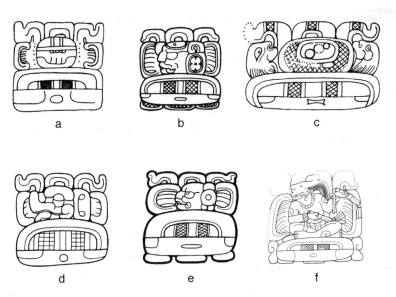

a   b   c

d   e   f

Fig. 3-7   Examples of the Initial Series Introducing Glyph: a) with patron of the month Xul; b) with patron of the month Yaxk'in; c) with patron of the month Ch'en; d) with patron of the month Yax; e) with patron of the month Mol; f) with full-figure patron of the month Mak.

Long Count

To keep track of individual years, as opposed to the day and month, the Maya developed an exceptionally sophisticated positional notation system. Usually, **Long Count** notations follow underneath the ISIG or extend horizontally towards the right. A typical notation begins with the highest order of time, just as our system records two multiples of 1,000 in the year 2000—or two thousand years since the beginning of our calendar. As our system expresses a date in terms of millennia, centuries, decades, and single years elapsed since the year of the Birth of Christ, or in terms of *decimal* positions, so too the Maya system counts in increments of twenty, or *vegisimally*, and provides the quantity of the **b'aktun** (400 years), **k'atun** (twenty years), **tun** (years of 360 days), **winal** (months), and **k'in** (days)—representing elapsed time since the calendar's mythological zero date on August 13, 3114 B.C.

B'AKTUN

B'aktun (400 tuns, or 20 k'atuns, or 360 × 400 = 144,000 days): (T528 reduplicated) Two **KAWAK** elements, each with an infixed "bunch of grapes" motif, overlap to form the symbolic variant. The personified form represents a bird, identified as the mythological composite bird called the Muwan, with a human hand that replaces its jaw in a manner similar to the head-variant "completion" sign (T1033). Since two **KAWAK** signs together have the logographic value **PI/PIJ**, most epigraphers accept that the *b'aktun* glyph reads **PI/PIJ** as well. On Yaxchilán Stela 11 the *b'aktun* occurs at A2.

K'ATUN

K'atun (20 tuns or 7,200 days): Very similar to the ISIG (Initial Series Introducing Glyph; see above), the *k'atun* consists of two **ka-** elements (T25) that flank the **KAWAK** sign (T528), and the **TUN** sign (T548). Like the *b'aktun* glyph the personified form probably represents the mythological Muwan Bird. The **k'a** element may derive from an abbreviation of *k'al* "twenty." On Yaxchilán Stela 11 the *k'atun* occurs at B2.

	Symbolic	Head Variant	Head Variant	Full Figure
B'AKTUN				
K'ATUN				
TUN				
WINAL				
K'IN				

Fig. 3-8   Period glyphs: geometric or symbolic forms, head variants, and full-figure glyphs.

TUN

Tun (360 k'ins, or 18 winals, or 360 days): (T548) The base element or main sign of the *k'atun* and ISIG, the **TUN** sign probably represents a wooden drum in cross-section, or *tun k'ul*. As in the *b'aktun* and *k'atun* glyphs, the personified variant is identified as the mythological Muwan Bird, which is sometimes replaced with a monster that wears the drum as its headdress. Notice that, because the system is vegisimal, the *tun* reflects a shortened form of the actual length of the solar year (360 days, which is divisible by twenty), rather than the standard 365-day period. On Yaxchilán Stela 11 the *tun* occurs at A3.

WINAL

Winal (20 k'ins or 20 days): (T521) Although the significance of the symbolic form remains unknown, the personified form portrays the head of a frog. Note that while the *winal* comprises twenty *k'ins* or days, it does so in only eighteen groups, not twenty as is the case for the other time periods. Thus the *winal* can take only numbers 0 through 17. On Yaxchilán Stela 11 the *winal* occurs at B3.

K'IN

K'in (1 day): (T544) Identified as the four stylized petals of a flower with a dot in its center, the symbolic form represents the "day." The personified variant depicts a zoomorphic creature or alternatively the head of the Sun God, with a square eye and the flower infixed to the forehead or concealing the ear. On Yaxchilán Stela 11 the *k'in* occurs at A4.

Bar-dot combinations multiply the periods of time. For example, "nine *b'aktuns*"—the *b'aktun* sign with either a bar and four dots or the personified form with beard and jaguar spots—equals nine times 400 years or nine times 144,000 days. Similarly, "sixteen *k'atuns*" equals sixteen times twenty years or sixteen times 7,200 days. All the tallied *b'aktuns, k'atuns, tuns, winals,* and *k'ins* count from the base date 3114 B.C., yielding the contemporary year, month, and day, just as we add 2001 from the birth of Christ.

Fig. 3-9   9 b'aktuns: a) symbolic form; b) head variant.

If we examine our text from Yaxchilán Stela 11, we see that its inscription expresses the following Long Count:

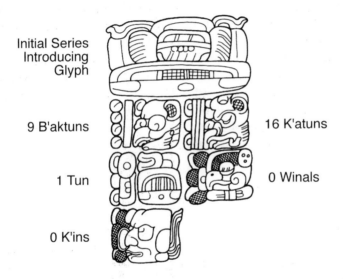

Fig. 3-10   Initial Series, Yaxchilán Stela 11, front, lower glyph panel.

b'aktun (A2)	**k'atun** (B2)
9	16
tun (A3)	**winal** (B3)
1	0
k'in (A4)	
0	

Epigraphers typically express Long Count notations like the one given above as a sequence of numbers from left to right, in this case 9.16.1.0.0 (A.D. 752).

Summary

Texts that include Initial Series were the product of the Classic Period, at the height of Maya civilization. Indeed, the span of dates during which the Maya recorded the Initial Series are those that scholars use to define the Classic Period itself, beginning with Tikal Stela 29 at 8.12.14.8.15, or A.D. 292, and ending with a set of monuments corresponding to 10.4.0.0.0, or A.D. 909, at sites that include Toniná and Tzibanche. But these are merely arbitrary parameters, and certainly earlier and later monuments remain to be discovered in the rain forests that blanket much of the Maya's ancestral homelands.

The Maya carved most of their dated sculptures during the ninth *b'aktun* (or Cycle 9; A.D. 435–830), but a few examples survive from the end of the eighth (Cycle 8; A.D. 292–435) as well as from the beginning of the tenth (Cycle 10; A.D. 830–909). Evidence indicates that the system encompassed thirteen *b'aktuns* (zero through twelve), theoretically due to end long after the Maya ceased keeping count. We entered the last *k'atun* or twenty-year period of these cycles on April 6, 1993, and Maya time will end in A.D. 2012. Lest the modern world tremble, all lower cycles start over, and the *b'aktuns* click over into higher orders of "epochs" and "eons," as the gods of time proceed along their roads.

NOTE

1. Indeed, evidence suggests that the formal count of fingers and toes—with the total "twenty"—may relate to the "tally" of an individual person, that is, a man or **winik**. Hence the term **winal** for the Long Count month of twenty days.

CHAPTER 4

The Calendar Round

After the five-glyph Long Count comes the much briefer, usually two-glyph block **Calendar Round** (abbreviated to CR). Our example from previous chapters, Yaxchilán Stela 11, includes the Calendar Round at B4 and D3. Epigraphers express the CR date as two sets of numbers and two sets of names, in this case 11 Ajaw 8 Sek. This dual-component Calendar Round gives the number and name of the day (11 Ajaw), and the position and name of the month (8 Sek), and functions as the general equivalent of the day and month in our own system when we write, for instance, January 1. The initial number and day sign (11 Ajaw), called the **Tzolk'in**, incorporates a calendar of 260 days, while the latter (8 Sek)—the **Ja'ab'**— incorporates a calendar of 365 days.

TZOLK'IN		**JA'AB'**	
number	day	number	month
11	Ajaw	8	Sek

It may be easiest to visualize the Calendar Round as sets of cogs or wheels interlocking to form a larger system (see figure 4-3). The various elements function like integrated gears perpetually repeating through time. The first set of cogs, corresponding to our Tzolk'in example 11 Ajaw, records a repetition of numbers one through thirteen in relation to twenty

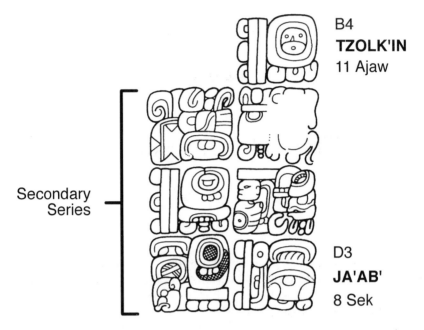

B4
TZOLK'IN
11 Ajaw

Secondary
Series

D3
JA'AB'
8 Sek

Fig. 4-1   Yaxchilán Stela 11, bottom, lower glyph panel, Tzolk'in,
Secondary Series, and Ja'ab', B4, and C1-D3.

TZOLK'IN   **JA'AB'**

11 Ajaw   8 Sek

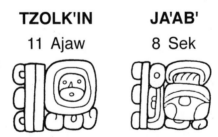

Fig. 4-2   Calendar Round from Yaxchilán Stela 11, front, lower
glyph panel, B4 and D3.

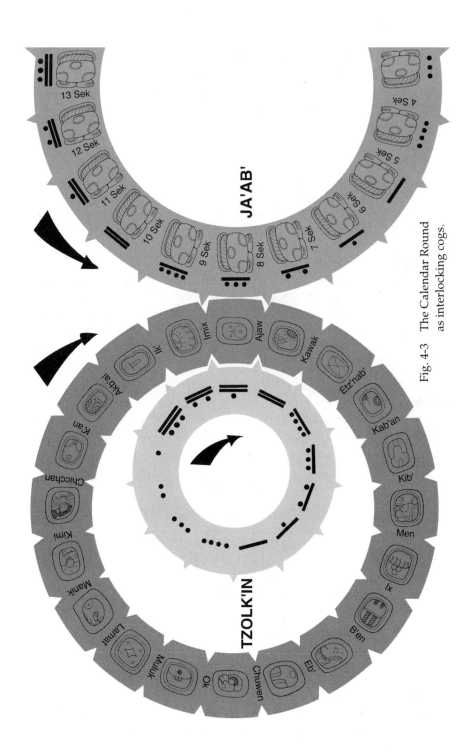

Fig. 4-3 The Calendar Round as interlocking cogs.

day names, with their number-day combination starting over once every 260 days (13 × 20 = 260). The second set of cogs, or the Ja'ab', corresponding to 8 Sek, records a series of eighteen months of twenty days each, together with an additional five-day period (18 × 20 + 5 = 365).

Tzolk'in

The **Tzolk'in**, or 260-day Sacred Almanac, was widely used in ancient times for divinatory purposes. Guatemalan Maya and other cultures in Mexico still use it as a means of "day keeping." The origins of the 260-day calendar are debatable, although a number of scholars have suggested it corresponds to the nine-month period of human gestation.

In the Tzolk'in, a series of twenty named days runs concurrent with the numbers 1 through 13. Since the numbers fall out of sync from fourteen onward, it takes 260 days to come back to where 1 coincides with the first day (13 × 20 = 260). For example, the sequence starts with 1 Imix, proceeds to 13 B'en (the thirteenth named day), then proceeds to 1 Ix (the fourteenth day), 2 Men, 3 Kib', and so forth, until 7 Ajaw, where the days will start over with Imix but this time with the number 8, or 8 Imix. Thus, on the second round of numbers and days, the two sequences have fallen out of step and will continue to fall out of step on the third, fourth, and fifth rounds and so on for 260 days, after which the sequences start back at 1 Imix again and another set of 260 days unfolds.

TZOLK'IN

11   Ajaw

Fig. 4-4   Yaxchilán Stela 11, front, lower glyph panel, Tzolk'in position, 11 Ajaw.

At first complicated, the **Tzolk'in** tally only takes practice. But eventually, like a juggling act, more and more number and period cycles must be added. These cycles require an exceptional memory or, better yet, a good computer. Cut through the difficulty and get one of several excellent computer programs listed in Appendix II.

Day signs typically occur within characteristic cartouches that frequently, but not always, rest atop nongrammatical "volute stands." In order, the twenty day signs are:

Imix: (T501/1031a,b)) Represents a stylized water lily. A circle impinges at the top, often crosshatched, with small circles in an arch underneath and several curving parallel vertical lines at the bottom. Outside its calendrical context, **Imix** has the phonetic value **b'a** when the impinged circle at top has a curving arch inside it, the value **ja'** when the circle contains crosshatching, and the value **ma** when infixed with T534 (the upside-down **AJAW** sign). The personified form of the day sign represents the Water Lily Monster.

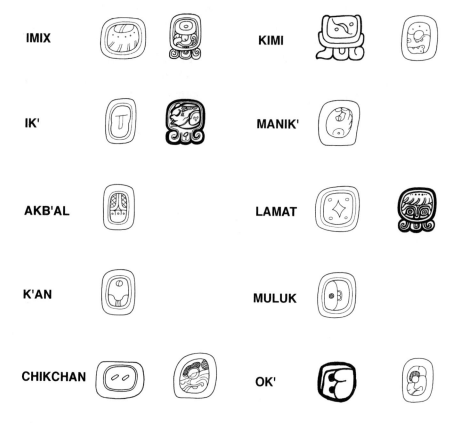

Fig. 4-5   Tzolk'in day signs, Imix through Ok'.

Ik': (T503) The T-shape in the middle of a plain background symbolizes the wind. The personified variant represents a young man with the T symbol infixed over the cheek or inside an ear ornament.

Akb'al: (T504) A segment of a serpent's body, with two opposed crescents at the top, sometimes crosshatched, that represent the serpent's body-markings, and undulating lower segments that depict the scales of the serpent's underbelly. In most contexts the **AKB'AL** sign symbolizes "darkness."

K'an: (T506) The **K'AN** sign depicts an oval with a lower curving or bracket-like band with vertical lines inside, and with an additional oval in the upper area. In the codices, the barkpaper books that the Maya wrote in, young corn plants are shown sprouting from the **K'AN** sign as if from maize seed. Therefore the symbolic variant of this sign probably represents a grain of maize. The word *k'an* means, among other things, "yellow"—the color of maize—and has the connotation "ripe." (Note, however, that another distinctive **K'AN** glyph (T281) actually represents "yellow," rather than the day sign **K'AN**.) T506 **K'AN** has the polyvalent values **WA** or **WAJ** outside of calendrical contexts, as in *waj* "tortilla," and **OL** "heart." But if it includes a series of diagonal dotted lines (T507), the **K'AN** sign reads **tsi-**. It closely resembles the day sign **B'EN** (T584), and also resembles an upside-down version of the day sign **KIB'** (T525).

Chikchan: (T508/764) Simply two parallel diagonal slashes, very short and blunt, against a plain field, the symbolic form resembles the top area of the **YAX** sign (T16). The personified form depicts a snake, which is called *chan* in Ch'olan or *kan* in Yucatec.

Kimi: (T509/1040) The symbolic form resembles a percentage sign—an undulating line between two dots—and signifies "death," while the head of the Death God serves as the personified variant.

Manik': (T671) A hand with an inner and outer circle at the wrist. No head variant currently known.

Lamat: (T510) Called the "star" or "Venus" sign, the symbolic form represents a field quartered by curved inner lines, with each quarter containing a circlet. The personified form represents an unidentified zoomorph, with half the "star" infixed at the back of the head or elsewhere. One head variant incorporates the lower "star" configuration as if representing a pair of eyes, over which hangs a fringe of "hair" or an element very much resembling **IMIX** (T501).

Muluk: (T513) A plain field divided by a curved vertical line with two parallel circlets attached along the right, and a circle in the left half that is sometimes crosshatched. The occasional addition of a mouth personifies the glyph, making it resemble a fish. Other variants include a plain field infixed with a single circle and a personified form that clearly corresponds to the phonetic sign T757 **b'a-**.

Ok: (T765) The head of a dog. The rare symbolic form, confined to the codices, has a field divided by two horizontal loops with spots attached.

Chuwen: (T521) Similar to the *winal* month sign (T521; see Chapter 3) or even the **K'AN** day sign (T506; see above), the **CHUWEN** day sign includes two curving lines that start from opposite sides and come towards each other but then curve down to the bottom of the cartouche. The personified form represents a monkey, and *chuwen* figures in the name of one of the twin monkey gods in the *Popol Vuh* (a postconquest manuscript written in the Mayan language using European letters). The monkey gods were notable scribes and artists.

Eb': (Tnn) Easily confused with the day sign **KIMI** (T1041), the personified form resembles the skeletal head of the Death God, replete with fleshless jawbone. One of its distinguishing features, however, is its **KAWAK** element, or "bunch of grapes," infixed at the back of the skull. Furthermore, since only four numbers can coincide with any given day sign (in the case of **EB'**, seating, 5, 10, and 15), the calendar provides a check that eliminates one or the other (see below, under "The Initial Series: Putting Everything Together"). Early examples of **EB'** depict only the jawbone.

B'en: (T584) Similar to the day sign **K'AN** except that, in place of a loop appended to the upper cartouche edge, **B'EN** has two narrow parallel loops. The personified form wears the "bracket" across the lower jawline.

Ix: (T524) The **IX** glyph includes an area of fringe above a trio of dots that are sometimes crosshatched. In certain dialects of Mayan, *jix* means "jaguar" and is the equivalent of the Quiché day name Balam "jaguar."

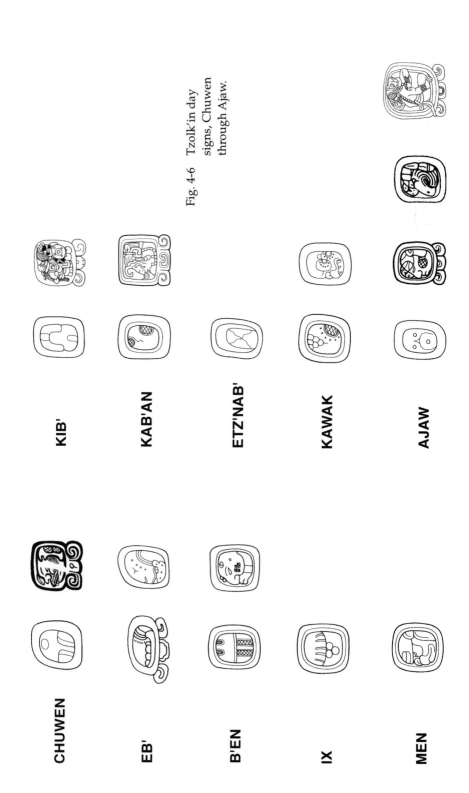

Fig. 4-6 Tzolk'in day signs, Chuwen through Ajaw.

CHUWEN

EB'

B'EN

IX

MEN

KIB'

KAB'AN

ETZ'NAB'

KAWAK

AJAW

Accordingly, the three circles probably represent the jaguar's spots. Alternatively, the fringe may represent an eyelash and the dots, the glint within an eye.

Men: (T1017v?) The head of an unidentifiable supernatural being. Has a squared loop under the eye, a beak-like snout and, in some versions, a distinctive jaw.

Kib': (T525) Essentially the **K'AN** day sign (T506) turned upside down, with the circle area converted to a triangle or a narrow loop and its location reversed. The whole may represent the cross-section of a univalve shell similar to "completion" in the Long Count (see Chapter 3).

Kab'an: (T526) Represents the "earth" and is commonly called the "earth" sign. Consists of upper and lower crosshatched semicircles or loops, with a curled line resembling a question mark suspended from the upper border. Similar to the features that identify the Earth Goddess of number eleven.

Etz'nab': (T527) Represents a pressure-flaked flint or obsidian blade. Essentially an X-shape with undulating lines shown superimposed upon a plain field.

Kawak: (T528) One of the most pervasive symbols in both Maya writing and iconography, **KAWAK** outside of calendrical contexts has the values of **TUN** and **JA'AB'** (logograms), and **ku-** and **pi-** (phonetic values), and therefore is said to be *polyvalent* or to have multiple values. Its value in any given text depends on the affixes attached, the context, or both. The upper area contains a "cluster of grapes," the sign's primary diagnostic feature and possibly a depiction of rain clouds, while the lower right includes a series of lines or circlets extending in a rainbow-like arch. The glyph is therefore intimately associated with rain, and the whole may represent the sky after a rainstorm.

Ajaw: (T533, T747a, or T1000d-e) The day of the Sun God. No other word occurs in Maya inscriptions more frequently than **AJAW**, rendered either in its day sign form or spelled out phonetically. The sign that most frequently represents *ajaw* resembles a stylized face in frontal view, with an inner and outer circle in the lower half for the mouth, a triangular "nose," and two little circles for eyes. The personified form represents an archetypal young lord in profile, usually wearing a headband or scarf (T1000d-g)—the headband of accession or *ajaw*-ship worn by Maya rulers. A vulture can replace both versions, although in these instances the bird usually wears the symbolic form over the forehead (T747a), a semantic determinative that changes the vulture's value from **TI** to **AJAW**.

Ja'ab'

The second half of the Calendar Round, the other set of cogs that occurs in our example 11 Ajaw 8 Sek, represents the **Ja'ab' cycle** and repeats a series of eighteen months that each have twenty individually numbered days (0 through 19). An additional five-day period brings the tally to 365 (18 × 20 + 5 = 365). The Ja'ab', based on an approximate solar year,[1] probably represents a "civil" or "secular" calendar more like the day-month calendar of Western culture.

JA'AB'

8 Sek

Fig. 4-7   Yaxchilán Stela 11, front, lower glyph panel, Ja'ab' position, 8 Sek.

In the following descriptions of individual months, **boldfaced** lower-case names at the beginning of each section represent the Yucatec month name given by Landa. Names given in **BOLDFACED CAPITALS** represent suggested hieroglyphic values for the month signs, based on the phonetic reading of individual components and the concurrence of their values with names of months in Ch'olan. Otherwise, names are given in **UPPER CASE** within the description regardless of whether they correspond to Yucatec or Ch'olan, as if each month sign functioned as a logogram.

Pop (K'ANJALAB'): (Usually T551:130, or T551:21) Includes as its main sign two entwined segments representing a woven *pop* or mat made of

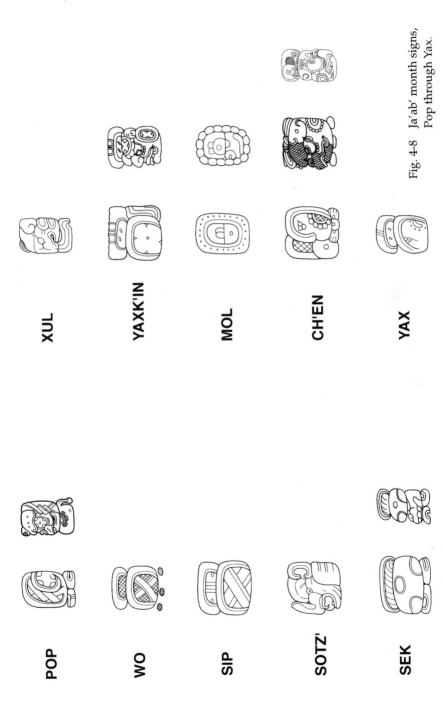

POP

WO

SIP

SOTZ'

SEK

XUL

YAXK'IN

MOL

CH'EN

YAX

Fig. 4-8   Ja'ab' month signs, Pop through Yax.

plaited palm fronds, with an infixed **K'AN** cross which is the symbol for "yellow" (T281; not to be confused with the **K'AN** day sign, T506).

Wo (EK' K'AT): (T95:552.142 or T95:552.103 or T552[95].96) **WO** and **SIP** include the same main sign, a cartouche with crossed bands (T552) that may have the value **K'AT**, part of the name in Ch'olan. The distinguishing features in each case are the color signs. **WO** takes the sign for "black," or **EK'** (T95), together with one of several subfixes that probably read **-ta**, giving both the initial word and final sound for the month's name. Since the word for this month is *Ik'k'at* "black cross" in the Mayan dialect of Ch'ol, we can be fairly sure that **WO** had this value in the inscriptions.

Sip (CHAK K'AT): (T109:552.103 or T109:552.142) Having the same crossed-bands **K'AT** sign as **WO**, the distinguishing feature of **SIP** is its affix **CHAK** "red" (T109), perhaps yielding **CHAK K'AT** "red cross." The sign can also include the subfix **-ta**, giving the final **t** sound of the name.

Sotz' (SOTZ'): (T756) The head of a leaf-nosed bat.

Sek (KATSEW): (T25:520.130) Significance unknown. The **SEK** month sign spells out the name phonetically: **ka-se-wa**.

Xul (TZ'IK'IN): (T757v) Represents a dog. The T116 tail-like phonetic complement **-ni** provides the final *n* sound to the Ch'ol name *Tz'ik'in*.

Yaxk'in (YAX K'IN): (T16:544.116 or T16:1010[544].116) Linguistically paired with the month sign **K'ANK'IN** (see **K'ank'in** below), the month sign **YAX K'IN** uses as its main sign the **K'IN** solar flower (T544), symbol of the Sun God, prefixed with **YAX** (T16), meaning "first," "blue," or "blue-green." Consequently, **YAX K'IN** most likely means "First Sun." The tail-like element, which reads **-ni**, functions as a phonetic complement and provides the final *n* consonant of *k'in*.

Mol (MOL): (T581 or T582[580]) A cartouche of circles (T582) with an infixed upright **MULUK** (T580) day sign.

Ch'en (EK JA'AB'): (T95:528.142 or T95:60:528.142 or T60:528[95].142 or T60:1030p[95].142) The first in a series of four "color-**KAWAK**" months that have T528 as the main sign (the "bunch of grapes" that may represent a rainy sky and stands for the day **KAWAK**). **CH'EN** takes one of four symbols for colors, in this case **EK'** "black" (T95; designated primarily by cross-hatching). Since the month takes a "knot" prefix with the value **ji-**, and because it lacks the T116 **-ni** sign, the **KAWAK** sign reads **JA'AB'** "year." Hence the complete sign reads "black year." A personified version from Tikal has the "black" crosshatching across the front half of the face.

Yax (YAX JA'AB'): (T16:528 or T16:528.142) The second "color-**KAWAK**" month. Like **CH'EN**, the month sign **YAX** includes the "bunch of grapes" **KAWAK** (T528) prefixed by the color symbol **YAX** (T16) meaning "blue" or "blue-green" and sometimes "first." Hence, **YAX JA'AB'**—the month sign's hieroglyphic name—means "blue year" or "blue-green year."

Sak (SAK JA'AB'): (T58:528 or T58:60:528 or T58:60:528.142) The third "color-**KAWAK**" month. Like **CH'EN** and **YAX**, the month sign **SAK** combines **KAWAK** (T528) with a color symbol, in this case **SAK** "white" (T58), with the whole perhaps reading **SAK JA'AB'**, "white year."

Kej (CHAK JA'AB'): (T109:528) The fourth "color-**KAWAK**" month. Like **CH'EN**, **YAX**, and **SAK**, the month sign **KEJ** combines the **KAWAK** (T528) sign with a color symbol, in this case the color "red." The complete glyph probably reads **CHAK JA'AB'** "red year."

Mak (MAK): (T74:556.25 or T502.25.25 or T74:626v or T74:566) The main sign of **MAK** can be the T502 variant of **IMIX** infixed with T533 **AJAW**, which reads phonetically **ma-**. Another closely related but confusing sign takes the T556 variant, which has an infixed crosshatched arch and reads **ja-**. Most versions "spell out" the month name **MAK**, as in T74:556.25 **ma-ja-ka** or T502.25.25 **ma-ka-ka**. In an alternate version, the elements T556 or T502 are replaced by a turtle shell that has the value **AK**, for **ma-AK**.

K'ank'in (UNEW): (T559.130) The symbolic form represents a tree flanked on the left by a crosshatched area, while the T130 phonetic complement **-wa** reflects the Ch'ol version of the name (*unew*). An unidentified animal serves as the personified variant.

Muwan (MUWAN): (T593b or T593b.116) As in a host of other examples where the name ends in **n**, the month sign **MUWAN** takes the T116 **-ni** phonetic complement. Known only in its head variant form and phonetic spelling, the depicted creature represents the mythological Muwan Bird, an owl combined with some other avian form.

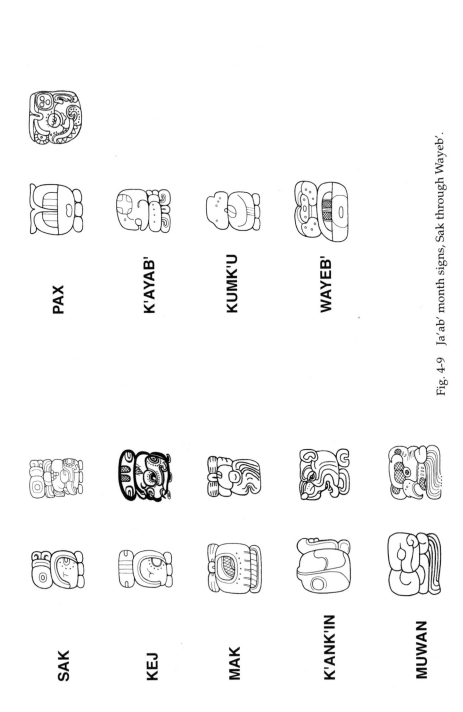

PAX

K'AYAB'

KUMK'U

WAYEB'

SAK

KEJ

MAK

K'ANK'IN

MUWAN

Fig. 4-9   Ja'ab' month signs, Sak through Wayeb'.

Pax (PAX): (T549 or T549.142) Incorporates the **TUN** year sign with a bifurcated plant-like element sprouting from the center and parting over the top. In the personified form the same element sprouts from the top of the head of a zoomorphic creature with jagged teeth, possibly a frog or iguana combined with attributes of the jaguar.

K'ayab' (K'ANASI): (T743[281].57.126) Generally identified as the head of a parrot or macaw and assigned the value **aj/AJ**, the main sign takes a T281 **K'AN** cross infixed over the eye, and rests above the sequence T57.126 or **si-ya**. This collocation renders **K'AN-aj-si-yi** or *k'anasi*, clearly spelling the Ch'ol version of the name.

Kumk'u (KUMK'U): (T155:506) Combines the **K'AN** day sign with the superfix T155 (of uncertain value), and hence would seem to spell something other than **KUMK'U**. Landa's version gives the prefixes **ku-** and **k'u**, a fairly sure indication that the Classic version used in the inscriptions had a different value than its form in Yucatec.

Wayeb' (WAYEB'): (T157:548) The final five-day period or "short month" of the Ja'ab' or 365-day calendar. Considered unlucky, the final days were looked to with dread. The glyph takes the **TUN** period sign, surmounted by the glyph for "hole" (T157)—signifying the "black hole" at the center of the night sky on the evening of Creation. *Way* has the connotation of "vision" and "spirit," or "dreaming," but with overtones of "to sleep." **WAYEB'** may be the "sleeping period" of the year, before the cycle starts over from the beginning.

How the Calendar Round Works

As described earlier, the two sets that comprise the Calendar Round intermesh to form a single statement, as in our example 11 Ajaw and 8 Sek. The combined cycles of numbers, days, and months identify a day within a month within a Long Count year.

The total number of permutations of the Tzolk'in-Ja'ab' combination is 18,980 days, or fifty-two years. In other words, there are 18,980 possible number-day-month combinations. What this means is that any given position, such as 11 Ajaw 8 Sek, repeats only every fifty-two years, lending the system its nickname, the "Fifty-Two Year Cycle." Fifty-two years will elapse until the calendar again reaches the position 11 Ajaw 8 Sek.

The following gives a short segment of Calendar Round positions to illustrate how the two sets of cycles progress:

TZOLK'IN	JA'AB'	
11 Ajaw	8 Sek	
12 Imix	9 Sek	
13 Ik'	10 Sek	
1 Akb'al	11 Sek	
2 K'an	12 Sek	
3 Chikchan	13 Sek	
4 Kimi	14 Sek	
5 Manik'	15 Sek	
6 Lamat	16 Sek	
7 Muluk	17 Sek	
8 Ok	18 Sek	
9 Chuwen	19 Sek	
10 Eb'	0 Xul	**First day of month Xul**
11 B'en	1 Xul	
12 Ix	2 Xul	
13 Men	3 Xul	
1 Kib'	4 Xul	
2 Kab'an	5 Xul	
3 Etz'nab'	6 Xul	
4 Kawak	7 Xul	
5 Ajaw	8 Xul	
6 Imix	9 Xul	
7 Ik'	10 Xul	
8 Akb'al	11 Xul	
9 K'an	12 Xul	
10 Chikchan	13 Xul	
11 Kimi	14 Xul	
12 Manik'	15 Xul	
13 Lamat	16 Xul	
1 Muluk	17 Xul	

Because of the Calendar Round's mathematical properties, the month number or coefficient can occur with one of only four possible day names. Thus, the "1st" of any month can occur only with the day signs **ETZ'NAB'**, **AKB'AL**, **LAMAT**, or **B'EN**. These limitations provide a useful check for damaged CR dates. You can have 5 Ajaw 3 Mol, but *never* 5 Ajaw 4 Mol, since only the numbers 3, 8, 13, or 18 occur with the day **AJAW**. The following chart gives a concordance of month coefficients and day signs. Only the four numbers shown to the right can occur with the four day sign names shown on the same line to the left.

Kab'an, Ik', Manik', Eb'	seating,	5th,	10th,	15th
Etz'nab', Akb'al, Lamat, B'en	1st,	6th,	11th,	16th
Kawak, K'an, Muluk, Ix	2nd,	7th,	12th,	17th
Ajaw, Chikchan, Ok, Men	3rd,	8th,	13th,	18th
Imix, Kimi, Chuwen, Kib'	4th,	9th,	14th,	19th

The Initial Series: Putting Everything Together

As we have seen, in a large number of hieroglyphic texts the Initial Series comes first, which consists of the Long Count year position (equivalent to the Gregorian year position, as in 2001) and the Calendar Round day and month (equivalent to January 1). The Calendar Round contains four components in two sets: Set 1 includes a series of thirteen repeating numbers (1–13) and twenty day names (**IMIX** through **AJAW**) ($13 \times 20 = 260$), while Set 2 includes a series of numbers 0 through 19 and eighteen named months with a final five-day unlucky period ($20 \times 18 + 5 = 365$). Both sets combine to form the 52-Year Cycle. In an Initial Series, the five-period Long Count comes first, then the usually two-part Calendar Round.

A few "subtleties" provide checks and balances on the Initial Series. First, only certain number-month combinations can coincide with certain Long Count days. Another handy feature is that whatever the number in the Long Count **K'IN** position, it will coincide with the order of the day sign. Thus, if the **K'IN** is 1, the day sign in the Tzolk'in position *has* to be **IMIX**. If the **K'IN** position is 2, the day sign *must* be **IK'**. When the **K'IN** position contains 0, the day position *must* be **AJAW**. Since the Long Count contains a total of 20 **K'INS** (0 through 19), the number in the **K'IN** position will *always* correspond to its appropriate day sign.

1 **K'IN**	Imix
2 **K'IN**	Ik'
3 **K'IN**	Akb'al
4 **K'IN**	K'an
5 **K'IN**	Chikchan
etc.	etc.

The Calendar Round functioned as a pervasive system in Maya inscriptions, and could stand alone without support from a preceding Long Count. Likely initiated outside the Maya area in relatively remote times, and perhaps first carved on monuments at Monte Alban around 600 B.C., the Tzolk'in had roots extremely deep in the past. It was adapted by a diverse assortment of Mesoamerican cultures that included the "Epi-Olmecs" and the central Mexican cultures of the Late Post Classic, including the Aztecs, Zapotecs, and Mixtecs, and continues to be used today among the modern Maya of highland Guatemala and Chiapas—a span of at least 2,600 years. So sacred was the Calendar Round that the Aztecs focused their most crucial ritual on the return of the 52-year period—the New Fire Ceremony, which insured the continuance of life on earth—an event most individuals saw only once in their lifetime. The 52-year Calendar Round lay at the heart of Mesoamerican civilization, representing its beliefs and its continuity. As Linda Schele once expressed, to be Mesoamerican *was* to use the Calendar Round.[2]

NOTES

1. The length of the year is approximately 365 days, 5 hours, 48 minutes, and 46 seconds, counted between one vernal equinox and the next. Hence an error accrues in the 365-day *ja'ab'* at the rate of slightly more than one day every four years, which our own Gregorian calendar accounts for by interpolating a leap year. As far as scholars know, no such interpolation, or "determinative," was allowed for in the Maya calendar, and hence the *ja'ab'* fell out of sync with the seasons at a regular rate.
2. Personal communication 1986, the Blood of Kings symposium, Kimbell Art Museum, Fort Worth, Texas.

CHAPTER 5

———

The Supplementary and Other Series

The Long Count and Calendar Round comprise most of the Initial Series, but an additional sequence called the **Supplementary Series** is usually placed between the Tzolk'in and Ja'ab' and separates them within the text. Hence, the two components of the Calendar Round only sometimes occur back-to-back. While a novice can make do with a thorough knowledge of the Long Count and Calendar Round, the Supplementary Series supplies important checks on the calendar system as a whole, vital to anyone attempting the decipherment of badly eroded texts.

The Supplementary Series consists of a cycle of nine days called the **Lords of the Night,** together with a **Lunar Series** that keeps track of the phases of the moon. Long inscriptions can also include a rare **819-Day Count** related to the cardinal directions, and an even more rare **Seven-Day Cycle**. Glyphs of the Supplementary Series were assigned letters by Sylvanus G. Morley in the 1910s, and occur in descending order from **G** through **A**. In addition, the variable **Glyph C** accompanies a sign group called **Glyph X** that "names" the particular lunation. The **Seven Day Cycle**[1] carries the letters **Y** and **Z**.

Lords of the Night

First identified by J. Eric S. Thompson in the late 1920s, the **Lords of the Night** sequence represents the equivalent of a nine-day week, where nine separate glyphs repeat in sequence and correspond to the nine governing lords of the Underworld. Since each Lord of the Night repeats endlessly without interruption, any given Long Count or Calendar Round combination has a corresponding glyph from the Lords of the Night sequence. Thus the Long Count and Calendar Round combination 9.17.0.0.0 13 Ajaw 18 Kumk'u takes the last in the series, God Nine or **G9**. The position 9.17.0.0.1 1 Imix 19 Kumk'u takes **G1**, and the following day, 9.17.0.0.2 2 Ik' 0 Wayeb, takes **G2**. The mathematical properties of the calendar systems are such that if the **K'IN** and **WINAL** positions of the Long Count are 0, the Lord of the Night has to be G9. Since any of the 18,980 possible Calendar Round dates in the 52-Year Cycle coincide with a given Lord of the Night only once in 467 years and slightly more than eight months (170,820 or $260 \times 365 \times 9$), the presence of a glyph from the Lords of the Night sequence can provide an extremely valuable check when attempting to decipher a partially damaged Calendar Round or Initial Series date. A given Lord of the Night can identify the date, even when one or more components are missing.

Each of the nine separate "G" glyphs or "gods" in the Lords of the Night series usually occurs with a constant glyph called **Glyph F**. Often, however, glyphs **G** and **F** merge to form a single **Glyph G/F** combination.

Glyph F: (T128:60.23 or T128:609b.125 òr T128:740.23 or T128:60:1000) In its most common symbolic form, **Glyph F** incorporates the T60 "knot" sign that has the value *jun*, superfixed by a bracket usually read **ch'a-** or **k'a-**, and subfixed with T23 **-na**. An additional symbolic variant replaces the knot with the depiction of a Maya book or codex replete with jaguar-pelt covers, thought to read **JUN** or "paper." The Maya clearly intended a visual pun or "rebus" of the word *jun*, and Glyph F therefore probably reads *ch'a jun*. Recent decipherments have shown that the T60 "knot" corresponds to the barkpaper headband tied over the ruler's forehead during installation as ruler, and that the Glyph G/F combination refers to the "tying on" of the "barkpaper headband of rulership" by each of the nine Lords of the Underworld in succession. Thus the glyphic sequence **CH'A JUN** means in effect "he tied on the barkpaper headband," with the subject—the person who did the tying on—being the Lord of the Night appropriate to the date. The sequence states that a specific Lord of the Night ruled over a particular date. The personified form of Glyph F merely substitutes for the knot or codex the head of the young lord who represents **AJAW**, the Sun God known as Jun Ajaw, or "One Ajaw." Still other personified forms of Glyph F use the "upended birth frog" read **ju-** (T740), or take the head of a zoomorphic creature.

Fig. 5-1   Lords of the Night: Glyph F.

The nine **Lords of the Night:**

G1: (TIX:41:670 or TIX:35:1016:670) A hand holding God C^2 (T1060) and one of the "blood group" affixes (T32 through T40).[3] **G1** always takes a coefficient consisting of a bar and four dots, or "nine"—not to be confused with G9, the last glyph in the Lords of the Night sequence.

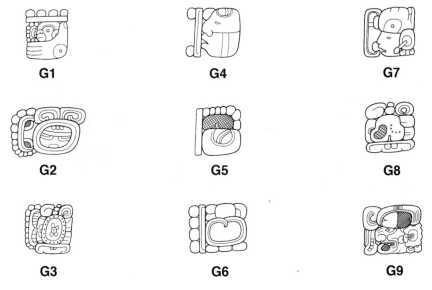

Fig. 5-2   Lords of the Night: Glyphs 1 through 9.

G2: (T1:86:675 or T45:86:709) Consists usually of a sign that resembles the **TUN** glyph of the Long Count, with the "centipede segment" T45 as its prefix. **G2** seems never to take a coefficient. (Alternatively, because of the bad preservation of existing examples, **G2** may take the number two or three.)

G3: (T583 or T624) All known examples appear conflated with Glyph F. Consists of either a "shield" or "propeller" glyph (T583 or T624) infixed within Glyph F. A zoomorphic head, which resembles a bird-like creature, can replace the "propeller" as the personified variant.

G4: (T506hv) In personified form the main sign resembles a head variant of the day sign **K'AN** (T506). The symbolic form can take either the same main sign as G2, or an element that resembles the "Moon Sign" (T181). **Glyph G4** always takes as its numerical coefficient a bar and two dots, or "seven."

G5: (TV:[617]:582) The main sign depicts an obsidian lancet or mirror either outlined with circles or infixed within a "blood group" sign or within an element similar to the day sign **MOL**. The arched bands in the "mirror" evidently denote the glint of the polished stone.[4] **G5** can sometimes take T45 as a superfix, while the "personified" form seems to represent a variant of God C (T1016). **Glyph G5** always takes a single bar for a coefficient of "five."

G6: (TIX:267:574.?) A very rare sign, **Glyph G6** incorporates the profile view of a univalve shell that usually signifies the **K'IN** position in **Distance Numbers** (see Chapter 6).

G7: (T4.?) Relatively rare, the single diagnostic feature of **Glyph G7** seems to be T4, which functions as an affix that reads **NA-** "first." However, the main sign can sometimes incorporate a conflation of T58 **SAK** "white" with T709 **SAB'AK**, a glyph that seems to refer to paint or ink (hence, "white ink"). Whether the "young man" head form represents a true variant or a conflation with Glyph F remains debatable, but another variant incorporates the head form of the number two—a male profile with hand on top. Since **NA-** signifies "first," T4 may function as **G7**'s numerical coefficient.

G8: (T155) The cross-section of a stylized shell, usually with an infixed crosshatched area on the left or right, which may be the same element used for the superfix in the month sign Kumk'u (T155). Shells represent the interior of the earth and by extension the Underworld. Never occurs with a numerical coefficient.

G9: (T135:544 or T135:544.116 or T86?:545.126) The most common of all glyphs in the Lords of the Night series because it will always correspond to zero *k'in*, **G9** incorporates a **K'IN** flower symbol that represents the Sun

God (T544) and is sometimes "darkened" with crosshatching (T545). The prefix may represent three *tamales* (T135), and the **K'IN** sometimes takes the "tail" T116 **ni-** as its phonetic complement. The head variant depicts an old man who wears the **K'IN** flower on his head and probably represents the "aged" Sun God. **G9** never takes a numerical coefficient.

While the two series of the Long Count and Lords of the Night do not advance continuously in step with each other as the **K'IN** position and Tzolk'in do, any given Lord of the Night can be predicted mathematically from a legible Long Count by adding the days recorded in the Long Count's **WINAL** position and **K'IN** position. Simply convert the **WINAL** position to days by multiplying the **WINAL** coefficient times 20 (the number of days in each **WINAL**), then add the whole numbers thus obtained with the coefficient in the **K'IN** position. For example, if the Long Count reads 9.15.5.6.2, multiply 6 × 20 for a total of 120, add the 1 and 2 in 120 to obtain 3, then add 3 to the **K'IN** coefficient of 2, for a total of 5. For the Long Count 9.15.5.6.2, the Lord of the Night has to be **G5**.

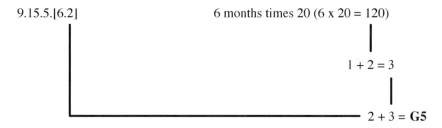

9.15.5.|6.2| 6 months times 20 (6 x 20 = 120)

1 + 2 = 3

2 + 3 = **G5**

Fig. 5-3   Lords of the Night formula.

Because they are linked with the royal headband, many features of individual glyphs in the Lords of the Night series have associations with barkpaper (out of which the royal headbands were made), to codices (which were made from specially prepared barkpaper), and to writing or painting. The cycle was first brought to notice when Thompson demonstrated a relationship with the Nine Lords of the Underworld series of the Aztecs of Central Mexico, further evidence of the close interrelationship of belief systems throughout Mesoamerica.

Since the **K'IN** position on Yaxchilán Stela 11 records the day **AJAW**, the Lord of the Night position should read G9, which is what we find at C1 (left half). Glyph F overlaps and partly obscures the sign.

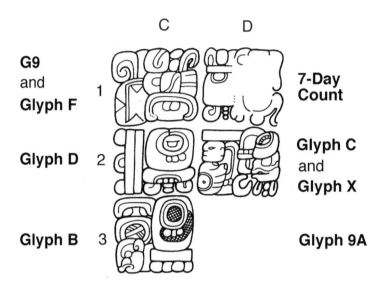

Fig. 5-4   Yaxchilán Stela 11, front, lower glyph panel, Supplementary Series.

Lunar Series

In addition to the Lords of the Night cycle, the Supplementary Series that follows the Tzolk'in can incorporate still other cycles, extending a date even longer. The more common cycles include a series of components referred to collectively as the **Lunar Series**, basically consisting of three lunar notations and their companion glyphs. One sequence indicates the "age" of the moon—that is, the number of elapsed days since the moon's dark period. Another sequence gives the completed cycles of the moon out of a series of six lunations. A final sequence tells how long the current moon will last—either 29 or 30 days.

The Lunar Series was perhaps the most accurate of the Maya calendars, keeping fairly regular track of the moon and often "recalculated" to keep the Lunar Series in step with actual lunar phases (similar to adding a leap year). In contrast, the Ja'ab' or solar calendar fell out of sync with the actual length of the year for lack of an interpolated day every fourth year   ·
(see Chapter 3).

CURRENT AGE OF THE MOON

Glyph E: Gives the age of the moon by combining a numerical coefficient up to and including nine (a bar and four dots) with a variant of the "Moon Sign" (T683) that has the value "twenty." Thus if **Glyph E** includes three dots together with the "Moon Sign," the age of the moon on the date recorded in the Long Count is twenty-three days.

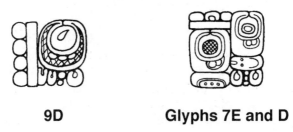

9D　　　　　　　**Glyphs 7E and D**

Fig. 5-5　Age of the moon.

Glyph D: Gives the age of the moon by means of an affixed numerical coefficient but only when the current moon is nineteen days or less. (Remember, this is a vegisimal system.) **Glyph D** stands alone in this case—in other words, without Glyph E. But when the moon's age exceeds nineteen, Glyph D occurs with Glyph E, described above, with the coefficient attached to the latter. Note that Glyph D may be confusing in this context because its standard form resembles the "Moon Sign" variant that represents "twenty." As the main sign of Glyph D, however, it carries an infixed "eye" and represents a different value altogether. This version reads **ju** and takes affixes that spell **ju-li-ya** or *juliy* "arrived," as do other variants of this sign. Thus Glyph D tells us that X-day of the current lunation has "arrived."

The "age of the moon" can be thought of as a "Distance Number" (see Chapter 6) that calculates so many units of a given sequence of periods, not unlike a specialized or abbreviated Long Count.[5] If the moon age is nineteen or less, Glyph D stands alone and carries the coefficient. When twenty days or more, Glyph E precedes Glyph D, and Glyph E carries the coefficient, which is added to the accompanying "Moon Sign" (T181 and 683).

On Yaxchilán Stela 11, Glyph D occurs at C2 and reads *kalajun juliy-* "the 12th day of the current lunation arrived."

LUNAR NAME

The Lunar Cycle rotates between a sequence of six lunations, or six lunar "months," and forms a calendar much closer to our own month which has an average length of thirty days. The fairly constant **Glyph C** indicates via numerical coefficient in which of the six months the Long Count falls, while the variable **Glyph X** names the month. **Glyph B** simply iterates that "this [the preceding glyph] was its [the moon's] name."

Glyph C: One of the verb or "action" glyphs that incorporates a "flat hand" (T713) preceded by a numerical coefficient, ranging from "nothing" (one of the "zero" signs) and two (instead of one) through six. Generally the "flat hand" holds one of several objects, which can be a female or male deity head, a skull, or an eye. **Glyph C** takes verbal affixes, most usually T181 **ja-** or **-aj**, marking it as a passive verb (see Chapter 8: Verbs, Verbal Inflection, and Grammatical Elements).

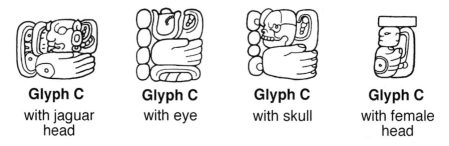

| **Glyph C** | **Glyph C** | **Glyph C** | **Glyph C** |
| with jaguar head | with eye | with skull | with female head |

Fig. 5-6   Lunar name: Glyph C variants.

Glyph X: The variable element accompanying Glyph C. Although **Glyph X** generally takes six basic forms and varies according to the month, it can take a wider range of affixes and may specify certain qualities of the moon. Recent decipherments have shown that Glyph X actually names the lunar month.

> **X1:**   A winged element (T709?) over an obsidian lancet?
>
> **X2:**   God C (T1016) with the "zero" sign (T173), usually within the maw of the Vision Serpent.
>
> **X3:**   Usually T622b above a "wing" element.

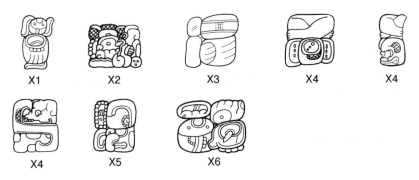

Fig. 5-7   Lunar name: Glyph X variants.

X4a: Crossed legs over a skull (T1010) or over a "Moon Sign" (T683).

X4b: The "square-nosed beastie," generally considered a symbol of Venus, and a skull.

X5:   A zoomorph usually wearing a **KAWAK** sign (T528).

X6:   Similar to **G7** of the Lords of the Night series. Sometimes includes T709, the symbol for "white" or **SAK** (T58), and a clenched hand.

Glyph B: (T1-3:187:287:110 or T1-3:187:757:110) **Glyph B** literally reads *uka'ab'a* "its name," in reference to Glyph X. Hence, Glyph X records a variable collocation that Glyph B tells us "was its name"—that is, the name of the lunar month. Consisting of the "bent elbow" glyph with crossed bands (T187) and the prefix **U** (T1) as the third-person possessive pronoun, Glyph B usually encloses a variable element or sequence of elements which are to be read separately and serve as adjectives to modify the phrase. The variable most often represents either a gopher head (T757) with T110 **ko**, which when combined read *ch'ok* "youth" or "youthful," or a pair of circles that look like eyes (T287) over T110, with the same reading. Thus the "elbow" with variable elements reads "was its youthful name." (An alternative form reads "was its divine name.")

Fig. 5-8   Lunar name: Glyph B.

The **Lunar Cycle** of six months represents a discrete phrase within the **Initial Series**, and identifies the current month by telling us metaphorically that "the headband of the Xth month was tied on," and that "X was its [the month's] name."

On Yaxchilán Stela 11, Glyph C occurs at D2a, Glyph X at D2b, and Glyph B *u k'ab'a ch'ok* "was its youthful name" at C3a.

MOON LENGTH

The final sequence in the Lunar Series, **Glyph A**, states the expected length of the current lunar month, since the month can range from twenty-nine to thirty days. Glyph A consists of the "Moon Sign" variant (T683) that incorporates a circle within its brackets and that indicates the value **K'AL** "twenty"—the same form of the "Moon Sign" that occurs in Glyph D. A coefficient of either nine or ten is added, always as a postfix—in other words, it *follows* the "Moon Sign"—for a total of either twenty-nine or thirty days. While Glyphs D–E tell how old the current moon is, and Glyphs C, B, and X name the lunation, Glyph A relates how long the current moon will last—29 or 30 days.

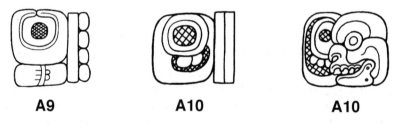

A9   **A10**   **A10**

Fig. 5-9   Moon length.

On Yaxchilán Stela 11 at C3b, Glyph A gives the length of the current lunation as twenty plus nine, or twenty-nine days.

819-Day Count

Another cycle that figures within the Initial Series notation in addition to the Calendar Round, Lords of the Night, and Lunar Series is the **819-Day Count**. The **819-Day Count** occurs very rarely (scholars know of only some fifteen examples),[6] and is based on the permutation of the important numbers 7 (the number of the earth), 9 (the number of levels in the under-world), and 13 (the number of heavens) ($7 \times 9 \times 13 = 819$). Its significance, other than its mathematical permutation, and exactly why it was used remains uncertain. What is understood is that the **819-Day Count** ties a monument's Initial Series date—which generally represents a significant historical or mythological event—to a specific "division of time." These divisions are a sequence of quadrants that each have a particular color and associated direction: east corresponds with red, west with black, north with white, and south with yellow.

To determine these quadrants the Maya calculated back in time from the Initial Series date (using what scholars call a Distance Number; see Chapter 6) to reach a Calendar Round date in the "past"—in other words, before the stated Initial Series. In this system the date "moves backwards" by so many periods (so many **K'INS, WINALS, TUNS**, and so forth) to reach the "past" or secondary Calendar Round, and the occurrence of an event that always involves a god named K'awil. The description of the event includes a reference to a particular direction and an associated color, therefore placing it in one of the four possible quadrants.

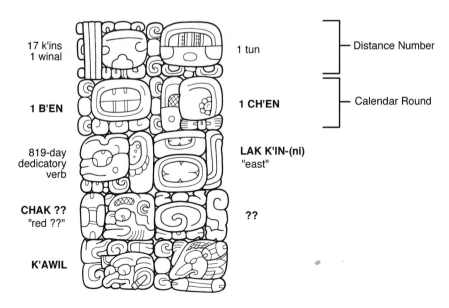

17 k'ins
1 winal

1 B'EN

819-day
dedicatory
verb

CHAK ??
"red ??"

K'AWIL

1 tun

1 CH'EN

LAK K'IN-(ni)
"east"

??

Distance Number

Calendar Round

Fig. 5-10   819-Day Count.

What is known of the properties of the **819-Day Count** is that each "K'awil event" happens during intervals of multiples of 819. As 13 is one of the multipliers of the 819-day factor, the day number of the Tzolk'in always remains the same for any of the 819-day events.[7] In addition, the Calendar Round associated with the count always falls in the most recent set of 819 days before the Initial Series date (and never before that). Yet while the day number of the Tzolk'in remains the same, the actual day name falls behind by one day with each set of 819 (instead of running Imix, Ik', Akb'al, K'an, it runs Imix, Ajaw, Kawak, Etz'nab'). Because any given day always co-occurs with the same color-direction, with only four possible directions, the color-direction sequence constitutes a separate cycle of four days. It follows that the 4-day color-direction cycle and the 819-day cycle create a permutation series of 3,276 days (4 × 819) that cycles as relentlessly as all other calendar systems in use, and that can be used to predict the nearest earlier 819-day station (the Calendar Round position) and its associated direction and color with respect to any given Initial Series, regardless of whether the Maya actually recorded the station or not.

No 819-Day Count occurs on Yaxchilán Stela 11.

Glyphs Y and Z

A **7-Day Count**, referred to by the letters **Y** and **Z,** ran concurrently with all of the other cycles of the Maya calendars. Even more rare than the 819-Day Count, Glyphs Y and Z cycle through coefficients 1 through 7 in a kind of secondary "week." Glyphs Y and Z, when present, generally follow the Lords of the Night series.

Glyph Y   **Glyph Z**

Fig. 5-11   Glyphs Y and Z.

Glyph Z: Consists of a coefficient 1 through 7, a cartouche (T580) infixed with T585 **b'i-**, and the verbal inflection T126 **ya-**, while the personified form depicts a skull with **b'i-** over the brow.

Glyph Y: Called the "flattened roadkill toad," **Glyph Y** functions as an optional compound that supplements Glyph Z.

On Yaxchilán Stela 11, the 7-Day Count occurs in the partially eroded position at D1, with "six" given as the coefficient of Glyph Z.

Glyph Z  **Glyph Y**

Fig. 5-12   Yaxchilán Stela 11, front, lower glyph panel, D1, Glyphs Z and Y.

Putting It All Together

To see how the Supplementary Series works within the context of the complete Initial Series, we can again turn to Yaxchilán Stela 11 where the Initial Series occupies the positions A1 to D3. A1–B1 carries the ISIG, while the Long Count runs just below it from A2 to A3 and reads "nine *pij* (*b'aktuns*), sixteen *k'atuns*, one *tun*, zero *winals*, and zero *k'ins*" (9.16.1.0.0). The Tzolk'in follows at B4, and because the *k'in* position of the Long Count stands at zero, the day sign is **AJAW**. Its coefficient includes two bars and one dot, or "eleven," for 11 Ajaw. Next comes the Lord of the Night (at C1), in this case G9 because the day sign reads **AJAW**, while Glyphs Z and Y occur at D1 and designate the sixth day of the 7-day week. The moon had arrived twelve days ago, as explained by Glyph D, with Glyph C following at D2a, then the undeciphered name of the lunation at D2b, and the statement *u k'ab'a ch'ok* "was its youthful name" at C3a. The expected length of the lunation, Glyph A (C3b) is given as twenty-nine days. The final statement of the Long Count, the Ja'ab' position at D3, reads 8 Sek.

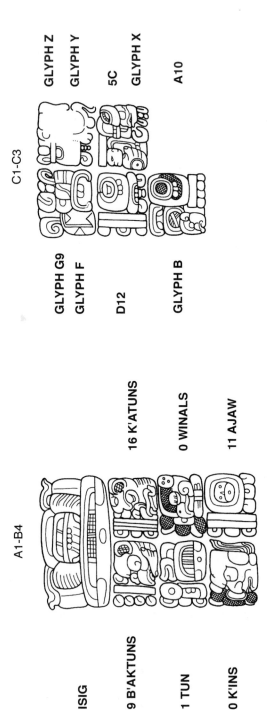

ISIG

9 B'AKTUNS

1 TUN

0 K'INS

A1-B4

16 K'ATUNS

0 WINALS

11 AJAW

GLYPH G9
GLYPH F

D12

GLYPH B

C1-C3

GLYPH Z
GLYPH Y

5C
GLYPH X

A10

Fig. 5-13 Yaxchilán Stela 11, front, lower glyph panel, Initial Series, Tzolk'in, and Supplementary Series.

NOTES

1. To my knowledge, the "Seven Day Cycle" was given this name by Tom and Carolyn Jones of Humboldt State University, Arcata, California. Jones and Jones (1997): 31.
2. Names of gods designated by letters of the alphabet refer to a system developed near the end of the nineteenth century by Paul Schellhas from studies of the surviving Maya codices.
3. The Thompson catalog number that expresses the combination of God C and a "blood group" affix can be rendered as T32-40:1016 or more simply T41. The "blood group" affixes incorporate dots usually interpreted as blood, water, grain, seed, or incense-pellets. Epigraphers usually identify the glyph as blood, although others, including certain art historians, disagree.
4. Such bands evidently symbolize "reflectivity" or a polished surface.
5. Jones and Jones (1997): 34.
6. Ibid.
7. Ibid.: 34–35.

CHAPTER 6

Period Endings and Distance Numbers

Period Endings

The majority of Maya cities recorded Initial Series or Long Count notations throughout most of the Classic Period. Others, such as Tikal, recorded relatively few Initial Series, providing instead only Calendar Round notations or simply the Tzolk'in position. Because the Calendar Round repeats every fifty-two years, the date sometimes remains uncertain when only the Tzolk'in and Ja'ab' have been given. The advantage of only writing the Calendar Round is the brevity achieved and the considerable space saved. The disadvantage is the potential for ambiguity.

Fortunately, the Maya often provided additional information to narrow the possibilities, specifying that the date—for example, 11 Ajaw 8 Sek—recorded an "end of *tun*" (when the lower positions stand at zero, as in 9.16.1.0.0). Other examples might supply the information "end of the tenth *k'atun*" and so forth. Because 11 Ajaw 8 Sek occurs as an "end of *tun*" only once per *b'aktun* cycle, or 13 × 400 years, and only one Calendar Round can hold this position, the Long Count must fall on the date 9.16.1.0.0, and no other. In this way, the Maya could tie a Calendar Round notation to a year unequivocally, without actually writing the Long Count itself. Epigraphers refer to this shorthand system as a **Period Ending**—any date where, at minimum, the *k'in* and *winal* are at "zero," but more often where the position represents a major calendrical node. The bad preservation of many monuments, however, can render such additions illegible, usually due to erosion or intentional damage by the Maya. And of course, not all Calendar Round dates express a Period Ending, and their corresponding Long Count must be discerned from context (see below: Distance Numbers).

All of the major nodes of the Long Count were potential Period Endings. Every *k'atun* completed, every fifth, tenth, and fifteenth *tun*, and every third *tun* of any *k'atun* became special occasions, frequently celebrated by the dedication and erection of stelae or other monuments.[1] Positions such as 9.15.0.0.0 (*k'atun* ending), 9.15.10.0.0 (half-*k'atun* or ten-*tun* ending), 9.16.5.0.0 (fifth *tun* of a *k'atun*), and 9.16.15.0.0 (fifteenth *tun* or "five *tun* lacking") are examples of Period Endings, where the *k'in* and *winal* stand at zero, and either the *k'atun*, half-*k'atun*, quarter-*k'atun*, or three-quarter-*k'atun* ending was memorialized.

Notice that all Period Endings, as multiples of twenty, fall on the day Ajaw, just as any instance where the *k'in* position stands at zero.

Period Completed: (T218.17) Consists usually of two glyphs. The first collocation includes a hand shown "flat" and from the back (T713a) or with fingers curled against the palm (T713b), together with a "tassel" postfix (T165) and the subfix **-yi** (T17). An alternative version substitutes for the hand and tassel the head of a leaf-nosed bat turned upside down. The whole reads **TZUTZ-yi** or *tzutziy* "it ended." The second collocation incorporates a period glyph, generally the **K'ATUN** or **B'AKTUN** sign, as well as a coefficient, with the whole expression prefixed by the third-person possessive pronoun **U** (T1-3) that also converts cardinal numbers to ordinals. Consequently the **Period Completed** glyph reads, "It ended, the seventeenth *tun*," "It ended, the fourteenth *k'atun*," and so on.

a   b

Fig. 6-1   **TZUTZ-yi**: a) hand with tassel variant;
b) leaf-nosed bat variant.

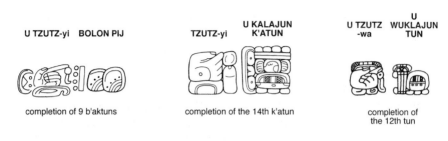

U TZUTZ-yi BOLON PIJ

completion of 9 b'aktuns

TZUTZ-yi U KALAJUN K'ATUN

completion of the 14th k'atun

U TZUTZ -wa U WUKLAJUN TUN

completion of the 12th tun

Fig. 6-2   Period Completed.

Ordinal-Numbered Periods: Incorporates the prefix **U** (principally T1-3, T13, and T204) and a numbered period glyph (**TUN, K'ATUN**). The presence of a *u* prefix converts any number to an ordinal: fifth, tenth, fifteenth, and so on, as opposed to five, ten, fifteen. Thus in **ordinal-numbered periods** we have "the thirteenth *tun*," "the fifteenth *k'atun*," "the tenth *b'aktun*."

the 13th tun   the 15th k'atun   the 15th k'atun

Fig. 6-3   Ordinal-numbered periods.

Tun Endings: The **KAWAK** sign (T528) functions as the *tun* in Period Endings (but never in the Long Count): "*tun* completed," "*tun* seated," "the *jotun*" (fifth *tun*), and "*jotun* lacking" (the fifteenth *tun*). While T528 represents the day sign **KAWAK**, it also functions, depending on context and the affixes it possesses, as **JA'AB'**. It can also function as the phonetic sign **ku**, and when doubled, as the phonetic sign for **pi**. Iconographically, when found in artistic, non-linguistic contexts, it functions as the symbol for "stone," or *tun*. Thus, the sign generally read **KAWAK** (T528) is said to be **polyvalent** and has different values depending on context (much as soft "ch" in "church" becomes hard "ch" in the last name Cocheran). In Period Endings, the **KAWAK** day sign takes an element that resembles a wing but more probably represents a tail and reads -**ni** (T116). Ni functions as a phonetic complement in "**TUN** ending" glyphs, to cue the reader that here **KAWAK** (which ends in *k*) becomes **TUN** (which ends in *n*). In other words, there are various ways to read **KAWAK**, but the Maya provided clues as to which was the intended meaning.

T528   **TUN-(ni)**

Fig. 6-4   T528 and **TUN-(ni)**.

Tun Completed: Represents a hand (T713) holding a "winged **KAWAK**" (T528 with -**ni**) and prefixed with the third-person possessive pronoun **U** (T1-3 or its variants). As explained above, the "tail/wing" phonetic complement indicates which of several values **KAWAK** has. The hand may read **K'AL** "bound, tied," likely referring to the process of binding the stone with hauling ropes preparatory to raising the stone upright. Early decipherments suggested that **Tun Completed** regularly accompanies Period Endings, and epigraphers have come to interpret the compound as a reference to the dedication of the monument itself—the erection of a stela—rather than a reference to the *quality* of the date.

Fig. 6-5   Tun Completed.

Tun Seated: Consists of the verb usually called the "Seating Glyph" (read **CHUM**) which otherwise functions as "zero" in the sense of "beginning" (as opposed to the other kind of "zero," which is "completion") in most contexts. In the **Tun Seated** compound, the Seating Glyph precedes or is conflated with the "winged" **KAWAK** or TUN sign (read **TUN-(ni)**). The whole therefore reads **CHUM TUN-ni** or *chum tun*. **Tun Seated** can also take **wa** (T130) and other suffixes as grammatical verbal inflections, and sometimes **ya** (T126) as the "background marker" indicating the event took place in the past. Thus we have such variations as **CHUM-wa TUN-(ni)** (*chumwan tun*), **CHUM TUN wa-n(i)** (*chum tun wan*), and **CHUM-wa-ni-ya** (*chumwaniy*).

CHUM-[mu]

TUN
-(ni)

Fig. 6-6   Tun Seated.

Ox Tun: Double **KAWAK** with the superfix T124 **tzi** from the ISIG (Initial Series Introducing Glyph) and the prefix T16 **YAX** "first," "green," or "blue-green." Although full decipherment continues to elude epigraphers, it remains clear that the collocation functions as a Period Ending glyph in a few rare instances of "three-**TUN**" dates (as on Tikal Temple I Lintel 3, with the date 9.13.3.0.0).

Fig. 6-7   Third Tun.

First Jotun: The "winged" **KAWAK** glyph (T528 with T116 **-(ni)** phonetic complement), prefixed with **na-** or "first" (T4 or T48) and incorporating a bar for "five." Scholars gloss the collocation as "the first *jotun*" or "the fifth *tun* of the current *k'atun*" (for example, 9.15.5.0.0).

Fig. 6-8   First Jotun.

Half Period Completed: Incorporates the lower half of the "completion" or "zero" sign (T173, in the sense of "ending"). Denotes "the tenth *tun* of the *k'atun*" (for example, 9.15.10.0.0), and may read **LAM-ja**.

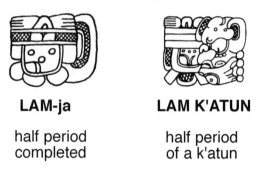

LAM-ja   **LAM K'ATUN**

half period   half period
completed   of a k'atun

Fig. 6-9   Half Period Completed.

Jotun Lacking: In effect, "the fifteenth *tun* of the *k'atun*," but evidently functions as "five *tun* lacking [until the completion of the *k'atun*]" (as in 9.15.15.0.0).

Fig. 6-10   Jotun Lacking.

As stated earlier, Period Ending glyphs occur when the scribe or sculptor recorded the Calendar Round by itself, without the Long Count. In this context, a Period Ending serves to anchor the Calendar Round without having to write out the **B'AKTUN**, **K'ATUN**, and so forth of the complete Long Count. A Calendar Round with a Period Ending fixes the date unequivocally, though occasionally a Period Ending follows the Long Count as redundant information.

Period Endings represent the great milestones of the Maya calendar, the pretext for commissioning monuments and other celebrations. Kings recounted their lives in terms of Period Endings, and Maya texts often focus on or "revolve around" such important nodes.

Distance Numbers

Most simply put, **Distance Numbers** add or subtract specific quantities of time from a previous date given in the text—so many quantities of the *k'atun, tun, winal,* and *k'in* positions—in order to reach a new date. Once the text provides an Initial Series (or alternatively a Calendar Round with a Period Ending), the text will characteristically move forward or backward in time to reach this new date. Such simple equations can occur repeatedly within a text, depending upon the length of the inscription, leading years and often epochs into the past and future. In this way a continuous narrative time sequence develops, without having to write additional Long Counts for every date recorded. The Long Count position of any "terminal" date reached by the Distance Number can be quickly calculated simply by referring to the original Long Count.

In the Initial Series, the Long Count proceeds in *descending* order—**B'AKTUN, K'ATUN, TUN, WINAL,** and **K'IN.** But as a rule, in Distance Numbers the time periods *ascend* in order—**K'IN, WINAL, TUN,** and so on. Like the Initial Series, the Distance Number has an "introductory glyph," and both introductory glyph and Distance Number stand out clearly within the text.

Distance Number Introducing Glyph: Like the ISIG (Initial Series Introducing Glyph), the **DNIG** "announces" in the manner of a "prologue" that a Distance Number calculation follows. In most cases it consists of the main sign that was earlier nicknamed the *"hel* glyph" (T573), but which has been deciphered most recently as **TZ'AK.** T573 resembles a swastika and generally has the meaning "change" or "succession." The DNIG also regularly takes one of the **U** possessive pronouns, and sometimes **ka** (T25), together with the subfix **-ja** (T12), and thus would read **U TZ'AK-ja** or *u tz'akaj* "its change was." Particularly interesting but rare DNIG variants

u TZ'AK-aj

u TZ'AK-(ka)-aj-ja

u IK' JA'-aj
wind and water

u EK' JA-aj
star and moon

Fig. 6-11   The Distance Number Introducing Glyph (DNIG).

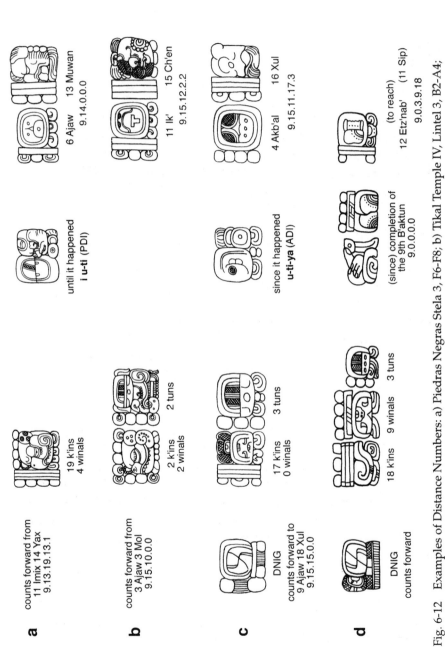

Fig. 6-12 Examples of Distance Numbers: a) Piedras Negras Stela 3, F6-F8; b) Tikal Temple IV, Lintel 3, B2-A4; c) Kuná-Lakanjá Panel 1, J5-K3; d) Tikal Stela 31, H24-G27.

a

counts forward from
11 Imix 14 Yax
9.13.19.13.1

19 k'ins
4 winals

until it happened
i u-ti (PDI)

6 Ajaw   13 Muwan
9.14.0.0.0

b

counts forward from
3 Ajaw 3 Mol
9.15.10.0.0

2 k'ins   2 tuns
2 winals

11 Ik'   15 Ch'en
9.15.12.2.2

c

DNIG
counts forward to
9 Ajaw 18 Xul
9.15.15.0.0

17 k'ins   3 tuns
0 winals

since it happened
u-ti-ya (ADI)

4 Akb'al   16 Xul
9.15.11.17.3

d

DNIG
counts forward

18 k'ins   9 winals   3 tuns

(since) completion of
the 9th B'aktun
9.0.0.0.0

(to reach)
12 Etz'nab'   (11 Sip)
9.0.3.9.18

replace T573 with "paired oppositions," for example the **IK'** "wind" sign (T503) with **JA'** "water" (T501v), and the "star" sign **EK'** (T510v) with T683 "moon" (the latter of uncertain value).

Anterior Date Indicator (ADI) (ut-i): What follow the DNIG are the periods of time that count from the preceding date. To indicate whether the periods must be added or subtracted, the scribe had a distinctive set of glyphs called the **Anterior** and **Posterior Date Indicators (ADI and PDI).** Both glyphs use the same main sign, either the glyph used as the day sign **MULUK** (T513) or the head of a fish (T738), both of which read **u** in this context. In addition, both indicators incorporate **ti** (T59), to be combined with **u** for the value **ut.** In this compound, **ut** has the meaning of an action that has already happened, as in "it happened" or "it came to pass." The variable element of the ADI, the "background marker" -**ya** (T126), expresses the concept "since," with the whole reading **u-ti-y(a)** "since it happened" or "since it came to pass." In many instances the ADI variable element **ya** attaches as a *suffix* to the following time period, for example the **WINAL** or **TUN.** In any event, **ya** as the "background marker" always occurs as a postfix, with occasionally only half the element visible and tucked away into the bottom right corner of the glyph compound.

 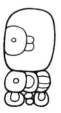 

Fig. 6-13   The Anterior Date Indicator (ADI).

In effect, the ADI has the function of telling the reader to count back-ward. Thus a Distance Number with an ADI states that a given date represents so many multiples of the **K'IN,** of the **WINAL,** of the **TUN,** and so on, between the original date and the earlier new date, enabling the Maya to discuss an event that happened in the past in relation to the Long Count or to another date. For example, the 819-Day Count discussed in Chapter 5 refers back in time from the Long Count to the closest, previous 819-Day station with its associated color and directional quadrant.

Posterior Date Indicator (PDI) (i ut): The variable element of the **PDI** (T679), which expresses the concept "until," occurs as a prefix or superfix and has the value **I**. The PDI reads *i ut* "until it happened" or "until it came to pass," indicating that a Distance Number counts *forward*. In this capacity, the PDI enabled the Maya to link several different events in a continuous chronological narrative. The PDI variable **I** element can occur as a prefix in additional compounds without the remaining PDI signs, in which case the compound functions as part of the verb with the implication that the narrative leads forward "until" the action—"until birth," "until sunrise," "until death," and so forth.

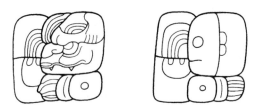

Fig. 6-14   The Posterior Date Indicator (PDI).

Future Date Indicator (FDI) (utom): Most Distance Numbers involve fairly short calculations in comparison with the Long Count, and usually link events that have taken place within a single person's lifetime. Less frequently, Distance Numbers extend over several generations and through epochs and ages that have either not yet occurred or that took place thousands, even millions of years in the past. Dates that occur in the future— that is, dates that had not *yet* taken place at the time the Maya wrote the text—have their own indicator, with the meaning "it will happen." Like *utiy* and *i ut*, the **FDI** takes either T1 or T2 **u**, but has **-to** as its superfix and a logogram with crossed-bands infixed as its main sign. The FDI reads **u-t(o)-OM-(ma)** or *utom* "it will happen."

Fig. 6-15   The Future Date Indicator (FDI).

K'IN VARIANTS IN DISTANCE NUMBERS

In addition to the usual symbolic **K'IN** "flower" sign (T544) which represents the sun, Distance Numbers make use of several specialized variants not found in the series. Each of the following can represent the period of one day:

1). An element similar to the day sign **K'AN**, which represents in this case a univalve shell in cross-section (T574), sometimes with T130 **wa**.

2). An upside-down **AJAW** day sign which may be doubled (T534, normally phonetic **la**), together with T565 **ta** or an allograph as a suffix, giving *-lat*.

3). An animal with crossbones in its eye (T765d).

4). A skull that wears T585 **b'i** over its head and has the suffix T126 **ya**. The skull-**b'i** elements probably read **B'IX**, a sequence normally confined to the 7-Day Cycle or Glyphs Y-Z.

5). The "Sunrise Glyph" that sandwiches the **K'IN** glyph between the signs for "sky" **CHAAN** (T561) and "earth" (the **KAB'AN** day sign T526). (See below, **Until Sunrise**.) The "Sunrise Glyph" probably reads **PAS**.

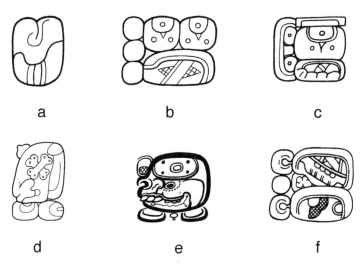

a   b   c

d   e   f

Fig. 6-16 *K'in* variants used in Distance Numbers: a) shell variant; b) **OX la-t(a)** (*ox lat*) "three days"; c) **U JO la-t(a)** (*u jo lat*) "five days"; d) animal head variant with crossed bones in eye; e) **BIX-ya**; f) "sunrise": **JUN PAS** (*jun pas*) "one day."

Until Sunrise: This especially brief Distance Number includes the PDI prefix T679 **I** "until," together with the "Sunrise Glyph" **PAS**, mentioned in the previous section, where the **K'IN** day sign that represents the sun is sandwiched between **CHAAN** "sky" and **KAB'AN** "earth" (T561:526). The combination therefore reads *i pas* "until sunrise." In effect a Distance Number of just one day, **Until Sunrise** leads forward from one day into the next, and may reflect that the day changed names at the time the sun comes up (rather than at sunset or midnight, for example).

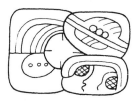

Fig. 6-17   Until Sunrise.

Suppression of Signs

For the sake of brevity, Distance Numbers will regularly delete one or more of their period signs (but retain the coefficients). In these cases the missing sign is understood as part of the count, but is "suppressed" and not shown. Generally only the **K'IN** and **WINAL** are suppressed, and more commonly just the **K'IN**. The coefficient that extends into the upper left corner of the glyph block almost always represents the number that should be read first (again generally the **K'IN** but sometimes the **WINAL**). Thus an inscription might render a two-part Distance Number such as the **K'IN** and **WINAL** by indicating the **WINAL** by itself but bracketed by its own coefficient across the top and by the **K'IN** coefficient along the left. If the coefficient missing its period sign extends all the way to the top of the glyph block, it should be read first.

Distance Numbers as Initial Series

On rare occasions Distance Numbers express an Initial Series (within the body of the text), probably for aesthetic reasons. An example occurs on the back of Tikal Stela 31, where an opening Initial Series sets the initial date

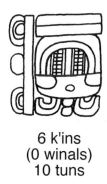

6 k'ins
(0 winals)
10 tuns

Fig. 6-18 Suppression of period glyphs in Distance Numbers.

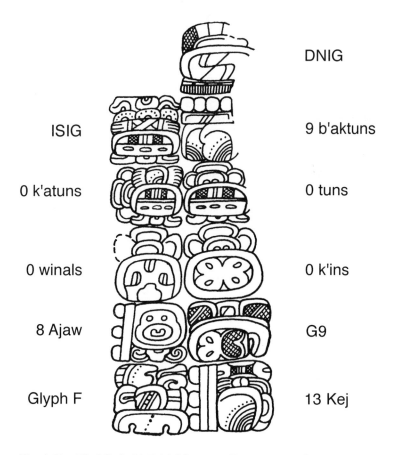

	DNIG
ISIG	9 b'aktuns
0 k'atuns	0 tuns
0 winals	0 k'ins
8 Ajaw	G9
Glyph F	13 Kej

Fig. 6-19 Tikal Stela 31, Initial Series as Distance Number, H9-H14.

of an enormous inscription of more than 200 separate glyphs. Nevertheless, the scribe provided a second Initial Series towards the end of the text, probably for the sake of variety. In such cases the Initial Series functions exactly like a Distance Number, but preserves the normal descending order of Long Count time periods (from **B'AKTUN** to **K'IN**, rather than **K'IN** to **B'AKTUN** as is the normal fashion for Distance Numbers).

Summary

Distance Numbers function as the closest counterpart that Maya writing has to punctuation marks, and structurally order the event line or sequence of events presented in the inscription. As such, Distance Numbers mark off the script's internal sentence structure or syntax and almost always indicate the beginning of an episode. The Initial Series introduces the starting event, for example a birth, and usually the protagonist, while Distance Numbers carry the narrative into a larger body of events. Around these markers of time the whole composition of an inscription revolves, as the frame or skeleton on which scribes and sculptors hung the flesh and bones of their mythic and historic epochs.

NOTE

1. New discoveries at Palenque indicate the Maya also celebrated one-eighth of a k'atun.

CHAPTER 7

Phoneticism in the Maya Script

Attempts to read Maya hieroglyphs phonetically, in terms of *language*, began almost from the first efforts to decipher the script. Some of these early endeavors were more or less successful, others failed dismally. In recent years, scholars have come to view Maya hieroglyphic writing as an independent, phonetic script that reflects spoken language in all of its complexity.

As described in the previous chapters, individual glyphic signs express either complete words (*logograms*), or function as syllables. Hence epigraphers classify the Maya script as **logo-syllabic**. Another term for this is **morpho-phonemic**, meaning that the script combines **morphemes**, units of meaning, with **phonemes**, units of sound that have no meaning by themselves.

Maya hieroglyphs combine linguistic sounds and grammar in much the same way as the Mayan language. Mayan can be classified as an *agglutinative* language, in which a succession of morphemes—the minimum units of sound that make a difference in meaning—combines to form individual words. Agglutinative languages such as those of Native Americans build up complex words from root words and attach affixes to modify or *inflect* them. In the Maya script, clusters of affixes and main signs similarly form written words.

Phoneticism most clearly distinguishes Maya hieroglyphs from other Precolumbian writing systems, including those of the Aztecs and Mixtecs.

The script not only incorporates a repertory of words, but combines these words to form complex sentences comprised of verbs, nouns, adjectives, pronouns, and so on, creating narrative texts that are phonetically "read" in the Mayan language.

While the beginner can probably best learn the phonetic signs and how these form words by plunging feet-first into the study of individual glyphs, some background on how decipherers came to understand this aspect of the writing system will help to explain how the script functions overall.

Landa's "Alphabet"

Our knowledge of the way Maya hieroglyphs function begins with the work of the sixteenth-century Franciscan priest, Diego de Landa, who recorded certain phonetic values. It was one of two singular achievements of Yuri Knorosov, the Soviet artillery spotter during World War II, to have convinced scholars of the essential correctness of Landa's hieroglyphic "alphabet," an inventory of signs erroneously repudiated for decades.

Diego de Landa, who is perhaps best known for having destroyed many of the Maya books, gathered information on the Maya while he was proselytizing in Yucatan, just after the Spanish conquest. Among his informants who offered details about Maya culture, one—a Maya lord named Gaspar Antonio Chi—provided signs for the sounds corresponding to sounds in the Spanish alphabet. This had led epigraphers to assume that Landa misunderstood the nature of the glyphs, because he was trying to render them as an alphabet. Landa, however, in his great treatise *Relación de las Cosas de Yucatan*, makes it clear that he was providing for his readers the Maya equivalent of the Spanish alphabet precisely because the script was too complex to describe anything more. In other words, Landa knew that his was a much-abbreviated version. Thus, in providing illustrations, Chi gave glyphs corresponding only to the sequence *ah*, *be*, *ce*, *de*, and so on, making no attempt to offer translations of any of the other thousand or so hieroglyphic signs.

Landa also provided, with Chi's assistance and illustrations, examples of how the script actually functioned, demonstrating the agglutinative process of the logo-syllabic system. In one case Chi wrote out the sentence "I don't wish to," rendering the signs **ma-in-ka-ti** and demonstrating how the glyphs were to be linked together to *spell out* entire ideas.

In addition, when Landa described the Maya day and month signs, together with their names, his scribe (who was probably Chi) provided a

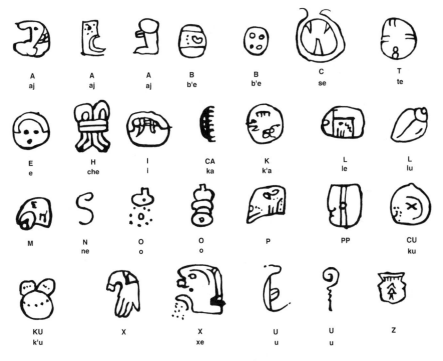

Fig. 7-1 Landa's "alphabet."

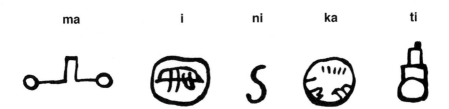

Fig. 7-2 Landa's spelling of *mainkati* "I don't want to."

series of phonetic complements to aid pronunciation. Apparently pronunciation of certain glyphs differed by the time of Landa from their Classic Period versions (see The Language of the Glyphs, below). His informant, Chi, consequently intended to write *Yucatec* Mayan, whereas originally the script reflected some form of Ch'olan. Thus Chi added complements to make them readable in Yucatec. Since we know the Yucatec values for the day and month signs, quite clearly these glyphs offer the first sound of the *Yucatec* word. Chi's phonetic complements therefore add a considerable repertoire of phonetic signs to Landa's alphabet, enabling epigraphers to roughly decipher about sixty separate glyphs from this source alone. Landa's work represents something of a Rosetta Stone, the most important clue to phoneticism in the Maya script available up to now.

Clues from the Codices

Armed with Landa's ammunition, several epigraphers during the nineteenth century tackled such inscriptions as the codices, often with impressive results. Many decipherments from this period stand the test of time, offering values based on a method that might be called "the principle of substitution" and confirming Landa's description that glyphs were strung together to form words.

Consider page 91a of the Madrid Codex as an example. There, some kind of bird dangles from a noose below a conventionalized representation of a tree that is bent toward the right. It so happens that among the four glyph blocks above the bird there occurs one of the combinations given by Landa in his explanation of the writing system. That combination, according to Landa, reads *le*, which means "noose" in the Mayan language of Yucatec. It can hardly be a coincidence that the glyphs provide the word for the noose depicted in the scene.

Similarly, the same text includes the sign given by Landa for the sound *cu* (written in today's orthography as **ku**), where it precedes an element incorporating a series of parallel horizontal lines. Suppose we assume for a moment that we will find in one of the text's glyph blocks a reference to the depicted action—in other words, a verb—and that an additional glyph functioning as a noun names to whom the action occurs. Based on the structure of Mayan languages today and in Colonial times, we know that the verb in Mayan sentences usually *precedes* the names of both the object and subject. Specifically, word order proceeds for the most part as VERB-OBJECT-SUBJECT. Therefore we would expect one of the earlier

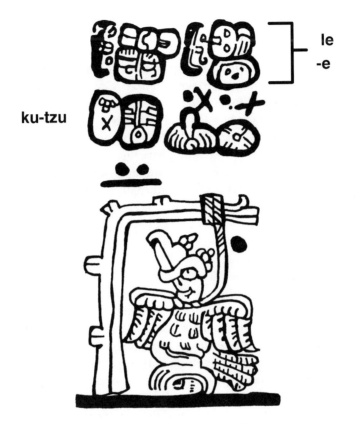

ku-tzu   le
            -e

Fig. 7-3   Madrid Codex, Page 91a.

e   le   e   le

Fig. 7-4   Landa's spelling of *le* "noose."

glyphs in the inscription to contain the verb and one or more of the following glyphs to contain at least one name. Since the accompanying picture depicts a single entity—the bird—with no other entity *acting* upon it, we can guess that this particular sentence lacks an object. That is, we are most likely dealing with an *intransitive* sentence construction.

So far, we've made a few intelligent guesses, but now let's test these suppositions. If we assume the T528:559 combination of **ku-?** represents the name of the bird, we have to find a type of bird whose name begins with the sound **ku**. One such bird is the *kuts*, or turkey, a common animal probably domesticated by the ancient Maya and also trapped or snared. Very possibly, the scene depicts a turkey caught in some type of trap.

It so happens that the second of the two glyphs in question—T559—occurs elsewhere in combination with the glyph Landa said records **lu**, in scenes depicting a dog-like animal. If we hypothesize that T559 represents the sound **tzu**, it becomes a simple matter to find, in one of the several excellent Maya dictionaries, the word which is spelled out glyphically **tzu-lu**, or *tzul*. Voilà! That word spells precisely "dog." This presents fairly conclusive evidence that not only does T559 carry the value **tzu** wherever we find it, but confirms our assumptions about how the glyphs convey language. Certainly, if in all examples of T559 the value **tzu** generates identifiable readings—that is, a word that makes sense—then there can be little doubt that this particular glyph has been correctly deciphered. Chances of coincidence remain much too astronomical, especially when other similarly generated values offer productive readings. It would be impossible that such readings could generate meaningful words "accidentally."

The history of decipherment abounds with not just a few similar examples, but literally hundreds. What is important here is that values can be *suggested* by their environment—that is, by the spelling of contiguous glyphs and by the images that accompany the text—and *tested* rigorously in all contexts. Epigraphers call this process "syntactic auditioning"—the trial or *testing* of suggested values to see if they generate other readings and hold up to all possible uses. As we will see, syntactic auditioning has allowed decipherers to identify the vast majority of syllables in the hieroglyphic script (roughly eighty percent), and to create a "syllabary" or syllabic grid.

The Principle of Synharmony

The second great contribution of the Russian epigrapher Knorosov was to propose a rule for spelling conventions, arguing that terminal vowels are

tzu-l(u) →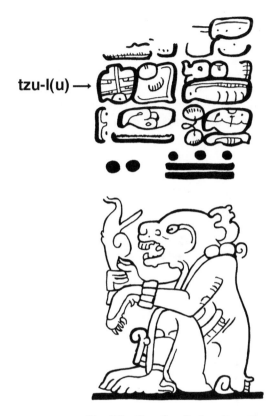

Fig. 7-5 Dresden Codex, Page 7a.

silent and that vowels in consonant-vowel syllabic signs agree with each other when spelling out words. He called the process of agreement **syn-harmony**. Such rules could explain the entire operation of Maya glyphs. Thus in our inscription from Yaxchilán Stela 11, at position I4 the Maya wrote **b'a-ka-b'a**, not **b'a-ka-b'i**, for *b'akab'* "standing one." The final consonant-vowel sign has to contain the same vowel as the preceding syllables **b'a** and **ka**, and cannot include **b'i** because it has **i** as its vowel. Only another syllable with **a** as its terminal vowel is acceptable.

b'a      ka-
b'(a)

Fig. 7-6 Phonetic spelling of *b'akab'*, Yaxchilán Stela 11, front, lower glyph panel, I4.

Actually, because in many cases the final vowel does *not* agree, Knorosov translated them with **disharmonious** vowels. An example of disharmony would be that of **mu-t(i)** for *mut*, meaning "bird." In fact, quite a few readings made their way into publications by Knorosov where the glyphs seemed to *disprove* his own rule, offering tremendous ammunition to critics—especially to Thompson. Consequently, either the values generated by Knorosov and other proponents of phoneticism were wrong, or epigraphers must have misinterpreted Landa, or another explanation had to be found.

Fig. 7-7   Disharmonious spelling: **Mu-ti**.

Again, finding reassurance from the impossibility of *accidentally* generating words, most early adherents of a phonetic approach assumed that the future would hold explanations for these exceptions to the rule, and ignored the apparent contradiction. That explanation has yet to come forward, although several attempts have been made. Most recently, David Stuart, Stephen Houston, and John Robertson have argued the principle of **disharmony**, suggesting that synharmonic agreement does not apply when the root word in Mayan contains a *complex* vowel, rather than a short one. The Maya therefore distinguished words with "irregular" vowels by spelling them with different terminal silent vowels. *Mut* "bird" therefore conforms to the sequence **mu-t(i)** rather than **mu-t(a)** because the vowel **u** should be extended and made long. In the system of Stuart, Houston, and Robertson, the word would be spelled *mu:t*, with the (:) expressing the "complexity" of the vowel. Whether this suggestion will prove correct remains to be seen, but it offers the first truly consistent explanation of an otherwise vexing problem.

Spelling Conventions

By and large, words can be spelled with either a combination of vowels and consonant-vowel syllables, or with logograms that have consonant-vowel syllables attached to them to reinforce or inflect the logogram's pronunciation. Often syllables attach as affixes to main sign logograms and function as **phonetic complements,** assuring the correct pronunciation out of one or more possibilities or—if Stuart, Houston, and Robertson prove correct—to signal a preceding complex vowel.

For most well-known glyphs, spelling conventions pose little problem. Trouble arises, however, with the considerable number of more obscure glyph combinations, and readers—even professional epigraphers—have trouble distinguishing in certain cases which glyph is to be read first. Moreover, not every glyphic element was meant to be pronounced, especially in the case of logograms that include what seem to be standard affixes, but which actually function as integral elements of the complete sign. Even more complicated, "bits" of logographic signs can stand by themselves, representing the *whole word,* though at first sight they tempt the reader to treat them as phonetic signs. Only familiarity with the script will help beginners resolve these difficulties.

Many written words are simply a chain of glyphic elements in straightforward succession, with syllables added to inflect the language. Nouns generally incorporate the simplest spelling conventions, while other parts of speech are distinguished by much more complex grammatical elements. For example, verbs are inflected for incompletive and completive transitive states, as well as intransitive ones, and can carry pronominal elements distinguishing third-person singular, first-person plural, and so on. (See Chapter 8: Verbs, Verbal Inflection, and Grammatical Elements.)

One useful example that illustrates spelling conventions in the Maya script is the word *b'alam* "jaguar." In its most common form, a pictograph representing the head of a jaguar stands for the logogram **B'ALAM,** two examples of which occur on Yaxchilán Stela 11 at F1 (below the bird sign) and I1 (next to a shield-like glyph). Other hieroglyphic spellings of *b'alam* include the subfixes T74 or T142, both of which read **-ma** and provide the word's final *m* sound. In the case of *b'alam,* the use of a phonetic complement may take into account the potential error of reading "jaguar" as *jix,* another name for this animal. When spelling the latter, the scribe would prefix the jaguar head with the "knot" sign T60, which reads **ji-** and clues the reader to the alternative pronunciation. A final way to spell *b'alam* is syllabically **b'a-la-m(a).**

One of the best illustrations of spelling conventions in Maya hieroglyphic writing is the word *pakal* "shield," already referred to in Chapter 2. The Maya could spell this word with simply a pictograph of a shield, with a pictograph subfixed by the phonetic complement T178 to render

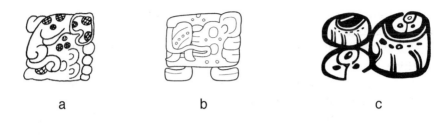

Fig. 7-8   Ways of writing "jaguar": *b'alam* as a) logogram, **B'ALAM**; b)
logogram with phonetic complement, **B'ALAM-(ma)**; c) phonetic
spelling, **b'a-la-m(a)**; *jix* as d) symbolic logogram and phonetic
complement, **ji-JIX**; e) head variant logogram and phonetic
complement, **ji-JIX**.

Fig. 7-9   Ways of spelling *pakal* "shield": a) logogram, **PAKAL**;
b) logogram with phonetic complement, **PAKAL-(la)**;
c) phonetic spelling, **pa-ka-la**.

the final *l* sound, or with phonetic signs completely spelling out the word as **pa-ka-l(a)**.

Still another way to spell words involves the use of **semantic determinatives**, special devices or conventions that indicate an alternative way to pronounce a sign. Although their existence in the Maya system remains debatable, a few epigraphers have proposed that the previously mentioned day sign cartouches signal a purely day sign value. Others have proposed that the addition of T533—the logogram for **AJAW**—or alternatively the so-called Jester God (T1030o), to the vulture and rodent heads that take headbands, may function as determinatives. In these latter cases, the presence of T533 on the headbands changes the value of the animal heads to the title *ajaw*.

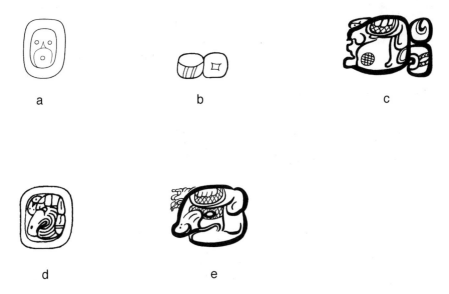

a   b   c

d   e

Fig. 7-10   Ways of spelling *ajaw*: a) symbolic logogram; b) T168 logogram; c) head variant with **AJAW** headband and phonetic complement; d) vulture with **AJAW** headband; e) rodent with Jester God headband.

An interesting convention involves a pair of dots attached to the edge of individual syllabic signs. When present, the two dots *double* the sign's value, as in the well-known collocation at P2 on Piedras Negras Lintel 3 that spells **ka-ka-w(a)** or *kakaw* "chocolate." Here the two dots attached to the forehead of a fish's head doubles the value **ka**, rendering **ka-ka**, which is then subfixed by **-w(a)** to add the final *w* sound.

Fig. 7-11   Doubler dots: **ka-{ka}-wa** for *kakaw*.

Morpho-syllables

David Stuart, Stephen Houston, and John Robertson have proposed very recently a category of signs that they refer to as "morpho-syllables." Essentially, the morpho-syllable consists of a consonant-vowel sign that can reverse itself to become a vowel-consonant. For example, the syllabic sign **-li** (T24) can function as **-il.** According to this proposal, a whole range of signs can function in this manner, especially when in word-final position. Thus we have **-il/li** (T24), **-al/la** (T178), and **-aw/wa** (T130), among many others.

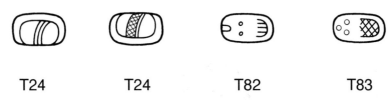

Fig. 7-12   The morpho-syllable **-il/la**.

Substitution Sets

Quite a number of signs freely interchange or *substitute* with one another in well-recognized substitution patterns. When glyphs interchange with other signs, in many cases they simply represent graphic variants of the same phonetic value. Such words having approximately the same pronunciation and meaning are called **allographs**. As mentioned earlier, the Maya scribe had a wide range of signs with which he or she could write the same thing. However, some substitutions reflect differences in grammatical function, as in the nominal affixing that distinguishes between first and second person (for example, first and second-person possessive pronouns; see Chapter 8).

Instances where glyphs of equivalent phonetic value freely interchange with each other are called **substitution sets**. What is probably the best-known set are the glyphs that represent the near-homonyms "four," "sky," and "snake." "Four," or *kan*, is represented by either four dots or the head of the Sun God (T1010 **KAN** or **CHAN**), while "sky" is rendered with T561 **KAAN** or **CHAAN**, and "snake" by T764 **KAN** or **CHAN**. Nevertheless, all four signs can stand in one for the other—outside of calendrical contexts, four dots may indicate the number "four," but they can also represent the logograms **KAN** or **KAAN** (or alternatively **CHAN** or **CHAAN**) for "sky" and "snake" (see below: The Language of the Glyphs). In these cases the reader discerns the meaning from the context of the surrounding words.

a   b   c   d

Fig. 7-13   Substitution sets: a) **KAN** "four," symbolic form; b) **KAN** "four," head variant; c) **KAAN/CHAAN** "sky"; d) **KAN** "snake."

The Syllabary

Drawing on Landa as their chief source, on evidence from substitution sets, and by using techniques of syntactic auditioning, epigraphers have deciphered a wide range of phonetic signs. Generally expressed in grid form, the inventory of securely deciphered phonetic signs comprises a "syllabary" incorporating all known vowel and consonant-vowel signs discovered so far in the writing system. Those squares left blank in the syllabary correspond to values for which no signs have yet been found.[1] Although syllabaries vary, only about twelve out of ninety possible squares remain empty—with roughly eighty-eight percent filled in. These findings illustrate the remarkable success achieved by epigraphers in "cracking" the Maya script.

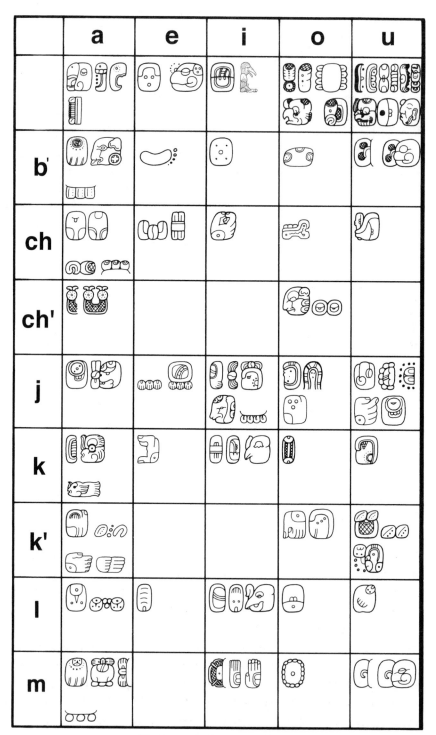

Fig. 7-14 Syllabary, left half.

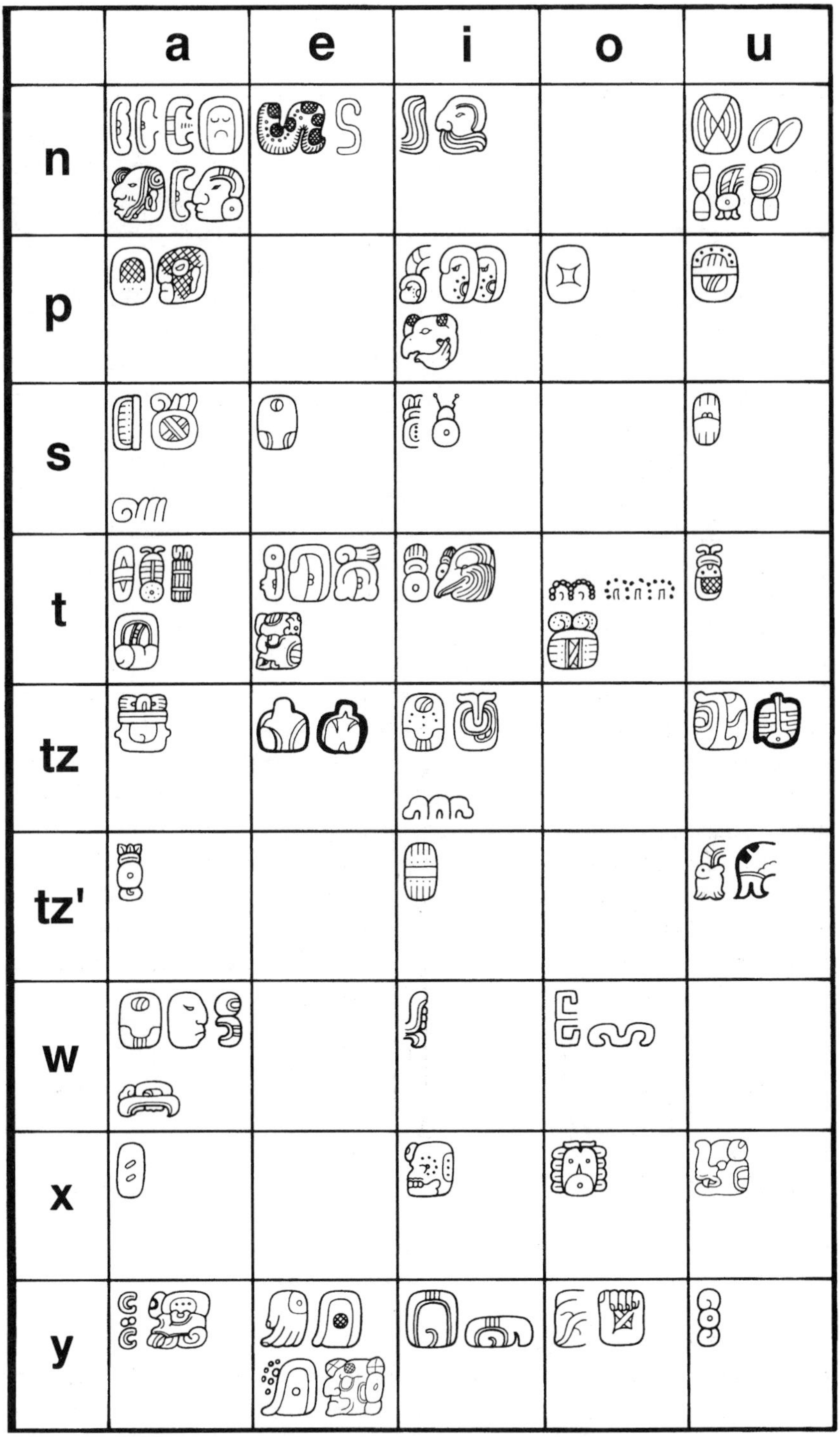

	a	e	i	o	u
n					
p					
s					
t					
tz					
tz'					
w					
x					
y					

Fig. 7-15 Syllabary, right half.

The Language of the Glyphs

Having established how the Maya wrote with logographic word signs and phonetic elements, it will help to clarify exactly which version of "Mayan" the scribes wrote. While Landa indicates that the glyphs at the time of his inquiries expressed the language of Yucatec Mayan, hieroglyphic inscriptions from the Classic Period record a fundamentally different dialect. That the glyphs were originally intended for another dialect was clearly indicated in Landa's examples of month signs, where his informant felt compelled to draw extra phonetic complements to help clue the reader to a *Yucatec* pronunciation.

The distribution of Mayan languages in ancient times suggests that the glyphs record specifically a Ch'olan dialect. Represented today by the dialects Ch'ol, Ch'ontal, and Ch'orti, and by extinct Ch'olti, the use of Ch'olan originally extended across the base of the Yucatan Peninsula as far as western Honduras, the heartland of the Classic Maya.

Historically, speakers of Yucatec and its sub-dialects have encroached or intruded upon this Ch'olan core, so that scholars have come to believe that many areas of the ancient Maya world included mixed or closely contiguous populations of both Ch'olan and Yucatec speakers.

Yet when we turn to spellings from Classic Period inscriptions, we find an ambiguous situation where inscriptions do not entirely conform to either language. In some cases, expected Ch'olan spellings have proven erroneous when the same glyphs turned up incorporating Yucatec spellings. One of the best examples is the name of the Palenque king formerly called Chan Bahlum, or Snake Jaguar, which was recently revised to Kan B'alam due in part to the explicit use of the phonetic complement **ka** for Yucatec *kan* rather than Ch'olan *chan*.

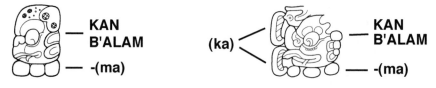

Fig. 7-16   Name of the Palenque king Kan B'alam.

Consider the following. Numerous examples of the glyph for "home" survive in ancient texts, read Yucatec *otoch* but Ch'olan *otot*. Hieroglyphs that designate "home" generally take the phonetic complement -**ti**, providing the final *t* sound that would indicate the Ch'olan form. Nevertheless, inscriptions from the same geographical area also contain the hieroglyph for the word *na* or *naj* "house," a term that survives in Yucatec but not Ch'olan. Thus the script would seem to record both Yucatec *and* Ch'olan words.

a   b

Fig. 7-17   Glyphs for buildings: a) **OTOT** "house"; b) **NA** "home."

Stuart, Houston, and Robertson have argued that the Maya hieroglyphic script records a distinctive, specialized "scribal language," a version of Mayan preserved only in ancient inscriptions, that they refer to as **Classical Mayan**. Although untested and as yet unconfirmed, their suggestion neatly solves one of the more puzzling problems of the script. Situations where a language represents a "high" or elite language are called "diglossia," and almost certainly a similar convention prevailed in inscriptions of ancient Egypt, where the Egyptian language expressed hieroglyphically peculiar traditions missing from the spoken language.

One advantage to introducing the idea of a "scribal language" is that it helps to explain the script's remarkable geographical uniformity, where—although each city had its own idiosyncrasies—the graphic form of the script preserved the same or very similar conventions and tended to change through time at approximately the same rate. We do not find, for example, any single city preserving a particularly archaic form of the script by Late Classic times, and presumably any inscription could be read by any scribe anywhere in the Maya world. How scholars resolve the issue of which language the glyphs record is one of the more exciting challenges faced by epigraphers today.

Summary

Maya scribes could write in a variety of ways using an extensive inventory of signs for complete words (logograms) and syllables (phonetic signs). In doing so they evidently preserved conventions of spelling that modern readers call synharmony, where the final vowel conforms to any internal vowels but remains silent. The Maya also may have used a principle of disharmony, where final unpronounced vowels fail to preserve internal vowel harmony when the internal vowels have a *complex* pronunciation. Maya scribes could choose from an array of glyphs that doubled as phonetic signs and grammatical elements, including pronouns and prepositions. With techniques of syntactic auditioning, identification of substitution sets, and Landa's "alphabet," a syllabary has been generated giving all known phonetic signs in grid form. One of the more curious aspects of Maya inscriptions is that they seem to spell both Yucatec and Ch'olan words, suggesting a specialized "scribal language" in use during the Classic Period.

We have seen how Maya hieroglyphic inscriptions incorporate basic principles of organization, and how they focus around sequential dates. Using some rather easy and straightforward spelling conventions (that nevertheless have their own set of difficulties), and possibly employing a special "scribal language," texts then lay out within the calendrical time frame a series of sentences that mark historical, mythological, and ritual events. These events are the subject and drama of Maya narrative texts.

NOTE

1. Most will likely be filled in as decipherment continues.

CHAPTER 8

• • •

Verbs, Verbal Inflection, and Grammatical Elements

When Bishop Landa compiled his "alphabet" during the latter half of the sixteenth century, included among his signs was the calligraphic-style **u/U**. Decipherers have long recognized the Classic Period sculptural and painted versions of this sign, T1 and its allographs, which figure among the most common glyphs of the script. Significantly, *u* functions as the third-person possessive pronoun "his/her/its" in most Mayan languages.

These facts confirm the language-based nature of Maya hieroglyphic writing, but they also have several profound implications that aid in reading the script. The presence of **U** allows us to identify in what *voice* the text was written, which was in most cases the third person—for example, "He captured so-and-so" (as opposed to "I captured" or "You captured"). More importantly, it means that, along with other evidence, the reader can identify verbs according to which affixes they carry. Thus both syntax and affixes help "predict" which glyph is the verb.

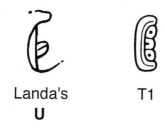

Landa's
U

T1

Fig. 8-1   **U** from Landa's alphabet and T1.

137

Actually, implications for the identification of **U** go much farther than this. Glyphic verbs should reflect the same or similar kinds of linguistic nuances as Yucatec, Ch'ol or another Mayan language spoken at the time. In practical terms, if *u* appears then other grammatical elements must also be present. It makes no sense for the script to have one grammatical element and not others.

Grammar is a fascinating yet hotly debated subject that holds the key to what Maya scribes had to say.

How to Identify Verbs

Hieroglyphic verbs undergo changes similar to spoken Mayan and can carry the same kinds of affixes, depending on context. Although the precise form of the language of the glyphs still eludes epigraphers, and the rules of verbal affixation continue to be debated, enough resemblance to modern versions of Mayan allows for an intelligible transcription in many instances. Syntax and associations with accompanying artistic scenes alone can render the general meaning of a text, although sometimes in a very oblique way, while in other instances only the text makes sense of an otherwise ambiguous artistic scene.

Syntax

We know from Mayan languages that word order largely follows the pattern verb-subject (abbreviated to VS) when only a subject is present, similar to the English construction "runs Bill." An action comes first (the verb), then the name of the subject (the noun) who performed that action. Linguists refer to verbs that express only an action followed by its subject as **intransitive**.

Other sentences express an action that someone or something (the subject) performs on someone or something else (the object), taking the form verb-object-subject (VOS) in Mayan. The equivalent in English would be "Feeds the baby Bill," where Bill represents the subject who feeds the baby. The verb comes first, then the name of the person fed, followed by the name of the one who does the feeding. Linguists call these kinds of action verbs **transitive**.

Just as Mayan follows these general constructions, the writing system reflects word order in the same way, generally using either the VS or VOS construction. Additionally, to a certain degree hieroglyphic verbs can be "predicted" by their location within an inscription. In the vast majority of cases, the verb immediately follows the last iteration of a calendrical statement. After all of the Long Count periods, the Calendar Round, the Supplementary Series, and any other temporal statements have been given, the verb follows and tells us what happened on that date. What we then have is date-verb-object-subject or more traditionally, temporal-verb-object-subject.

Like many hieroglyphic collocations, the verb can be expressed simply within one glyph block or a portion thereof as essentially a single "word," or more elaborately in two or more blocks that form a **verb phrase**. Examples of the latter include the *"ti* constructions," where the locative preposition T59 **TI** indicates the sense of "in," as in "in office."

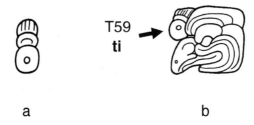

Fig. 8-2   The locative preposition **ti**; a) T59; b) vulture head variant.

We can see how the syntax of the verb works in our example from Yaxchilán Stela 11. If the Long Count, Tzolk'in, Lords of the Night, Lunar Series, and Ja'ab' end at D3, then C4 ought to contain our verb, and so it does—the well-known "toothache" glyph denoting "accession." In this case, however, the verb spills over to fill both D4 and E1 as well, incorporating a complex

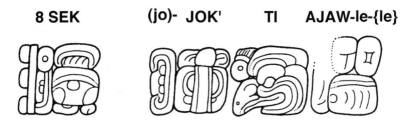

Fig. 8-3   Ja'ab' and verb phrase from Yaxchilán Stela 11, front, lower glyph panel, D3-E1.

verb phrase that states, "he took office." Therefore, the glyphs on Stela 11 inform us that on the Long Count date 9.16.1.0.0 11 Ajaw 8 Sek someone took office as ruler, an action that was equivalent in importance to the coronation of a European monarch. The verb phrase specifically reads (jo)-JOK TI AJAW-LE, "acceded in lordship."

AFFIXATION

Lengthy narrative inscriptions often introduce more than one event associated with the same date, so that in many instances syntax alone does not allow identification of all of the verbs present in a single episode. In such cases affixes provide identifying markers—not necessarily distinct or discrete ones, but ones that form distinctive *patterns*. An exhaustive or even in-depth discussion of the full range of verbal inflectional patterns lies outside the scope of the present book, and more properly belongs to a grammar of Maya hieroglyphs. But to read the inscriptions the beginner must recognize these patterns and how they function, and learn their phonetic transcriptions.

In English, speakers regularly communicate in terms that reflect past, present, and future, as well as the "number" of entities involved. For example, to indicate the past we most often convert a verb by adding an **-ed** ending—"walk" becomes "walked," "pick" becomes "picked," and so on. We also conjugate many irregular verbs by changing them internally—"run" becomes "ran," "sit" becomes "sat," and so forth. To indicate generally how many entities are involved, we add an **-s** ending to nouns to distinguish between singular and plural, although like irregular verbs, certain nouns change internally. "Sister" becomes "sisters," but "man" becomes "men."

The subtleties of English, however, also allow for nuances such as "will run" or "has walked," or we can cast sentences in an existential ongoing **aspect** corresponding to the **-ing** ending, for example "running." We can even speak in this way of running *in the past*—"he was running for his life." Actions in this ongoing aspect are said to be **incomplete**, as opposed to actions already accomplished, or **completed**.

Mayan languages differ in this sense from English chiefly in that tense is less important than whether an action is ongoing or finished. Rather than past, present, or future, sentences are molded based on **completive** or **incompletive** action. In practical terms, Mayan language takes an action or verb and either marks it or does *not* mark it, according to its completive or incompletive aspect and the kind of verb involved, such as transitive or intransitive.

In this same way, hieroglyphic verbs carry special affix patterns to mark their completive or incompletive aspect, and any additional verbal inflections. Moreover, like the language, the glyphs carry aspect patterns according to whether the sentence involves a subject or both a subject and an object. Thus what we have are intransitive completives and incompletives on the one hand, and transitive completives and incompletives on the other.

Because Mayan language and hieroglyphic writing function as agglutinative processes, both mark verbs by stringing together prefixes and suffixes that indicate transitivity and aspect depending on voice and number—first-person singular ("I"), first-person plural ("we"), second-person singular ("you"), third-person singular ("he/she/it"), and so on. Such constructions also reflect possession—his, your, my, and so forth. Therefore, many of these markings involve pronouns, one of which we already encountered in the third-person possessive **U**.

PRONOUNS

Unlike pronouns in English, which always stand alone as discrete words, Mayan pronouns attach themselves to both the beginning and ending of words, like affixes attach to main signs in the writing system. Also unlike English, Mayan pronouns take a wide range of forms, with their deployment depending on the quality of the verb. While the complexity of verbal inflection should not overly concern the beginner, the main thing to remember is that the different kinds of verbs take hieroglyphic affixes corresponding to pronouns from one of two *sets*, and that these pronouns vary depending on *person*—first-person singular, second-person plural, and so on. These two sets are called Set A or the **ergative** set, and Set B or the **absolutive** set. Pronouns of the ergative set mark the subjects of transitive verbs and possessors of nouns, whereas those of the absolutive set mark the subjects of intransitive verbs and objects of transitive verbs. The following chart reconstructs both sets of pronouns for Classical Mayan. Note that "-" before the pronoun indicates a suffix, while afterwards it indicates a prefix. (* indicates a reconstructed language.)

Set A (The Ergative Set)

1sing.	"I"	*in-
2sing.	"you"	*a-
3sing.	"he/she/it"	*u-
1pl.	"we"	*ka-
2pl.	"you"	*i-
3pl.	"they"	*u-

Set B (The Absolutive Set)

1sing.	"I"	*-en
2sing.	"you"	*-et
3sing.	"he/she/it"	unvoiced
1pl.	"we"	*-on
2pl.	"you"	*-ox
3pl.	"they"	*-ob'

Quite a range of pronouns has been detected in the hieroglyphic script, in addition to Landa's *u*. For example, David Stuart and Stephen Houston have argued recently for first and second-person pronouns, allowing the possibility of hieroglyphic quotations such as "it is his saying," and direct addresses, such as "my clothes" and "my earth." In this respect, identification of pronouns lies on the cutting edge of glyph decipherment.

Third-Person Pronoun

As previously mentioned, the third-person possessive pronoun **U** (most commonly T1, T2, T3, or T13) figures among the most common hieroglyphic signs, corresponding to "his/hers/its." In Maya hieroglyphic grammar, *u* occurs in initial position with incompletive and completive transitive verbs, incompletive intransitive verbs, and possessed nouns. In the latter case its presence tells us that an object belongs to someone, as in the well-known collocation found in dedicatory ceramic texts, **U la-k(a)** or *u lak* "his plate." At least seven separate signs function as the third-person possessive marker **U**, and, as far as is known, all are freely interchangeable.

A distinctive feature of both the script and the language is that since two different vowels back-to-back tend to clash, pronouns that consist of vowels become *y* when prefixed to words already beginning with a vowel. Thus instead of *u ajaw* we find *yajaw*, "his lord."

Possessive pronouns offer the reader major clues to syntax and grammar, and in many cases indicate the presence of verbs. (See Chapter 9:

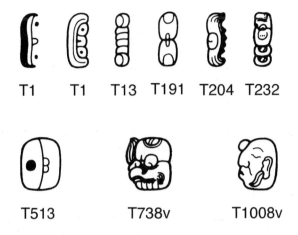

Fig. 8-4   T1 **U** and its allographs.

Fig. 8-5   The **U la-k(a)** spelling for *u lak* "his/her plate."

The Major Events, and Chapter 15: Discourse and Structural Analysis.) Picking out examples of **U** in Maya texts can provide a useful first step in glyphic analysis.

Second-Person Pronoun

Among the more exciting proposals of recent years concerns what David Stuart has identified as the second-person pronoun **AJ** (T228) meaning "you," which marks both possession ("your") and the subjects of transitive verbs. Although rare, notable examples occur on pottery vessels and "caption" texts on monuments, where they seem to introduce direct statements or quotations of actors in narrative scenes. In most other contexts, the glyph for **AJ** functions as the masculine agentive possessive pronoun "he of" (see Chapter 10: Names and Titles).

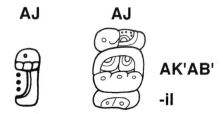

Fig. 8-6   Second-person pronouns: T228 **AJ** "you, your" and
AJ AK'AB' "your darkness."

First-Person Pronoun

Another possible pronoun, T116 most commonly occurs in final position
as the phonetic complement **-ni**, as in the calendrical glyph T528:116 **TUN-
(ni)**. However, David Stuart recently proposed that, when prefixed to
nouns, T116 serves as the first-person possessive pronoun *in-*, with consonant and vowel reversed. In these contexts the sign reads logographically
IN-, meaning "my," as in *in b'uk in pat* "my clothes, my tribute." Evidently
scribes invoked the first-person pronoun only in extremely rare conditions, and Stuart warns that his proposal remains very tentative.

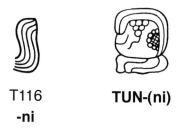

T116   **TUN-(ni)**
-ni

Fig. 8-7   T116 **ni** and **TUN-(ni)**.

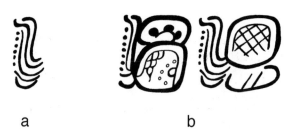

a   b

Fig. 8-8   First-person pronouns: a) T116 **IN** "my"; b) **IN b'u-ku
IN pa-ta-na** "my clothes, my tribute."

Demonstrative Pronouns

Demonstrative pronouns such as "this," "that," or "those" single out or specify an item under discussion. Unlike ergative or absolutive pronouns from Sets A and B, demonstratives stand alone as separate words, and can be spelled out using conventional techniques of glyphic word formation. Two recently identified demonstratives are glyphs corresponding to **ja'-i** (*ja-i*), meaning "this," "that," or "one," and **ja'-o-b'a** (*ja'ob'*), meaning "they," "these," or "they are." Notice that *ja'ob'* takes the third-person plural suffix *-ob'* from Set B.

ja'-[i]   **ja'**

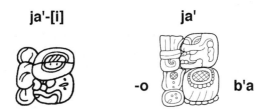

Fig. 8-9   Demonstrative pronouns: **ja'-[i]** "this," "that," or "one," and **ja'-o-b'a** "they."

QUOTATIVE PARTICLES

As the term "quotative" indicates, certain particles attribute phrases to individuals in Maya iconography as though these were the figure's utterances or actual speech. At least two have recently been proposed for the Maya script: *che'en*, spelled phonetically either **che-je-na** or **che-e-na**, which means "so it says" or "so he says," and *yalij*, spelled **ya-la-ji-ya** and meaning "it is his saying."

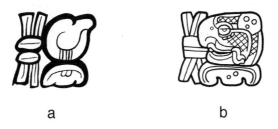

a   b

Fig. 8-10   Quotative particles: a) **che-je-na**; b) **che-e-na**.

ya   -la

-ji   -ya

Fig. 8-11   Quotative particles: **ya-la-ji-ya**.

Direct statements of individuals marked either as quotative particles or with first-person pronouns often have "speech scrolls" connecting them with the mouth of the figure speaking, similar to "balloons" in cartoon cells. For example, on one notable ceramic vessel the aged and nude God L explains to the Sun God, K'inich Ajaw, that a mythical rabbit has just stolen "my clothes, my tribute" (see Plate 7).

PLURAL ENDINGS

The plural ending *-tak* or **-TAK** has recently been proposed by Alfonso Lacadena and Garcia Campillo, who cite the example **CH'OK-TAK** or "the youths." An excellent example involves the logogram **AJAW** which, together with **-TAK**, means "the lords," while the sequence **KAN ch'o-k(o)-TAK** means "the four youths."

a   b   c   d   e

Fig. 8-12   Plural endings: a) **-TAK**; b) **CH'OK-(ko)-TAK**; c) **AJAW-TAK**;
d) **KAN ch'o-k(o)-TAK**; e) **-ob'**.

Perhaps far more significant is the plural ending from pronoun Set B, corresponding to the third-person plural suffix *-ob'* "they." Although David Stuart, the decipherer of this suffix, cautions not to accept it without reservation, he cites a number of cases where multiple objects named in succession carry the suffix (T142), incorporating three dots like a tripod stand. Usually read **-ma**, the suffix makes no sense with that value in these examples, since in one case the specific named objects refer to *witzob'* "mountains," and lack an *-m* ending sound. It makes more sense, Stuart argues, that T142 *pluralizes* these subjects. In this interpretation, the three dots behave not unlike the two-dot doubler mentioned in Chapter 7 that serves to multiply the value of any contiguous sign.

THE PARTICLE SUFFIX *-IL*

Among the most frequent terminal endings on glyphs, the suffix *-il* functions in Mayan where something exists as an inalienable part of something else. For example, bark bears an inextricable relationship to the tree, and a door relates to its building in such a way that a door by itself makes no sense. In such cases the thing it belongs to *possesses* it, and the object itself takes both the third-person possessive pronoun **U-**, as in "its doorway," and any of the consonant-vowel glyphs that read **li**. A good example from Yaxchilán Lintel 23 reads **U-pa-si-il yo-OTOT-(ti)**, "its doorway (or opening), (of) his house."

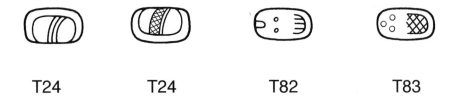

T24   T24   T82   T83

Fig. 8-13   Examples of **-il/li.**

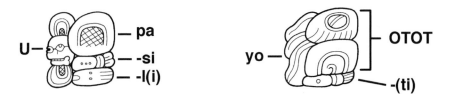

Fig. 8-14   "Its doorway, (of) his house":
Yaxchilán Lintel 23, B2-C1.

Prepositions

One other class of hieroglyphs includes signs that double as phonetic and grammatical elements. These signs represent the prepositions generally called locatives or indicators of position, including the signs for "at," "on," and "in." The most common of these prepositions, T59 **TI**, represents the positional "in"—for example, "in the house." Like the possessive pronoun **U**, **TI** can figure in the construction of verbs (but not always), as in the so-called *ti*-verbal constructions, discussed below. Note that T59 can have a purely phonetic function, serving as the syllable **ti**. Similarly, T565 **TA** can indicate "at," depending on context.

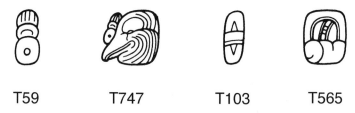

T59   T747   T103   T565

Fig. 8-15   Prepositions: T59, T747 **TI** and T103, T565 **TA**.

Verbal Inflection

Signs that function as verbs take pronouns from Set A or Set B depending on transitivity and aspect. However, they also incorporate additional signs in specific patterns, whose meaning and function remain in debate but most of whose values have been known for years. Four major patterns have emerged from decipherments of the last few decades. While arguments rage over these patterns, the beginner need only be concerned with the patterns themselves, their values, and their traditionally accepted linguistic categories. These categories are transitive, intransitive, positional, and passive.

Transitive Completive Verbs

Casts sentences that have both subject and object in the completive aspect—that is, the action is *completed*. Verbs of this class generally consist of a consonant-vowel-consonant (CVC) root word sandwiched between the third-person pronoun **U** and either the suffix **-wi** (T117) or **-wa** (T130).

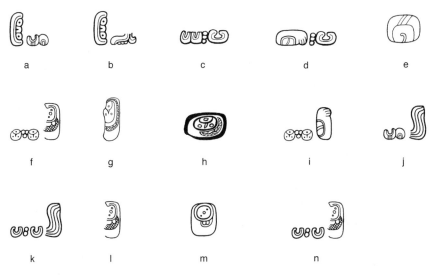

Fig. 8-16   Verbal inflectional patterns: a) T1 . . . 130, **U . . . -wa**;
b) T1 . . . 117, **U . . . -wi**; c) T246, **-ji-ya**; d) T88.126, **-ji-ya**;
e) T17/18/575, **-yi**; f) T178.181, **-la-ja**; g) T181[178], **[-la]-ja**;
h) T683[178], **[-la]-ja**; i) T178.17/18, **-la-ji**; j) T130.116, **-wa-ni**;
k) T126.116, **-ya-ni**; l) T181, **-aj**; m) T683, **-aj**; n) T126.181, **-ya-ja**.

INTRANSITIVE COMPLETIVE VERBS

Verbs that take only a subject carry affixes to mark the completive aspect, and generally consist of a CVC root with the conflated suffixes T136 **ji** and T126, which is most probably **ya**. This forms ROOT-**ji-ya**, with the latter signs yielding something like **-jiy**. Intransitive completives can also take the combination T88 **ji** and T126 **ya**, again yielding **-jiy**. Exactly how these suffixes should be read in terms of the principles of synharmony and disharmony remains unclear. Another common sign thought to represent the intransitive completive marker, and equally problematic, is T17 **yi**.

POSITIONAL VERBS

Certain intransitive verbs function in neither the completive nor incompletive, but in reference to the subject's position. Called **positionals**, these verbs refer to the condition of sitting, rising up, lying down, and so forth.

The most common and best known of these is the "seating" glyph discussed in Chapter 3. At least five positional completive suffixes have been proposed, including T178.181, T178.88, and T181 with T178 infixed, all of which probably read *-laj*, and the combinations T130.116 **-wa-n(i)** and T126.116 **-ya-n(i)**. Again, the precise spelling vis-à-vis vowel synharmony-disharmony remains unresolved.

PASSIVE VERBS

A final class of verbs, called passives, involves an action done *to* the subject, rather than a subject acting alone or upon an object. The so-called passives take the suffix T181 or its main sign equivalent T683, both of which read **-ja** or **-aj**.

MISCELLANEOUS

One final pattern, another difficult arrangement, incorporates T126 **-ya** and T181 **-aj**. The combination would seem to yield *-yaj*. Evidently of much more limited range, the sequence commonly occurs with the roots **JUL** "to arrive," especially in the Lunar Series, and **SIJ** "to be born."

General Verbs

A class of "general" verbs that stand alone or function as auxiliaries to main verbs render a meaning close to "he/she/it goes" or "he/she/it was going," or "here is so-and-so." They also may carry the meaning "his/her/its doing." The most common expression of these is the *u b'a* glyph portraying the head of a rodent, possibly a gopher (T757), infixed with the sign for "yellow," **K'AN** (T281). Other verbs of this class will be described in Chapter 11 under "Political Relationships."

Fig. 8-17   The "general verb" **U B'A**.

TI Constructions

Before exploring the actual events recorded in the inscriptions, one last class of verbs should be noted, the so-called *ti* constructions. In these cases, a general verb commonly precedes a more specific verb or noun, linked by the preposition *ti* meaning "on" or "in" and forming in essence a verb phrase. One of the best examples of this kind of construction are verb phrases that refer to "dance," where the **AK'OT** "dance" glyph precedes the dance's actual name and is linked to it by T59 **TI**, for example **AK'OT TI xu-ku-p(i)** (*ak'ot ti xukpi*) "He/she/it dances the xukpi."

U B'A   TI AKOT-t(a) TI xu-[ku]-pi

Fig. 8-18   The "**ti** construction" dance phrase from Yaxchilán Lintel 2, F1-H1.

Summary

While exploring the nature of grammar in hieroglyphic inscriptions, we have seen how the Maya script reflects some far-reaching and subtle nuances of Mayan language, even if those nuances remain obscure in some cases. Of course, verbs have meaning—run, walk, dance, and so forth. Beyond grammatical function, they actually *say* something. What hieroglyphic verbs tell us—the events of history—will be explored in Chapter 9.

Plate 1   Copán Stela A, Side. Carved from trachyte, a compacted volcanic mud, this sculptured shaft depicts Waxaklajun U B'a K'awil, the thirteenth ruler of Copán in the line of the "founder" Yax K'uk' Mo'. Hieroglyphs along the side refer to rulers from four of the primary regional capitals of the Classic Period—Copán, Tikal, Calakmul, and Palenque—associating them with the directions east, west, south, and north. Photograph courtesy of Pictures of Record.

Plate 2   Laxtunich Lintel 1 (the Kimbell Panel). Carved from limestone, this
exquisite panel—probably a door lintel originally—depicts the local
ruler Aj Chak Max (right figure) presenting three prisoners (lower
left) to the Yaxchilán ruler Chel Te Chaan. The scene takes place
within a palace chamber, indicated by overhead swag curtains and
two terraces, within which the ruler of Yaxchilán pontificates from
his throne (upper left). Hieroglyphs along the edge of the throne's
seat name Chel Te Chaan, while inset texts name the prisoners and
the sculptor who carved the monument. Between Chel Te Chaan
and Aj Chak Max a double-column text gives the date of the prisoners' capture and describes their adornment—their "dressing up"
for ritual sacrifice. Photograph © Justin Kerr (K2823).

Plate 3   Piedras Negras Throne 1. A backrest, seat, and two legs comprise this unprecedented limestone throne. Found in pieces by archaeologists, it originally occupied a niche within a royal palace that probably constituted the "throne room." The screen incorporates a full frontal view of the Witz or "Mountain" Monster with young lords who replace the monster's eye pupils. A continuous narrative inscription along the edge of the seat and covering three sides of each leg relates key events in the life of Ruler 7, the last king of Piedras Negras before the Maya collapse. Photograph © Justin Kerr (K4899).

Plate 4   Unprovenanced Jade Celt. Delicately incised with wooden drills and carved with other primitive tools, this small-scale jade plaque was rubbed with powdered cinnabar to color the lines of the hieroglyphs red. The plaque was carved early in the Classic Period, and functioned as a dangler or tinkler suspended below a belt ornament that was worn as part of a ruler's costume. The topmost glyph, rendered much larger than the others, gives the Tzolk'in position in the calendar, while the glyphs below refer to an individual named Chaan Yoat "Sky Penis," and recount his death. Photograph © Justin Kerr (K199).

Plate 5   Tortuguero Wooden Box. Few objects of carved wood survive the rain forest environment of the Maya, but this marvelously rendered little box remains in remarkably good condition. Found in a cave in Mexico, the box includes all-glyphic sides and ends that supplement a figural scene of a striding lord carved on the lid. The glyphs refer to two "seating" or accession events, one involving an *ajaw* or ruler, the other an *itz'at* or "learned one," both of whom were from the site of Tortuguero just to the west of Palenque. According to the inscription, the seating of the *itz'at* took place on the Calendar Round date 9 Manik' "end of" Pop, in the Late Classic Period. Photograph © Justin Kerr (K339a).

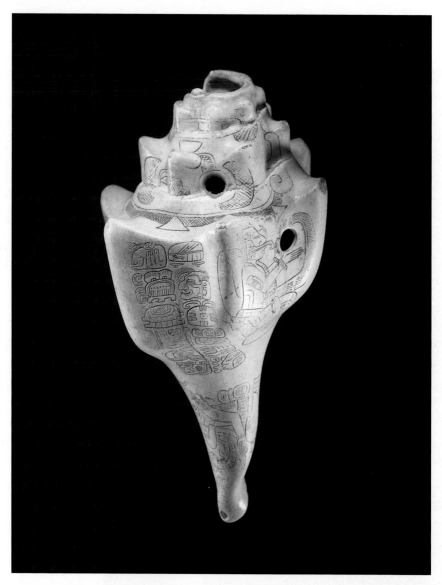

Plate 6   Incised Conch Shell. Used as a trumpet replete with finger holes to vary
the tone, this unusual conch shell was modified around its wider upper
end so that the contours depict an image of a face (shown in the photograph upside down). One of the finger holes doubles as the eye. Two sets
of incised hieroglyphs in double columns include the name of the
trumpet ("Moon-Conch"), the name of the trumpet's owner, and the designation of the owner's father as a "singer." Other glyphs may refer to the
"conjuring" of the trumpet's sound. Additional images depict a moon
deity inside a "moon" cartouche, and at the bottom on the narrow stem a
figure known as Wuk Sip Winik or "Seven Deer Man." Photograph ©
Justin Kerr (K519).

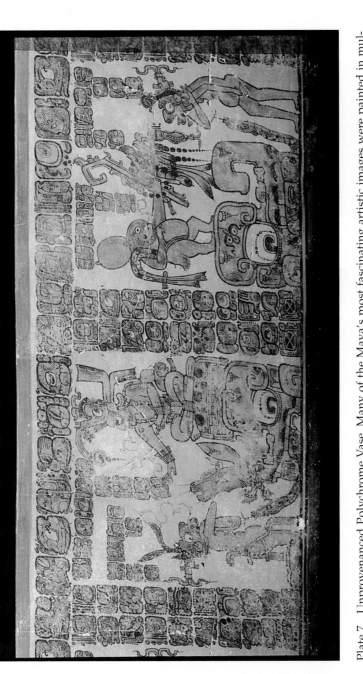

Plate 7 Unprovenanced Polychrome Vase. Many of the Maya's most fascinating artistic images were painted in multiple or "polychrome" colors on cylindrical vases and other pottery vessels. The scene shown here comes from a vase that has been "rolled out" with a special camera so that the entire curved surface may be viewed in one glance. With an almost comic sense of humor God L of the Underworld has been "relieved" of his clothing by a rabbit perched upon the head of a long-nosed Kawak monster (right scene), after which the same very naked God L explains to the Sun God that the rabbit has stolen "my clothes, my tribute" (left scene). Photograph © Justin Kerr (K1398).

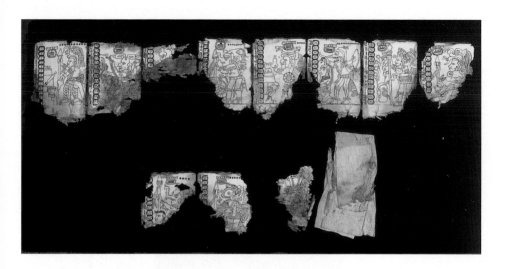

Plate 8

Grolier Codex. Maya hiero-glyphic books were typically made from barkpaper pounded flat and folded accordion-fashion to form pages, then whitewashed with stucco for a clean white writing surface. The most recently discovered Maya book, the Grolier Codex (so named for the location where it was first exhibited) contains cal-endrical and astronomical infor-mation, including data related to Venus. Only four of these hieroglyphic books survive, as many of the Maya books were burned during the sixteenth century on the orders of the Franciscan priest Diego de Landa, who went on to write the most significant early account of Maya hieroglyphic writing. Photographs © Justin Kerr (K4822 & K4822.7).

CHAPTER 9

●●●●

The Major Events

It must have been an impressive war. From surviving sculptures and murals we can envision cadres of javelin-throwers, dart-slingers, club-wielders, warriors arrayed in ferocious animal-helmets, in feather-crested shields and quilted cotton armor. Drawn up perhaps in a surprise attack, they descended upon the minor but important town of Pakab' in the present-day Mexican state of Tabasco, inflicting upon the enemy a resounding military defeat on January 18, A.D. 794. In the ensuing chaos the king's captains and others of the army managed to secure at least nine illustrious captives, binding them around the biceps with rope and dragging them back to the regional capital at Yokib'. There, bloodied and dazed, they were presented to the ruler as battle trophies destined for ball game sacrifices and other forms of torture.[1]

That Maya inscriptions record battles and other momentous events scholars can no longer deny. Indeed, as early as the beginning of the twentieth century, a few enterprising epigraphers had suggested the presence of historical narrative and personal names—suggestions ignored by scholars for nearly half a century. Breakthroughs by Heinrich Berlin and Tatiana Proskouriakoff proved definitively that Maya texts incorporate important historical information.

Event glyphs, or more formally the verbs of Maya discourse, reflect an exciting array of actions undertaken by the principal subject of Maya inscriptions, who was usually the *ch'ul ajaw* or king. Whether in reference to capture, war, birth, death, or some other action, hieroglyphic verbs relate what happened on the recorded Long Count or Calendar Round dates, followed by the name of the person who engaged in that action and, more rarely, the object toward which the individual's action was directed.

Verbs describe two broad categories of events. The first category consists of the more common episodes in life, ranging from birth to death. These events happen to or otherwise involve in some specific way rulers, mythological or legendary ancestors, or important deities. In the second category of events, the same performers or subjects participate in ritual or ceremonial events, including bloodletting and the dedication of monuments and buildings. While inscriptions can record a whole range of different "minor" actions, many of them poorly understood, the "larger" or "major" events documenting important milestones have long been successfully deciphered, either in terms of meaning or phonetic translation, or both.

Birth

In the 1960s, while hunting for glyphs related to "sacrifice," Tatiana Proskouriakoff noticed that at Piedras Negras stelae fell into chronological groups that never exceeded a reasonable length for a human life span. These spans of time, she argued, were the life spans of the persons whom the monuments portrayed. In addition, she observed that the earliest date in any group preceded a sign resembling a toad or frog turned "upright," the so-called "upended frog" (T740). This "initial" event, she reasoned, must have occurred close to the protagonist's birth, if not signifying birth itself. Epigraphers now accept for this sign the logographic value **SIJ**, which yields *sij* "birth."

a   b

Fig. 9-1   Expressions for "birth": a) T740 **SIJ**, "to be born"; b) **SIJ-ya-ja** "was born."

The "upended frog" represents the most common "birth" expression in the inscriptions, usually inflected as an intransitive completive verb and sometimes suffixed with T181 **-ja** for a passive construction. Most often the sign with its several possible affixes reads, "was born." The beginner should remember that while the "frog" reads logographically "birth," in phonetic spellings it has the value **ju**.

Another, much less common form meaning "birth" takes the logogram for "earth," or **KAB'**, superfixed by an extended or "flat" human hand. Spelled syllabically, the same expression takes the hand with the sequence **ka-b'(a)** instead of **KAB'**. The signs most likely spell *u kab'*, while their graphic arrangement suggests the gloss "he touched the earth," not inappropriate since Landa describes mothers as squatting over the ground during parturition, rocking and straining until the child dropped to the ground.

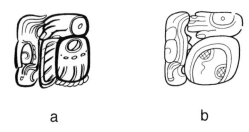

a   b

Fig. 9-2 Expressions for "birth": a) **U** hand **ka-ba**; b) "hand over earth."

Heir Designation

The next major event in an individual's lifetime would be "baptism," as described by Landa. However, since in the majority of cases the subject or protagonist was a ruler, or *ajaw*, usually his earliest event involved "heir designation," an occasion that combined secular ceremonies with blood-letting and warfare. Heir designation was especially common at Palenque, represented in some texts by the "flat-hand" verb supporting a deer hoof. While the deer hoof may read **MAY**, the hand in this position very likely reads **K'AL** and takes the inflectional suffixes **ji** and **ja**. The verb may read *k'al-jij may* (or some variation thereof), meaning "was presented" or "was bound, the offerings."

More commonly, "heir designation" takes the form of an extended two-part phrase centered around the verbal root *och* "enter." In these col-locations what follows is the "location" or "condition" or "state of being" that the individual "enters into," usually involving a "tree" of some sort. Thus we have *och te'* "entered the tree" or more elaborately *och ch'ok te' na* "entered the tree house." Even more extensive phrases can relate these

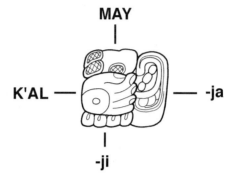

Fig. 9-3   The "deer hoof" event as "heir designation."

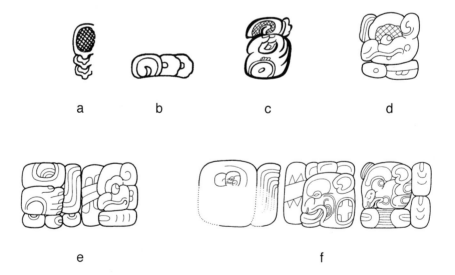

Fig. 9-4   "Enter" and expressions for "heir designation":
a) rattlesnake tail; b) rattlesnake tail; c) **OCH-(chi)**;
d) **OCH/OK TE'**; e) **K'AL . . . -wa-ni-ya TA OCH-le-{l}**;
f) **CHUM-[mu]-{wa}-n(i) TA B'A ch'o-k(o)-le-l(e)**.

events, varying the theme by adding auxiliary verbs and other expressions, for example *k'al . . . wan ta och te'lel* "was placed in entering the tree." Other forms include the "seating" glyph, as in *chumwan ta b'a ch'oklel* "was seated, he did it, the First Sprout," where a preaccession ceremony becomes the equivalent of an office that the protagonist is "seated" in.

Accession

The high point of an individual's life was to accede to the position of ruler, an office usually designated as *ch'ul ajaw* in the inscriptions, and celebrated with the erection of monuments. The twenty-year *k'atun* anniversary of the date of accession was often celebrated, and inscriptions recording this anniversary were added on the original monument and elsewhere in the city.

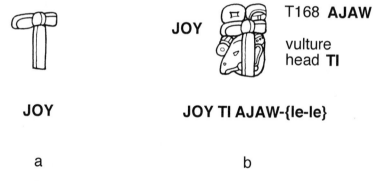

Fig. 9-5   Accession: the "toothache" glyph and affix cluster;
a) **JOY**; b) Piedras Negras Stela 25.

In Proskouriakoff's original analysis, she noted that one date stood out as the major focus of an inscription, emphasized by the following "toothache" glyph. The "toothache" collocation signifies accession and incorporates an actual head variant bound up in cloth strips like someone who has a toothache. The recounting of the ceremony of accession, the Maya equivalent of coronation, usually involves this two-part verbal phrase, or a variant thereof, that can fill a single glyph block or can spread across two or more glyph blocks.

The first part consists of one of several statements equivalent to "taking" or "accepting" or "being placed into," while the second part incorporates

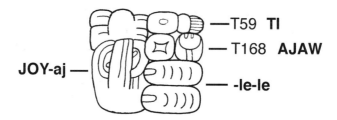

JOY-aj —
—T59 **TI**
—T168 **AJAW**
— **-le-le**

Fig. 9-6   Accession: the affix cluster from Piedras Negras Throne 1:
JOY-ja TI AJAW-le-le.

the actual office taken or accepted. Both parts can vary considerably. For example, the first part can include the common toothache form **JOY TI**, while the second part reads **AJAW-le-{le}**. Alternatively, the first part can incorporate the well-known "seating" glyph, securely read **CHUM-[mu]**, then followed by the title **KALOMTE'**, an office of unknown meaning. Also used is an important but rare "seating" variant, apparently carrying the same value, that depicts the lower half of a human body actually in the act of "sitting down."

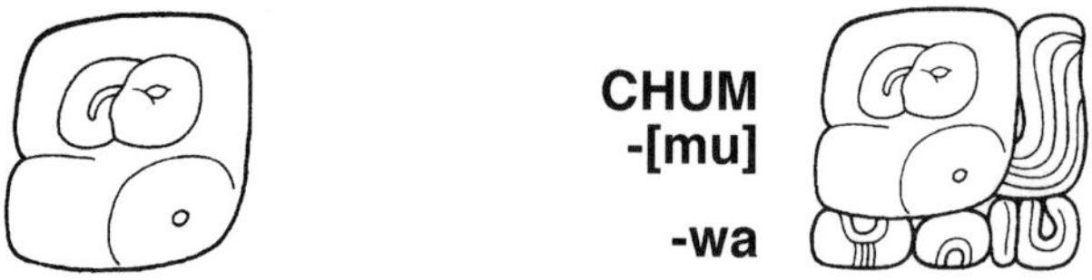

CHUM-[mu]

**CHUM
-[mu]**

-wa

-ni

-ya

Fig. 9-7   Accession: the "seating" glyph:
a) T644b; T644b with affixes.

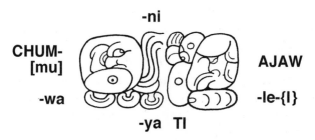

-ni

**CHUM-
[mu]**

-wa

-ya TI

AJAW

-le-{l}

Fig. 9-8   Accession: the "seating" expression from Chinikihá Throne, top:
CHUM-[mu]-wa-n(i) TI AJAW-le-{l}.

Fig. 9-9   Seating variant from Yaxchilán Lintel 37.

-ja   TI KALOM

CHUM

-la

TE'

Fig. 9-10   Accession statement from Tikal Stela 21:
CHUM-la-ja TI KALOMTE'.

The "toothache" image may refer to the "binding" or "tying" of the ruler in office, as in "he was tied in the rulership." More properly it refers to "tying on" the headband of royal office, a bandanna-like affair evidently made of barkpaper painted red or another sacred color and affixed with an image of the "Jester God," a little deity that wears a headdress resembling the apparel of a medieval jester. Sculptural scenes show the ruler's mother or wife or some other individual proffering royal headbands and head-dresses in an act symbolic of taking office.

The second part of the "toothache" collocation, the office portion, is generally called the "affix cluster" because of its grouping of *ajaw* "lord" with the affix T188 **LE**. Scholars have interpreted the latter as meaning "lineage," but examples that include the double **-le** signs or "doubler dots" suggest that it likely represents the suffix *-lel* (with the final *l* sound suppressed in the hieroglyphs) and has the function of transforming the noun that it is attached to into a quality or state. *Ajawlel* thus means "lord-ness" or "lordship."

Fig. 9-11   T188 **le**.

Fig. 9-12   Bonampak Sculptured Stone 1, man offering Jester God headband.

Any form of *ajaw* can serve in the context of "accession," either its logographic versions, the vulture with *ajaw* headband, or its phonetic spellings. The whole expression approximately signifies, "was tied in rulership." Alternatively, the "seating" glyph refers to the act of sitting on the ruler's throne, or being "seated in rulership," an event that the Maya graphically portrayed in artistic scenes.

We can see how accession statements work by turning to Yaxchilán Stela 11, where C4-E1 gives the complete verbal phrase. Initially we have the "toothache" glyph (C4), followed by the vulture head with T59 **TI** over its forehead (D4), and finally the office acceded to, in this case the "affix cluster" giving the combination . . . **AJAW-le-{l}**, or *joy ti ajawlel*—"was tied on, [the office of] lordship." The primary name of the ruler who accedes is given at F1.

(jo)-JOY-ja   TI

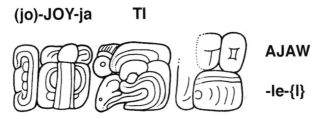

AJAW

-le-{l}

Fig. 9-13   Accession statement from Yaxchilán Stela 11, front, lower glyph panel, C4-E1.

Alternative expressions for accession include a variety of glyphs based on an outstretched human hand that points towards the right, which is probably read **K'AL** and which holds different objects as if to present them. The held objects can include the Jester God mentioned above, a knotted headband, the syllabic "upended frog" **ju** with the syllable **na**, the sign for "white" or **SAK**, and a variant that resembles the **WINAL** glyph. Recent study has shown that all of these interchangeable objects present

a   b   c   d   e

Fig. 9-14   Alternative accession expressions: a) **K'AL JUN**; b) **K'AL-ji-ya SAK JUN**; c) **K'AL SAK JUN-(na)**; d) **K'AL ju-n(a)**; e) **K'AL SAK JUN**.

the word *jun* "headband," or more specifically *sak jun* "white headband," again referring to the headband of rulership received upon accession. The basic phrase therefore reads *k'al sak jun*, approximately "the binding of the white headband."

Secondary lords, called *sajal*, also acceded to office. *Sajalob'* generally ruled over secondary "satellite" centers dependent upon the larger regional capital. The office of *sajal*-ship was confined largely to the Usumacinta River Valley, and was generally carried out "under the authority" of the local *ch'ul ajaw*, the "divine lord" of the regional capital.

Fig. 9-15   Accession to *sajal*-ship: **CHUM-la-ji-ya TI sa-ja-li**, "was seated in *sajal*-ship."

House, Monument, and Object Dedications

Rulers regularly erected monuments proclaiming their accomplishments in office. The erection of stelae, wall plaques, lintels, and other sculptures were occasions for celebration, and numerous hieroglyphic passages include formulaic dedications giving the date a particular monument was erected and often the monument's name.

The most common of these dedication events was the erection of stelae, which are called *lakam tun* "banner stone" in the inscriptions, evidently equating the carved shafts with a specific kind of cloth standard or banner. Based on the word *tz'ap* meaning "set up" or "erect," dedication verbs for these events precede the name of the class of object so erected, signified here by the common collocation **TUN-(ni)** "stone." Thus **U TZ'AP-wa TUN-(ni)** yields *u tz'apaw tun* "his set up stone," with the understanding that it was the ruler who was responsible for commissioning that particular work of art.

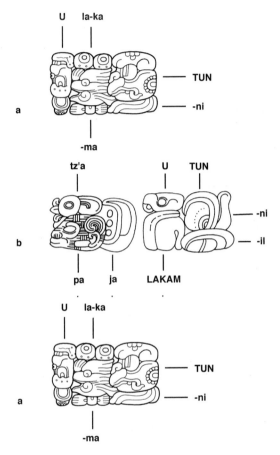

Fig. 9-16   Monument dedications: erection of stelae: a) *lakam tun* "banner stone";
b) *tz'apaj u lakam tun* "set up his banner stone"; c) *u tz'apwa tun* "his
set-up stone."

Another common dedication verb is represented by the head of the
deity called God N, whom the Maya depicted as a grizzled old man wearing
a crosshatched net headdress. God N, best known as a dedicatory verb from

Fig. 9-17   Dedication verbs: God N.

the Primary Standard Sequence (see Chapter 14), is linked with the *pawatunob'*, the gods who held up the sky. God N frequently replaces the "step" glyph, a sign that depicts architectural steps with an ascending "footprint." Both glyphs may read logographically **T'AB'**, "to rise up," "prepare," or "present,"[2] and can substitute freely for each other. Typically found in "house dedication" inscriptions honoring new houses and temples, the God N-Step set may refer to the act of "making sacred" or even to the physical act of "climbing up" the house steps to reach the temple, not unlike actual presentation scenes found on pottery.

Fig. 9-18   Dedication verbs: Footprint-on-Step.

Still another standard dedication verb combines the signs for **OCH** "enter" (T207), and the glyph for **K'AK'** "fire" (T122 and T1035)—or "enter the fire." Most epigraphers equate the event with the ritual cleansing of buildings and objects with smoke from burning incense braziers, a common ceremony attested ethnohistorically. (See Chapter 12: Locations and Objects.) The *och* "enter" glyph takes the form of a rattlesnake tail.

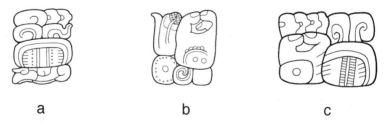

a   b   c

Fig. 9-19   Dedication verbs, "enter the fire": a) **OCH-(chi) K'AK'**;
b) **o-ch(i) K'AK'**.

Both the God N-Step set and the **OCH K'AK'** glyphs generally occur in dedication clauses that actually name the specific house or object involved and its "owner" (see Chapter 12). Thus we have a sequence opening with one of the dedication verbs, the name of the object dedicated (for example, a house or sculpture), a glyph that *tells* us this is the name, the class of object thus named but in possessed form (for example, "his house"), and the name of the object's owner.

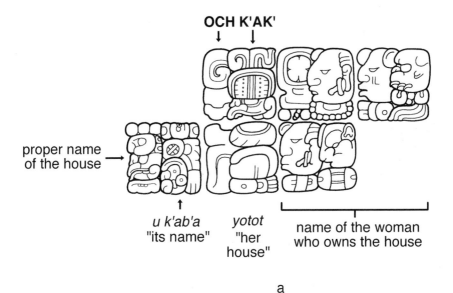

Fig. 9-20   House dedication phrases: a) Yaxchilán Lintel 56, I1-H2; b) Piedras Negras Throne 1, D'5.

Several verbs, that are still not securely deciphered, also serve to dedicate houses, monuments, and even plazas. Most of these take the prefix T79 attached to variable elements, but how these correspond is not fully understood. **PAT** is the most commonly accepted reading for T79, but the value **K'A** or **K'AL** has also been suggested for this sign.

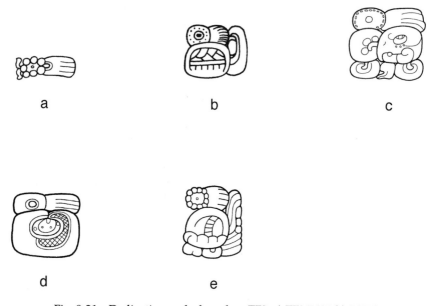

Fig. 9-21   Dedication verbs based on T79: a) T79 **PAT**; b) **PAT-ja**;
c) **PAT-bu-ya**; d) **PAT-[la]-ja**; e) **PAT-wa-n(i)**.

Another interesting form takes the profile view of a common ceramic plate infixed with the **K'IN** sign that symbolizes the sun or the concept of "day," followed by a sign previously read **NA** "house" but that may read **NOJ** "great." The combination of **LAK** "plate" and **K'IN** spells *lak'in*, "east."

Fig. 9-22   Dedication verbs: **K'IN**-plate variant, Piedras Negras Lintel 12, L1.

A wide range of objects can be dedicated using formulaic texts based on these combinations. Epigraphers refer to such dedicatory phrases as "name-tagging," the marking of objects for the primary purpose of identifying who owned them. Dedicated or "tagged" objects comprise not only "houses" or monuments, but earflares, ceramic vessels, textiles,[3] carved bones, jewelry, and other small-scale portable objects. We will review some of these dedication formulas in the Chapter 14 discussion of the Primary Standard Sequence.

Arrival and Departure

Among the more interesting recent decipherments are glyphs that refer to rulers and other members of the nobility who "traveled" outside their respective cities. The discovery that individuals "moved" from one place to another has had enormous impact on the way scholars view Maya political structure. Rulers did more than just stay put and govern internal affairs. Not only did nobility "travel" for the purpose of fulfilling marriage contracts, they visited each other to engage in mutually beneficial ceremonies or to "witness" accessions and other rites. As we will see in later chapters, rulers oversaw the installation of *sajal* underlords at secondary centers, perhaps placing their own puppets on the throne or otherwise ensuring the loyalty and prestige of their new underlord. In extreme cases, rulers were forced to flee their towns, driven out by political forces arrayed against them.

The most common of the verbs used to describe "movement" are the variants incorporating the "upended frog" sign seen in the "birth" glyph, but used here with the sign's phonetic value **ju**. Combined with the phonetic sign **li** (T24), the "upended frog" spells *jul* "arrive" (intransitive incompletive). *Jul* also can be spelled with the symbolic form of **ju** (T45) together with **-li** (T24 or T82). Other variations of *jul* include the **JUL** hand-variant

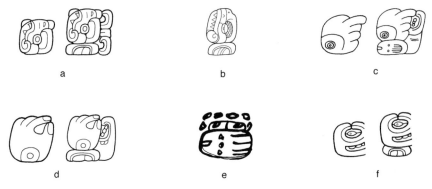

Fig. 9-23 "Arrive": a) "upended frog" variant; b) "upended frog" variant; c) hand variant; d) hand variant; e) symbolic variant; f) "Moon Sign" with infixed eye variant.

logogram (T220) with the usual **-li** (again T24 or T82), giving **JUL-(li)**. To make this a passive construction, the suffix T181 **-ja** gets tacked on. A final **JUL** takes the form of the well-known "Moon Sign" (T181 and T683) but with an infixed eye (T683v).

A less common sign for "arrive" takes the form T113.82ms or **ta-l(i)**, rendering *tal* or *tal-i* "come to" (incompletive), "arrived, came" (completive).

Fig. 9-24   The **ta-l(i)** "to arrive" verb.

Another infrequent glyph designates the act of "going," "traveling," or the general sense of "journeying." Composed of the somewhat rare form of T585 **b'i** with infixed crosshatching, and the well-known suffix **-na** (T23), possibly yielding the word *b'ixan*, the sign occurs in only a few texts, where the movement of an individual from one location to another is described, seemingly in a context of hostilities. A variant prefixed by **xa-** (T114) "again" may indicate "another journey" or "his/her/its journeying."

Fig. 9-25   *B'ixan/xan* "to walk, travel": **B'IX-na**.

Appear, Emerge

Individuals can "arrive" in other ways than actually traveling over ground, principally by being invoked supernaturally through rituals of manifestation. Thus supernatural creatures, gods, ancestors, and fantastic zoomorphic forms can "come out" and "make appearances." Verbs that relate these

JAL   **LOK'**

a   b

Fig. 9-26   Glyphs for "appear" and "emerge": a) **JAL** "appear";
             b) **LOK'** "emerge."

actions include the "crossed bars" **JAL** (T153) "to make manifest" (and alternatively, "to say"), and the logogram **LOK'** (Tnn) "to come out, emerge, escape."

Miscellaneous Actions

One of the main purposes of "movement" from one place to another was to participate in various events, such as major rituals. Not only did rulers visit other locations as a matter of state policy or of personal courtesy, they also invited illustrious guests from neighboring cities to come visit *them*. Some traveled considerable distances for these events.

Glyphs have been deciphered for quite a range of miscellaneous actions, performed by either local nobility or invited guests, providing a rich array of verbs of fascinating scope.

"Witness": An important and rather frequent glyph that implies the physical presence of someone as "witness" to an event, an oblique reference that this person has "traveled" from some other place. Composed around the root *il* "to see," the sign represents a human eyeball with "sight-rays" sometimes emanating in the direction that the eye is looking. When possessed, the root takes the prevocalic third-person pronoun *y* (generally in the form T17 **yi**), since two vowels back-to-back tend to clash, plus inflectional suffixes, yielding **yi-IL-ji**. Alternatively the glyph can be spelled out phonetically as **yi-la-ji**.

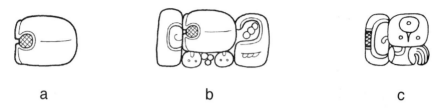

Fig. 9-27   "Witness": a) **IL**; b) **yi-IL-la-ja**; c) **yi-la-ji**.

"Open": Rituals can involve the opening of things, especially caches buried in the ground during the dedication of monuments, houses, and the tombs of ancestors. Most commonly the glyph takes the form **pa-sa** or *pas*.

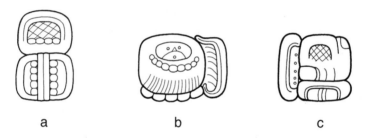

Fig. 9-28   "Open" and "close": a) **pa-sa**; b) **ma-ka**; c) **U k'a-li**.

"Close": The word exactly opposite of "open" can be written as **ma-ka** or *mak* "to close." *Mak* and *pas* can be combined for "to close and open." The glyph **k'a-l(i)** or *k'al* also means "to close."

"Enter": As mentioned above under "House, Monument, and Object Dedications," people and things can "enter" locations, an action expressed by glyphs representing either the rattles on a rattlesnake tail (T207), a hand grasping some sort of blade (T361), or by a leaf (T213v?), or the head of a dog-like animal (T765), each of which read **OCH**.

"Give": In many instances, visitors arriving before lords bear gifts and tribute and various rituals involve the exchange of a variety of objects. Thus we have a verb that reads *yak'wa* or *yak'aw* (**ya-k'a-wa**), meaning "he gave it."

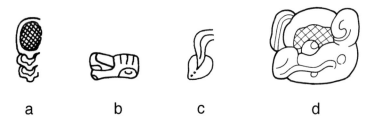

Fig. 9-29 **OCH** "Enter": a) rattlesnake tail; b) hand-grasping-blade; c) leaf; d) head variant.

Fig. 9-30 "Give": **ya-k'a-wa**.

"Take": Just as you can give something, you can take or receive. Expressed visually by an open hand that holds the familiar **AJAW** sign (T533), the glyph reads **CH'AM** or **K'AM** "to take, receive." What was taken usually follows in the immediately adjacent glyph, or replaces the **AJAW** within the hand. In most cases the object represents a variant of K'awil, referring to the "K'awil staff" or "Manikin Scepter" that rulers hold in their portraits. Other received objects include **lo-m(a)** or *lom* "staff, spear," and a twisted cord or knot of unknown value.

"Carry": Objects can also be carried, as expressed by the logogram T174 **KUCH**. Examples of "something carried" are the palanquins named on the carved wooden lintels of Tikal.

"Turn, Rotate": Something can be "turned" or "rotated," expressed as the logogram **PET** that consists of concentric circles, or as **PET** with verbal inflections for the incompletive, as in **PET-ji-ya** "turning, rotating."

"Face Down, Doubled Over, Fold": A positional verb based on the root *pak*, "fold" can read **pa-ka-la-ja** or *paklaj*, a passive form meaning "It was faced down, it was doubled over."

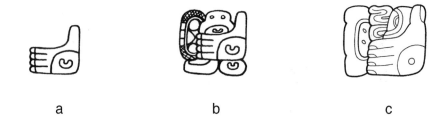

a   b   c

d   e

Fig. 9-31   "Take": a) **CH'AM/K'AM**; b) **U CH'AM-wa**;
c) **YAX CH'AM K'AWIL**; d) **U CH'AM-wa lo-m(u)**;
e) **CH'AM-(ma) K'AWIL-(la)**.

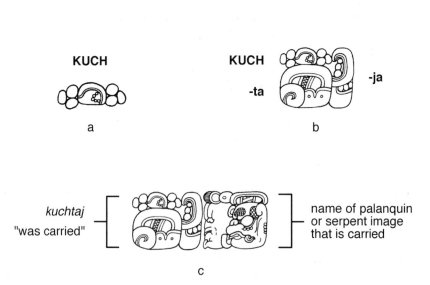

KUCH   **KUCH**

-ta   -ja

a   b

kuchtaj
"was carried"

name of palanquin
or serpent image
that is carried

c

Fig. 9-32   "Carry": **KUCH**.

Fig. 9-33 "Turn": **PET-ji-ya**.

Fig. 9-34 "Fold, face down": **pa-ka-la-ja**.

"Hurl": To indicate the action "throw" or "hurl," that was mostly used in the context of battle, scribes could employ the verb **ya-la-ja** or *yalaj*.

Fig. 9-35 "Hurl": **ya-la-ja**.

"Mold, Form in Clay": Things can be molded, especially objects of clay or "images." A common expression thought to describe this, T79 either by itself or with verbal affixes or other components of uncertain function, may read **PAT**. The same verb seems to be expressed in syllabic form as **pa-t(i)**. Another version meaning more specifically "forming in clay" takes the form **pa-k'a-ji-ya** or *pak'ajiy*, followed by the name of the molded thing.

"Create, Awaken": Objects formed in clay, either idols or ceramics, lead us to the notion of "creating something," which may be expressed by the sequence **ya-aj-ji-ya** and can also signify "awaken" or "awakening."

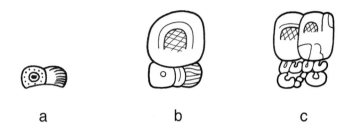

Fig. 9-36   "Mold, form in clay": a) T79 **PAT**; b) **pa-ti**; c) **pa-k'a-ji-ya**.

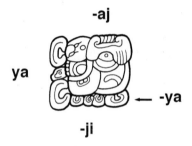

Fig. 9-37   "Create, awaken": **ya-aj-ji-ya**.

"Bathe or Water": Although seemingly restricted to references where names of the Paddler Gods follow, the sequence **ya-ti-ji** evidently refers to "bathe," and seems to indicate that these gods were immersed in blood.

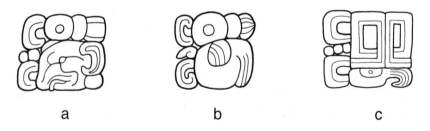

Fig. 9-38   "Bathe, water": variants of **ya-ti-ji**.

"Adorn": People can "dress up" or receive items for display, described as **na-wa-ja** or *nawaj*, "was adorned." Prominent captives taken in battle were referred to as "adorned" with ritual cloth and other items, before meeting their fate under the sacrificial blade.

Fig. 9-39   "Adorn": **na-wa-ja**.

"Cut Up": Things can also be cut up, perhaps in reference to dismemberment of victims of human sacrifice. The glyph that expresses this action reads **su-sa-ja** or *susaj*, a passive verb inflected as "it was cut up," or "it was rasped."

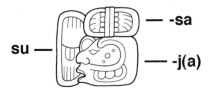

Fig. 9-40   "Cut-up": **su-sa-j(a)**.

"Eat": Not only can things be cut up or dismembered, it seems they can also be eaten, a possible reference to ritual cannibalism. This complex glyph expressing the act of "eating" takes the form **U-WE'-ya** "his eating of," incorporating a "sign cluster" that visually appears to have several different signs grouped together as the main sign but that in fact forms the logogram **WE'**.

Fig. 9-41   "Eat": **U-we'-ya**.

"Wrap": To express that something was wrapped, for example the royal headband in the sense of "tying it on," the sequence **pi-xo-ma** or *pixom* "to wrap" is used.

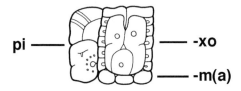

pi —————— -xo

—————— -m(a)

Fig. 9-42   "Wrap": **pi-xo-m(a)**.

"Rest, End, Finish": Of course, occasionally one has to stop and rest, and things come to an end. Separate from calendrical "completion" or "ending" glyphs, the concept "rest, end" can take the form *jil*, represented as a knot over the day sign **KAWAK** that together form the non-calendrical sign **ji** (T60:528), along with the suffix **-li**.

Fig. 9-43   "Rest, end, finish": **ji-l(i)**.

Contract, "Betrothal"

One event that took place when nobility came together was the formulation of marriage contracts. While no known glyph denotes marriage *per se*, we have the sign for "wife" that was most commonly used in the codices of Post Classic and Colonial times. (See Chapter 11: Relationships.) However, one collocation used in conjunction with a young woman on Piedras Negras Stela 1 reads **ma-ka-j(a)** or *makaj* "she made a contract," and doubtlessly refers to her betrothal upon reaching the age of twelve.

Fig. 9-44 "Contract, betrothal": **ma-ka-ja**.

Get Drunk, Dance

Having departed, traveled, and arrived, the guest could "witness" or take part in a wide assortment of events as described, or he or she could have what we in Western culture would call "a little fun." This might include "getting drunk," a reference known from Lintel 3 of Piedras Negras in what was certainly an all-night drinking bout celebrating the twenty-year anniversary of the accession of Ruler 4. Far from frivolous or merely for amusement, these were important rites solidifying relationships and "alliances" between cities. The principal collocation on Lintel 3 meaning "to get drunk" takes the shape **ti-ka-l(a)**, or *tikal*, followed by the inebriating substance—in this case, **ka-ka-w(a)** or fermented chocolate drink.

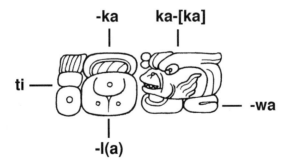

Fig. 9-45 "Get drunk": **ti-ka-l(a) ka-{ka}-w(a)**.

Before "getting drunk," an individual mentioned on Lintel 3 is said to have performed the "Descending Makaw" dance, expressed by the verb **AK'OT-(ta)-j(a)** or **AK'-ta** and followed by the dance's name. As used here, the verbal phrase incorporates the "**TI** construction" mentioned previously. Examples of the "dance" glyph are fairly common, especially in texts at Yaxchilán that accompany scenes of individuals dancing.

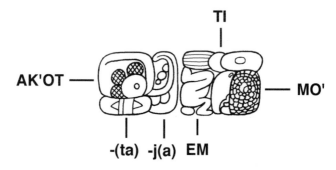

Fig. 9-46   "Dance": **AK'OT-(ta)-j(a) TI EM MO'**.

Bloodletting and Sacrifice

Not all was fun and games, so to speak, nor innocuous rituals of glorification. Blood was shed, and pain was inflicted. The Maya and other Mesoamerican civilizations indulged in human sacrifice, which included the extraction of human hearts, decapitation, flailing, and evidently the ripping off of the lower jaw from the face. War captives could be "softened up" through beatings, cutting, and other forms of torture. As we have seen, sacrificial victims were perhaps eaten. One figurine in the "Jaina style" of Campeche depicts a contorted, bound prisoner who howls in pain as he burns from the fasces of firewood strapped to his back.

But most important were certain forms of bloodletting that individuals performed on *themselves*. Women regularly slashed their tongue then drew barbed cords through the incision to draw blood that dripped and spattered on to barkpaper strips. In similar fashion, men communally slashed the foreskin and shaft of their penis, then tied themselves to the others' members with straw or cords.

Blood was the essence of the human spirit, the substance in which the soul resided. As such, it was important to draw some of this sacred essence and offer it as nourishment for the gods. The act of bloodletting also produced visions, induced through blood-loss and the weakened condition of the body. In these bloodletting "vision quests," supernatural spirits and renowned ancestors appeared and offered their "strength" and wisdom.

The signs for "blood" in Maya inscriptions (T32 through T41) consist of a stream of "blood droplets," the same convention used in sculptural depictions of bloodletting. Read **K'UL** or **CH'UL**, "blood glyphs" sometimes take the "monkey face" **k'u** element meaning "god." Together with the flowing stream, the principal glyph for "sacrifice" incorporates a down-turned hand that reads **CHOK** "to scatter," with the suffix T93 **CH'A** "drops," forming **CHOK CH'A** "to scatter drops."

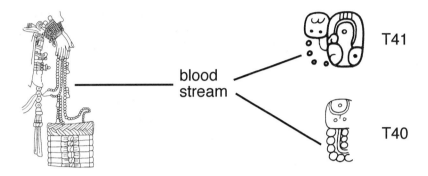

Fig. 9-47   Blood signs and their iconographic origins.

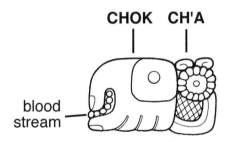

Fig. 9-48   "Scatter drops": **CHOK CH'A**.

Another common glyph for "sacrifice" depicts the obsidian lancet used to inflict wounds, read **CH'AB'**, "to harvest," "to sacrifice," "to pierce with a lance," and "to do penance." The sign for **CH'AB'** forms part of the "**TI** construction" verbal phrase *u b'a ti ch'ab'il* "he/she let blood."

Fig. 9-49   "Pierce": a) **CH'AB'**; b) **U B'A TI CH'AB'-il**.

When committing autosacrifice, one of the goals was to receive some type of vision, an act that frequently involved the conjuring of the "dead" spirit of an ancestor or a supernatural creature. The principal verb for this type of manifestation incorporates an upright hand that grasps a fish (T714). The hand by itself reads **tza**, but becomes **tza-ka** when holding the fish, yielding the word *tzak* "to conjure, to make manifest." Gods were also conjured, and often the specific god K'awil, patron deity of royal bloodlines.

Fig. 9-50   "Conjure": **tza** and **tza-ka**.

War

After Pakab'—ancient Pomoná, Tabasco—fell victim to the raid described at the beginning of this chapter, the victors commemorated their attack by carving one of the most spectacular monuments ever conceived by the Maya.[4] Packed with no less than nine prisoners arrayed below the Piedras Negras ruler and across the terrace risers of a pyramid, Stela 12 provides an extraordinary window into the consequences of war. Each captive, portrayed with sensitive realism, meets his fate in his own way, terrified, dazed, hopeful, dejected, or groveling shamelessly. And not only do the side inscriptions provide the dates of the conflict and the origins of the two factions, captions give each prisoner's name.

Monuments like these offer convincing proof that war was waged "for keeps," with vigorous aggression and little mercy for prisoners' lives. Not far from Piedras Negras, the Bonampak Murals actually depict war in action, a wild fray where two armies clash, waged evidently on a battleground rather than within the walls of any particular city. Other information suggests that towns were the principal objects of war, and that cities were sacked and the collection of tribute enforced.

The most dramatic of the events described in ancient Maya texts, war was also among the most frequently commemorated acts, particularly in the Late Classic Period when incidents of violence increased and eventually wide areas were engulfed in conflict. Not surprisingly, texts abound with a variety of expressions for different kinds of war, warriors, captives, and victory celebrations, while artistic scenes portray a plethora of bellicose and martial themes.

GENERAL WAR-RELATED TERMS

A general term for "warrior," **b'a-te'** (spelling the word *b'ate'* or *b'ate'el*) functions as a title of rank, while another title indicates how many captives a warrior has taken in his lifetime as a mark of valor (the Count of Captives Epithet). Warriors also take honorifics naming them "captor" of an especially renowned prisoner (*u chan* or *u b'ak*). (For all of these terms see Chapter 10: Names and Titles.)

A descriptive term for war—one of the most frequent war-related nouns encountered in Maya texts—reads **TOK' PAKAL** "flint-shield." The counterpart to Central Mexican and especially Aztec inscriptions which pair a shield and spear, or a shield and makannah (a type of wooden sword edged with obsidian), the combination that is sometimes called the *lechuzas y armas* motif functions as a metaphor, invoking the idea of war through the display of its principal weapons. Since Mesoamericans for the most part lacked metal blades, they employed instead varieties of flint and volcanic glass, or obsidian, which produced surgically sharp edges for lances, throwing-darts, swords, axes, and knives. Mesoamerican warriors also used shields of basket weave and other material, some of which were rectangular in shape and flexible and could be rolled up for storage or ease of transport.

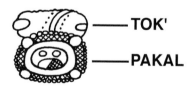

Fig. 9-51   "His flint, his shield": **TOK' PAKAL**.

In Maya inscriptions, "flint" takes the form of a lozenge-shape often marked with an X-motif of squiggly lines. Shields most commonly occur as oval forms with an outer band of crosshatching and with what may be the flayed face of a sacrificial victim in the middle. The logographic "shield" sign reads **PAKAL** (T624), while "flint" reads **TOK'** (T257), yielding the phrase *tok' pakal* "flint-shield"—an appropriate emblem for Maya warfare.

"CAPTURE"

Tatiana Proskouriakoff, who greatly contributed to unraveling the intricacies of the Maya texts, had only recently published her groundbreaking article on Piedras Negras when she turned to the inscriptions at Yaxchilán, in some respects the "queen" of Maya cities. There, on a low-relief doorway lintel that depicts the capture of two prisoners by the king and his cohort, Proskouriakoff noticed hieroglyphs that were carved both on the prisoners' legs and in the lintel's text. One phrase, the subject of the main clause, followed a sign-set that she argued must describe the action portrayed—the taking of captives. Thus, without knowledge of its phonetic value, she identified the "capture glyph" on structural and visual grounds alone.

Epigraphers now know that the glyph Proskouriakoff identified as "capture" reads just that: **chu-k(a)** or **chu-[ku]** or *chuk* "to seize." The standard collocation takes the passive form **chu-ku-j(a)** or **chu-ka-j(a)**, "he was seized." Because the collocation represents an intransitive verb, the name of the subject then follows, which is the prisoner's actual name.

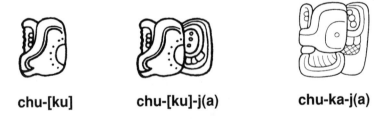

chu-[ku]   **chu-[ku]-j(a)**   **chu-ka-j(a)**

Fig. 9-52   "Capture": **chu-ku, chu-ku-j(a),** and **chu-ka-j(a).**

There are abundant examples of the capture glyph in inscriptions, and through the names of prisoners, toponymic references, and Emblem Glyphs, decipherers can piece together who conquered who, which kings dominated Classic Period politics, and the political fortunes of an array of Maya towns and cities.

"Bring Down"

Maya texts can convey considerable excitement, and nowhere more so than among those inscriptions that described warfare. Perhaps the most important discovery of recent years in this respect has been the phonetic decipherment of the verb **ju-b'u-yi** or *jub'uy,* "was brought down," "fallen, collapsed." Widely recognized for years as a verb for aggression, the compound figures in the expression *jub'uy u tok' pakal* "was brought down, his spear [and] shield" (or, "his spear, his shield"). In this sense, *jubuy* refers to the "conquest" of specific locations such as towns, cities, or even districts.

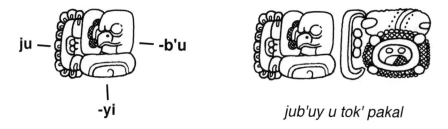

jub'uy u tok' pakal

Fig. 9-53 **Ju-b'u-yi** "bring down" and *jub'uy u tok' u pakal* "bring down his flint-shield."

"Burn"

To leave no doubt about Maya objectives in waging war, another related term reads **pu-lu-yi** (*puluy* or *puliy*) from the root *pul* "to burn." Personified variants include a young lord's face infixed with **K'IN** (T544) and topped with "smoke scrolls," graphically depicting an individual on fire.

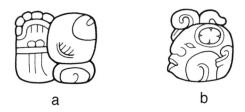

a   b

Fig. 9-54 "Burn": a) **pu-lu-yi**; b) **PUL-[yi]**.

In Maya texts both people and places burn, no doubt in reference to the sack of towns and other locations.

"Drive Out"

Individuals were also driven out of places, or made an "escape," indicated by the glyph that may read **LOK'** (see "Appear, Emerge"). The sign represents a little serpentine figure as it emerges from a glyph resembling a split **yi** (T17), sometimes prefixed with T580 **lo**. The most prominent person thus driven out was the Late Classic Tikal king Nuun U Jol Chaak, who was defeated during a civil war with his apparent half-brother, the ruler of Dos Pilas. Under pressure from Tikal's main rival, Calakmul, aggression from Dos Pilas succeeded in "driving" U Jol Chaak into exile and sent him packing west to Palenque. U Jol Chaak's misfortune continued, his life ending in oblivion before his son, Jasaw Chaan K'awil, was able to reinstate Tikal's former glory.

LOK'

Fig. 9-55   "Drive Out": **LOK'**.

Star-Shell, Star-Earth, and Star-Emblem Glyph

Most prominent and best known of all war glyphs, the "Star-Over-Shell," "Star-Over-Earth," and "Star-Over-Emblem Glyph" complex figures as one of the first war compounds identified, but among the last to be deciphered phonetically. The correct reading remains disputed. Perhaps read *jub'uy* "to sink, go down, fall, collapse," as suggested by David Stuart, the signs in this complex may simply function as variants of the aforementioned, more standard *jub'uy*.

The complex includes the sign for "star," significant because ethnohistoric accounts relate that war was common during first appearances of

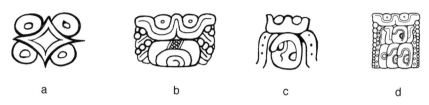

Fig. 9-56 Star variants: a) star; b) star-over-**yi**; c) star-over-earth; d) star-over-Emblem Glyph.

the morning star. For this reason, epigraphers have long argued that the *jub'uy* glyph bears an intimate connection with the planet Venus.[5] More recently, however, David Stuart raised doubts about these assertions, suggesting that the shower or streams of dots found with the glyph relate to meteor showers.

The "Star-Over-Shell" complex depicts a star—probably read **EK'** when by itself—and a stream of dots, above and laterally around the **yi** sign, which provides the final *y*. The sign used for the day **KAB'AN** (T526), read in this case **KAB'**, can replace or surmount the **yi**, as can the main sign of Emblem Glyphs that denote individual cities or the lineages that ruled them. (See Chapter 12: Locations and Objects.)

The "star-shell" complex seems to denote war against a city, as opposed to aggression against a person. (In the latter case, the sign for "war" takes the form of an axe, as discussed below.) As with other verbs, the following glyph indicates the object of the war, in general a town represented by an Emblem Glyph, although as mentioned the Emblem's main sign can replace the **yi** or **KAB'** signs instead.

AXE GLYPH

One final glyph denotes "war," graphically depicting an axe and read **CH'AK** "to chop, decapitate." Such was no doubt the fate of unlucky warriors in battle or prisoners destined for sacrifice.

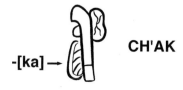

-[ka] → CH'AK

Fig. 9-57 "Axed": **CH'AK**.

Death

Of course every life culminates in death, and the Maya took great pains to mark the deaths of rulers and other individuals. Sumptuous tombs were built and dedicated for the most illustrious *ajawob'*, stocked with mortuary goods of high aesthetic quality—exquisitely carved jade jewelry, powerful polychrome narrative scenes painted on pottery, sculptured human and animal bones, and wooden objects. Over the burial sites of the highest ranked noblemen, enormous multi-tiered pyramids reached skyward, crowned with sculpted lintels and painted roof displays. The Maya reverently sent their dead into an afterlife of different grandeur, one of supreme glory where the gods and ancestors resided.

Several expressions for death figure in Maya inscriptions, beginning with the bluntly stated "death" verb representing a skull, or **CHAM** (T736v), sometimes postfixed with **-mi—CHAM-(mi)** "death of" or **CHAM-(mi)-ya** "he dies." A more elaborate and poignant version is the "wing-shell" expression which reads *u ch'ay u sak nik ik'il* (**U ch'a-y(i) U SAK NIK IK'-il**), "it diminished, his white flowery soul," in reference to a flower-blossom that has faded in death.

a   b   c   d

Fig. 9-58   "Death": a) **CHAM**; b) **U CH'AY SAK NIK IK-il**;
c) **OCH JA'**; d) **OCH B'I-ji-ya**.

The most interesting and complex expressions for death are focused around the act of "entering." Evidently the Maya believed, among other related concepts, that a person or soul actually voyages through life in a canoe, and that death involves sinking beneath the surface of a primordial sea to enter the Underworld. Thus, **OCH-JA'** means "to enter the water," or "to die." The canoe itself represents the Milky Way, a great *sak b'e* or "white road" that sweeps across the nighttime sky. In the Maya's most dramatic expression for death, when one dies one travels the Milky Way, journeying along its celestial brilliance. The appropriate glyph for this final act is **OCH-B'I** "entered the road." In this way, the most renowned of

Palenque rulers, Janab' Pakal the Great, left this world to join his ancestors along the great white road of the stars.

Burial

The final rite of passage is when the body is placed in its grave—in the case of Maya rulers, a tomb stocked with the king's personal possessions and funeral gifts. Carefully noting this last formal event on earth, Maya scribes recorded the place of the burial and the fact that the king was *mukaj*—"was buried" (**mu-ka-ja**)—marking the date and circumstance. Only ceremonies of anniversaries—the commemoration of former greatness—then remained to be told.

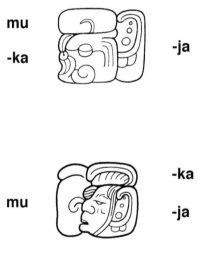

Fig. 9-59   "Burial": **mu-ka-ja**.

NOTES

1. I've reconstructed the Piedras Negras-Pomoná wars primarily from the inscriptions of Piedras Negras Stela 12 and La Mar Stela 3 (now in the Los Angeles County Museum of Art), including details of the dates involved and the names of some of the captives taken. Details concerning the prisoners' torture derive from the iconography of Stela 12, while evidence of warrior uniforms comes from painted and sculptured iconography on a variety of Maya monuments.
2. The God N-Step set was previously read **JOY** by epigraphers, but although still viable as a transcription the signs have been taken more recently by David Stuart and others to read **T'AB'**.
3. Shown in paintings such as the Bonampak murals, which depict hieroglyphically tagged clothing.
4. Monuments at both Piedras Negras and nearby La Mar commemorate a series of coordinated attacks on Pomoná.
5. Apparently based on an incorrect reading of a Calendar Round found with the battle scene in Room 2 of the Bonampak murals.

CHAPTER 10

‗‗

Names and Titles

Robust for his race, he stood about five feet, six inches tall to judge from his earthly remains, and was fairly well nourished. About eighty years old when he died, he lived an especially long life—not as long as certain other *ajawob'*, but impressive nonetheless. His name was Jasaw Chaan K'awil I, and he reigned for at least forty years—the equivalent of two *k'atunob'*.[1]

For more than one hundred years, archaeologists, travelers, and the simply curious have wondered who were the subjects of the portraits that graced the ruined cities, who built the huge pyramids at sites like Tikal, Copán, Palenque, and dozens of other locations. Part of the answer lies in the Maya script, the signs the Maya themselves recorded.

Linda Schele publicly expressed her hope that history books would one day include the names of Maya kings alongside those of European luminaries such as Alexander the Great or Henry VIII. That wish has since become reality. Modern textbooks designed for art history and architecture classes, and history books themselves now speak of the Tikal "sky-sweeper" Jasaw Chaan K'awil I and the Palenque "flower-shield" Janab' Pakal the Great. Their names, their titles, and their political affiliations have all yielded to the decipherer's pursuit of the past.

From the calendars, the structure of the script, and the events related, we now turn to the subjects of the inscriptions, those who dominated Maya civilization and ranked in the highest echelons of society.

Exactly how stratified a society the Maya developed remains uncertain, but we know from hieroglyphic inscriptions that there were at least two tiers of nobility, and possibly even four or five. At the apex stood the *ch'ul ajaw*—the "holy lord"—and his immediate family, including wives, princes, and princesses. Very rarely did women accede as ruler. Underneath ranged the *sajalob'* (*sajal*, singular) or "underlords," and the *itz'atob'* or "learned ones," the artisans such as scribes and sculptors. Together with titles of rank and prestige, each individual had his or her personal names, often based on those of deities or derived from locations. Name strings— or extended name phrases—recorded such crucial data as the names of one's mother and father, especially if these were important persons.

Personal Name Clauses

Private or "personal" names can range from one or two simple "core" glyphs to extended nominal phrases that include complex strings of titles and parentage statements. When we turn to our Yaxchilán example, Stela 11, we find that one-half of the entire text—the right half—is taken up by a single, elaborate name phrase that can be broken down into the ruler's name (F1–F4), and the names of his mother (G1–G3) and father (H3–I4).

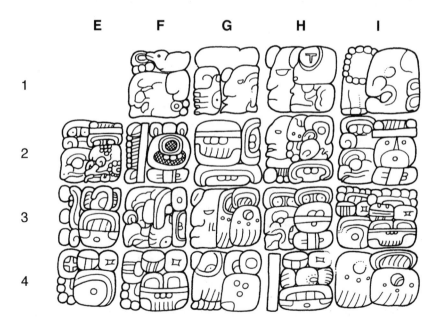

Fig. 10-1   Name phrase of protagonist, Yaxun B'alam, Yaxchilán Stela 11, front, lower glyph panel, F1-I4.

Extremely high-placed individuals used "pre-accession" names that changed to formal designations after "coming of age" or designation as heir. On Stela 11, the subject's personal post-accession name occurs at F1. Also, rulers in particular were distinguished by titles that could vary from inscription to inscription for any given name and were often used by more than one individual. Titles of the ruler on Stela 11 extend from E2 through F4.

Fig. 10-2   Principal name glyph of Yaxun B'alam, Yaxchilán Stela 11, front, lower glyph panel, F1.

Over time rulers accrued additional titles perhaps not present in earlier texts. Moreover, certain dynasties tended to recycle royal names—for example, Yaxchilán saw a host of high kings named "Shield Jaguar" (Itz'amná B'alam) and "Bird Jaguar" (Yaxun B'alam), while Tikal inaugurated at least two sets of rulers with the names "Stormy Sky" and "God Who Sweeps the Sky" (Jasaw Chaan K'awil) and three or four "Jaguar Paws." Consequently, some uncertainty arises over which ruler an inscription is describing, usually resolved by any dates present. For the most part, however, personal names include at least one "core" component specific to that individual, and epigraphers tend to "name" the person based on this constant sign or signs. In the early stages of decipherment, people were given nicknames—Curl Snout, Eighteen Rabbit, Lady Great Skull, and so on—but as decipherment progresses these sobriquets are being replaced by more genuine phonetic ones.

On Stela 11, the "core" sign in the ruler's name includes the prefix T126 **ya**, the full figure of a bird (**XUN**), and a jaguar's head as the main sign (**B'ALAM**), giving *Yaxun B'alam*—Bird Jaguar.

MALE NAMES

One specific glyph, the male agentive *aj* meaning "he of," marks names of men. (An example can be seen on Stela 11 as the first element at F2.) Usually taking the form T12, **AJ** serves in other contexts as a "relationship" glyph that ties the name of the person to a toponym or occupation or some other quality. (See Chapter 12: Locations and Objects.) Thus certain glyphs that carry T12 designate male individuals as "he of such and such a place" or "he of such and such an occupation"—for example, "he of water" (*aj naab'*), "he the scribe" (*aj tz'ib'*), and so forth.

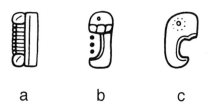

a   b   c

Fig. 10-3   The male agentive **AJ**.

FEMALE NAMES

The female article, usually a woman's head in profile, distinguishes the names of female subjects and objects from male ones. (Several examples occur on Stela 11, at G1, H1, H2, and G3.) Long thought to represent the value **NA** "mother," the female profile more likely has the value **IX** or **IXIK**, based on the presence of phonetic complements and its use as a title (in the form *ix*) in conquest period and early colonial documents. Some problems arise, however, since the female profile, and the entire female figure, function as the head and personified variant of the number "one," or **JUN**, in calendrical contexts, and may function with this value in certain names. Again, the reader has to rely on context in such cases, which is not always an easy task.

Fig. 10-4   The female article **NA** or **IXIK**.

Another key and fairly constant component of names that designate females is sometimes called the "female introductory glyph" and includes an upturned vase over dots that resemble the "water group" prefix (T32–41), generally with an infixed **K'IN** within the vase. At present, the sign remains unreadable, although suggestions include the value **JOY**.

Fig. 10-5   The female introductory glyph.

Titles and Offices

Just as royalty of the medieval and ancient Old World had prodigious strings of honorifics, or titles of glory, such as King of Kings, His Caesarean Majesty, Great Caesar, and so on, exalted Maya kings accrued their own epithets, sometimes a multitude of them. Lesser nobles also received titles of rank, setting them apart from other courtiers and official underlords. Although epigraphers often refer to titles by nicknames, numerous honorifics have yielded phonetic translations. Not all of them, however, can be understood.

Ajaw: By far the most important general title assumed by any member of the nobility, *ajaw* in all of its various guises served to rank the highest echelon of Maya society, those occupying the top rung of the social ladder. Both men and women were born into this strata and can carry the title in their hieroglyphic names.

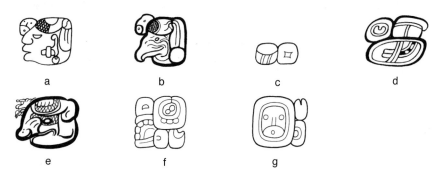

Fig. 10-6   The *ajaw* title: a) head variant; b) vulture variant with **AJAW** headband; c) T168; d) T168:518; e) rodent variant with Jester God headband; f) phonetic spelling; g) symbolic variant with **-(wa)** phonetic complement.

K'ul Ajaw: While the title *ajaw* could be used by anyone of the highest social rank, only kings became the *ch'ul* (Ch'olan) or *k'ul* (Yucatec) *ajaw* and took this designation. Individuals who acceded as supreme ruler acquired the title affixed to Emblem Glyphs naming the city they ruled or the dynasty to which they belonged. (See Chapter 12: Locations and Objects, Emblem Glyphs.) Thus the compound reads *ch'ul* "Tikal" *ajaw* or *k'ul* "Yaxchilán" *ajaw*. Note that the **CH'UL/K'UL** component has more recently been identified as **CH'UJUL/K'UJUL**, which likewise means "holy, divine."

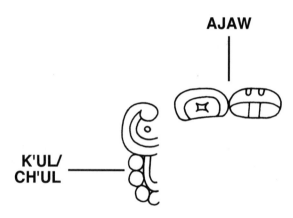

Fig. 10-7   **K'UL/CH'UL . . . AJAW.**

K'inich: Once thought to read *mak'ina* because of its **ma-** prefixes, then later just *k'ina*, the **K'INICH** sign (T74.184) means "sun-faced one" in reference to the ruler as Sun God. An alternative version has the **chi** hand infixed with the four-petaled flower that stands for "day" in the Long Count calendar and that reads **K'IN**, together with the **K'IN** sign's usual T116 phonetic complement **-ni**. The **K'INICH** head variant depicts the Sun God himself, often postfixed with the symbolic **K'INICH** in reverse

a   b   c   d

Fig. 10-8   Variants of the *k'inich* title: a) logogram; b) head variant;
c) head variant with **-ni** phonetic complement;
d) phonetic spelling **[K'IN]-n(i)-ch(i)**.

(T184.74). *K'inich* signs help to identify kings, especially in particularly long texts, where the sign offers an immediate clue to the presence of a royal name. Look for the *k'inich* sign and you have already found the name of the king, who is almost always the subject of the clause.

Kalomte': A convoluted history has led to at least three separate phonetic readings for this title—*b'atab'*, *chakte'*, *makuch*—none of which have proven durable. Currently epigraphers accept David Stuart's transliteration, *kalom* or *kalomte'*, based on phonetic spellings at Copán (**ka-lo-ma-te'**). Its meaning, however, is uncertain. Although both males and females could use the title, only the highest lords, the *ch'ul ajawob'*, acceded to this office, and only at Tikal, where *kalomte'* was the supreme social rank. Whether *kalomte'* sets Tikal rulers apart from those controlling other cities remains to be seen. As an aside, not infrequently individuals who take *kalomte'* also use the title *och k'in* meaning "west," as in "west *kalomte'*." Again the meaning remains unclear, but at least one such individual may have literally come from the west, the renowned Tikal war captain Siyaj K'ak' or "Smoke-Frog," who was perhaps from Teotihuacan in Central Mexico. Our text from Yaxchilán Stela 11 contains one example of *kalomte'*—the head variant that holds an axe beside its eye—at F3.

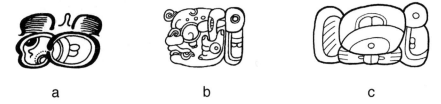

a   b   c

Fig. 10-9   The *kalomte'* title: a) symbolic variant; b) head variant; c) phonetic spelling.

B'akab': Meaning "Stood-Up One," *b'akab'* designates extremely important men and women of royal status, and generally occurs as one of the last

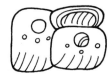

Fig. 10-10   The *b'akab'* title.

titles in the name string. What it refers to, however, currently remains unknown. Two *b'akab'* titles are present on Yaxchilán Stela 11, each associated with Bird Jaguar's mother and father respectively (G3 and I4).

Numbered K'atun Glyphs: Royal names frequently carry titles equivalent to the person's age, counted in terms of *k'atunob'* or twenty-year periods. Although sometimes counted from *accession*, the so-called Ben-Ich K'atun (misnamed from an incorrect reading of the *ajaw* component) gives a quantity of *k'atuns* (one, two, three, and so forth) generally counted from birth. For example, if the title reads "two *k'atun*," the individual has entered his second *k'atun*, and would have been between the age of twenty and forty. In this way, age was given merely in broad terms of aggregates of twenty years. On Yaxchilán Stela 11, the text records that Yaxun B'alam (Bird Jaguar IV) was a "three *k'atun ajaw*" (E3), or a "*kalomte'* ruler" between forty and sixty years of age at the time when the inscription was carved. His father, Itz'amná B'alam II (Shield Jaguar the Great), carries the remarkable title "five *k'atun ajaw*" (H4)—that is, an extraordinary eighty to a hundred years old. Any title acceded to can occur in numbered *k'atun* titles, and consequently we have "X-*k'atun ajaw*," "X-*k'atun kalomte'*," or "X-*k'atun sajal*."

a   b

Fig. 10-11   Numbered *k'atun* titles from Yaxchilán Stela 11, front, lower inscription: a) **JO K'ATUN AJAW**; b) **OX K'ATUN KALOMTE'-(te')**.

"Successor" Glyphs: The Distance Number Introducing Glyph appears with numerical coefficients in contexts that clearly have nothing to do with the calendar. Nicknamed the *hel* glyph, this compound functions as a title that designates the order of rulers *in succession*. The "numbered *hel*" title documents whether the king was the first, second, third, or twenty-third ruler, and so on, in line of succession at a particular site. "Successor titles" count from the legendary founder of the ruler's dynasty who was usually, but not always, the founder of the city itself. In this way we know that, in his line, Jasaw Chaan K'awil was the twenty-sixth king of Tikal, and

Yax Pasaj the sixteenth at Copán. (Curiously not all sites record succession, and not all counts within cities continue unbroken. For instance, we have no formal record at Yaxchilán designating which number Itz'amná B'alam was, though we have the appropriate numbered title for most of the early kings at the site.) Now read **TZ'AK** meaning "put in order," instead of *hel*, the "successor title" vaguely resembles a swastika, and carries inflectional affixes for completive and incompletive forms.

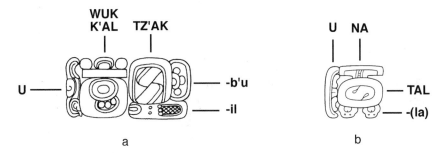

a   b

Fig. 10-12   Successor titles: a) **U WUK K'AL TZ'AK-b'u-li** "the twenty-seventh successor"; b) **U NA TAL-(la)** "the first successor."

A closely relayed sign, the numerical classifier **TAL**, functions in other glyphs that also indicate successors, as in **U OXLAJUN TAL** "the thirteenth [successor]."

Ch'ajom: As performers of sacred bloodletting ceremonies, rulers were designated *ch'ajom* or "dripper," a reference to Period Ending rites that involved the scattering of blood with the hand. Intimately associated with the "scatter" verb **CHOK** discussed in the previous chapter under "Bloodletting and Sacrifice," the glyph takes the same prefix—the sign **ch'a** or "drops"—followed by **jo-m(a)**. *Ch'ajom* replaces titles of rank that include *ajaw*, *kalomte'*, and *sajal* when paired with "numbered *k'atun*" glyphs, thereby giving the individual's age as *"X-k'atun ch'ajom."*

Fig. 10-13   The *ch'ajom* title.

Penis Title: Blood drawn from the penis served as the primary source of "drops" flung in male "scattering" rites. As such, the penis became a title in its own right, represented by a penis (**AT**) with foreskin slashes (**xa**) and scrotum and prefixed with T115 **yo-**. The compound yields **yo-xa-AT**, often subfixed with the phonetic complement **-(ta)**, or *yoxat* "scarred penis." As identified by Tom Jones, symbolic variants may simply read **yo-AT-(ta)**, with other forms reading **to-XAT-(ta)** (*toxat*) "bled penis" and **yo-to-XAT-(ta)** (*yotoxat*) "very scarred penis." Head variants include a rain god deity or jaguar head, both of which hold up a stone or curled element with one hand.

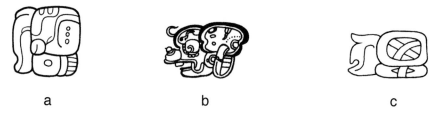

a   b   c

Fig. 10-14   The "penis" title: a) with "penis" as main sign;
b) head variant; c) phonetic spelling.

"He the Youthful": Originally read "ballplayer," *aj pitz* or *aj pitzal* signifies "of the youthful" or "he the youthful" and usually takes the form **AJ pi-tzi-la**. The title often precedes **OL-(la)** "heart," rendering "He of the Youthful Heart."

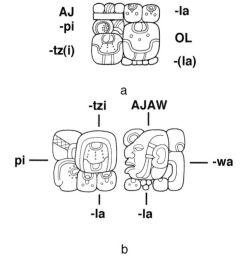

Fig. 10-15   "He the Youthful": a) **AJ pi-tz(i)-la OL-(la)**; b) **pi-tzi-la-AJAW-wa-la**.

"Warrior": Because the Maya placed so much emphasis on war and the taking of captives, the title **b'a-te'** or *b'ate'*, meaning simply "warrior," accrued to individuals who were prominent or successful on the battlefield.

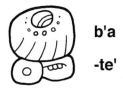

b'a

-te'

Fig. 10-16   "Warrior": **b'a-te'**.

"Captor Of": When successful at capturing very important or famous lords, a warrior could take a title that named him "captor of so-and-so." On Yaxchilán Stela 11, Yaxun B'alam takes the title *"u chan Aj Uk"*—"Captor of He of Uk" (at E2). (**u-ku** or *Uk* in this case refers to an unknown location somewhere in or around the Usumacinta River Valley from where the prisoner came.) This same text later calls Bird Jaguar's father *u chan Aj Nik*, or "Captor of He of Nik," another unknown location in the vicinity. Warriors caught during the campaigns of father and son, Aj Uk and Aj Nik were high enough in rank that their captors forever afterwards commemorated their conquests with these special titles.

Fig. 10-17   Examples of "Captor of" from Yaxchilán Stela 11, front, lower glyph panel: a) E2 **U CHAN AJ u-k(u)**; b) I2 **U CHAN AJ NIK-(ki)**.

"Count of Captives" Epithet: The number of warriors taken in battle determined one's "warrior status." Just as Aztec warriors advanced in rank according to the number of captives they took during their years of service, Maya warriors kept track of their own prisoners, tallying these in special numbered titles. Thus, F2 on Yaxchilán Stela 11 names Yaxun B'alam "He of Twenty-One Captives," with the "Moon Sign" functioning as "twenty." The

"Count of Captives" epithet probably reads **AJ-X-B'AK** or "He of X-number of captives" (for example, *aj jun b'ak* "He of One Captive").

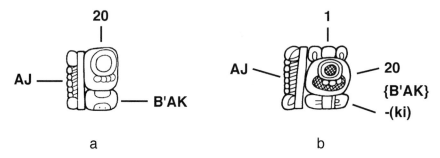

Fig. 10-18   "Count of Captives" Epithet: a). Yaxchilán Lintel 17, F4, **AJ K'AL BAK** "he of twenty captives"; b) Yaxchilán Stela 11, front, lower glyph panel, F2, **AJ JUN K'AL {B'AK}-(ki)** "he of twenty-one captives."

"First Staff": A rare title related to the status of warriors indicates perhaps a captaincy or status similar to "king's champion." In this sense the title **B'A-LOM** or *b'a lom* "First Staff or Spear" names a position equivalent to "head warrior" or "high war chief."

Fig. 10-19   "First Staff": **b'a-lo-m(u)**.

Ch'ok: Young people take the special title *ch'ok* "youth, sprout." Superficially similar to the **B'A** or **U B'A** "he does it/the image of" compound that may depict a gopher, the collocation nevertheless reads **ch'o-k(o)** or U **ch'o-k(o)**, with a variant resembling two round eyes frequently replacing the "gopher" head. Occasionally the sign becomes an adjective, followed by the term *winik* "person," or *ch'ok winik* "young person." Rulers seem to take the *ch'ok* title before accession, but are designated by more formal "adult" titles after ascending the throne. Use of the plural marker **-TAK** converts the sign to "youths." *Ch'ok* may also have the general meaning of "lineage member" so that, in combination with the **CHAK** prefix meaning "great," the compound refers to "great lineage member."

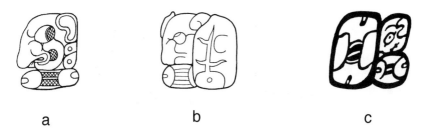

a   b   c

Fig. 10-20   *Ch'ok*, "youth, sprout": a) **ch'o-k(o)**; b) **ch'o-k(o)-TAK**;
c) **CHAK ch'o-k(o)**.

Sajal: Among the formal political titles denoting "rulership," *sajal* was an office to which both males and females could accede, especially in the regions of the Usumacinta and Pasíon Rivers. Unlike the positions of *ajaw*, *k'ul ajaw*, and *kalomte'* that designate rulers of major political centers, the position of *sajal* corresponds to "underlord" and represents a second or third-tier status. *Sajalob'* did, however, rule over lesser sites, generally referred to as "secondary" or "dependent" centers, and regularly erected monuments in their own right. *Sajalob'* commonly appear in portraits alongside rulers, with ruler and *sajal* formally interacting as they perform important state ceremonies. *Sajal* means roughly "one who fears," but how this meaning relates to the status of "underlord" remains debatable.

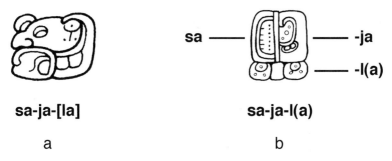

sa-ja-[la]   **sa-ja-l(a)**

a   b

Fig. 10-21   *Sajal*: a) head variant; b) phonetic spelling.

Itz'at: Meaning generally "wise person," "sage," and "artist," the *itz'at* title can be spelled phonetically **i-tz'a-t(i)** or **i-tz'a-t(a)**. Alternatively, the title may be represented by the portrait of a young lord with a quill writing instrument used by scribes tucked into his headband. The personified variant reads **ITZ'AT**.

a   b

Fig. 10-22   *Itz'at*: a) head variant; b) phonetic spelling **i-tz'a-t(a)**.

Aj K'ujun: Over the years the *aj k'ujun* title has had various readings ranging from *aj k'u-na* "He of the God House," to *aj k'ul na* "architect, mason." Recent decipherments indicate that the compound reads *aj k'ujun* "He of the Books," a possible reference to someone who cares for or preserves the sacred hieroglyphic codices, in effect a "librarian." In our example from Yaxchilán, Stela 11, the mother of Bird Jaguar takes this title (H2), incorporated in the sequence *chaanal ixik aj k'ujun*, or "Heavenly Woman of the Books."

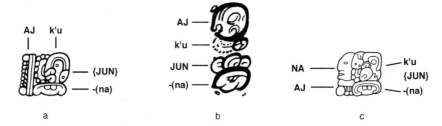

a   b   c

Fig. 10-23   *Aj K'ujun*: a) **AJ k'u-{jun}-na)**; b) **AJ k'u-JUN-(na)**;
c) **NA AJ k'u-{JUN}-(na)**.

Ordinal-Numbered Titles: When we count "one, two, three" and so on, we use "cardinal" numbers that express quantity. Ordinal numbers, on the other hand, such as "first, second, third," express degree, quality, or position in a series. Many different titles, as well as other hieroglyphic signs, take ordinal numbers, predominantly some form of "first." Thus we have *b'a sajal* "first underlord," *b'a lom* "first staff," *b'a ch'ok* "first youth," *b'a* *ajaw* "first lord," and *b'a uxul* "first sculptor." **YAX** "first" sometimes replaces **B'A-**, as in *yax ch'am* "first bloodletting," or Yax Mutul "First Bird (Tikal) Place." T23 **NA-** also can serve as "first," as in **NA cha-k(i)** "First Chaak" (*na chaak*). However, since all three—*b'a*, *yax*, and *na*—have secondary meanings (*b'a* functions syllabically, *yax* can mean "blue-green," and *na* means "house" and "mother"), caution should be exercised against a misreading. By implication, titles that receive *b'a*, *na* or *yax* may indicate the highest position in the kingdom corresponding to that title, for example, the "king's own artist." Individuals that carry "first" titles have achieved the highest level of their profession.

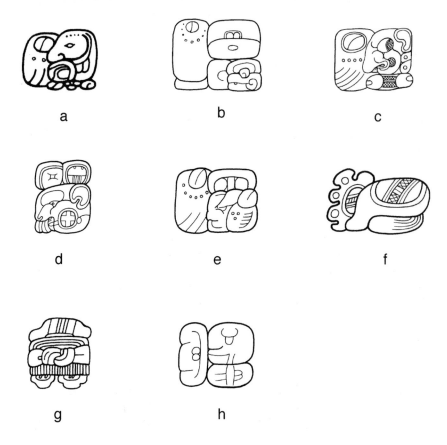

Fig. 10-24   Ordinal-numbered titles: a) *B'a Sajal* "First Underlord"; b) *B'a Lom* "First Staff"; c) *B'a Ch'ok* "First Youth"; d) *B'a Ajaw* "First Lord"; e) *B'a Uxul* "First Sculptor"; f) *yax ch'am* "first bloodletting"; g) *Yax Mutul* "First Bird Place"; h) *Na Chaak* "First Chaak."

Maya inscriptions incorporate dozens of additional titles, mostly unique or personal ones associated with specific lords and often functioning as descriptive references. Such epithets as Aj Payal ("He the Leader"), Mo' Witz Ajaw ("Macaw Mountain Lord"), and Yajaw K'ak' ("Lord of Fire") all attest to a remarkably rich legacy of personal epithets for individuals.

Royal Names

The names of literally hundreds of kings, royal consorts, and princely offspring were recorded in Maya inscriptions. Indeed, most major towns saw the accession of at least a dozen separate kings. Tikal, for instance, had well over thirty individual rulers during a period of roughly six hundred years, beginning in the third century A.D. and ending around A.D. 869. Many have taken their place among the great kings of history, with lasting fame for at least a handful of these rulers, including Pakal the Great, Shield Jaguar the Great, and Stormy Sky. While royal names alone could fill volumes, the following list includes the best-known Maya kings of the Early and Late Classic Periods.

TIKAL

Yax Nuun Ayin I (ruled ca. A.D. 379–426): Originally nicknamed "Curl Snout" or "Curl Nose," Yax Nuun Ayin reigned during a period of unrest, when Tikal may have come under the sway of the Central Mexican highland kingdom of Teotihuacan. Possibly himself the son of a Teotihuacan ruler who subjugated Tikal, Yax Nuun Ayin in turn was father to Tikal's most important Early Classic ruler, who was known euphemistically as Stormy Sky.

a   b   c

Fig. 10-25   Tikal rulers: a) Yax Nuun Ayin I; b) Siyaj Chaan K'awil II;
c) Jasaw Chaan K'awil I.

Siyaj Chaan K'awil II (ruled ca. A.D. 426–456): The most important of Tikal's Early Classic kings and one of Maya civilization's greatest rulers, Siyaj Chaan K'awil reigned during a time when Tikal prospered significantly—possibly under the direct control of Teotihuacan. The city's political fortunes would soon wane, with Tikal in decline for the next two centuries.

Jasaw Chaan K'awil I (ruled A.D. 682–ca. 734): After an especially low period in Tikal's fortunes, in the wake of outright conquest by Caracol and the ascendancy of Calakmul, Jasaw Chaan K'awil ushered in Tikal's most prominent period of growth. From this point on, Tikal dominated much of the Maya lowlands, the direct result of Jasaw Chaan K'awil's effective control and astute military campaigns.

PALENQUE

Janab' Pakal the Great (Pakal II) (ruled A.D. 615–683): Best known for his unprecedented funeral monument, the Temple of the Inscriptions, and the spectacular tomb and sarcophagus located underneath, Janab' Pakal initiated Palenque's meteoric rise to superpower. Like most kings at their respective cities, Pakal's descendants followed him in office.

a   b

Fig. 10-26 Palenque rulers: a) Janab' Pakal the Great;
b) Kan B'alam II.

Kan B'alam II (ruled A.D. 684–702): Son of Janab' Pakal, Kan B'alam continued the architectural development of Palenque begun under his father, completing the Temple of the Inscriptions, the Cross Group, and numerous other major buildings and sculptural programs.

COPÁN

Waxaklajun U B'a K'awil (ruled A.D. 695–738): The thirteenth ruler of Copán, Waxaklajun U B'a K'awil, also known as 18 Rabbit, ruled over a period of remarkable prosperity like many Late Classic kings. Unfortunately, midway through his reign Waxaklajun fell prey to an upstart lineage located a few dozen miles to the northwest at Quirigua, and was evidently captured by that city's ruler K'ak' Tiliw. Copán thereafter entered a slump, until reinvigorated under its last great ruler.

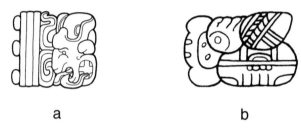

a   b

Fig. 10-27   Copán rulers: a) Waxaklajun U B'a K'awil; b) Yax Pasaj.

Yax Pasaj Chan Yoat (ruled A.D. 763–820): The greatest of all Copán kings, Yax Pasaj saw architecture culminate during his reign, though signs of unrest underlay the veneer of prosperity. Under Yax Pasaj, secondary lords achieved power and influence well beyond past traditions, creating a situation that may have contributed to the Maya civilization's collapse.

YAXCHILÁN

Itz'amná B'alam (ruled A.D. 681–742): Known as Shield Jaguar the Great, Itz'amná B'alam also helped his city reach its architectural peak, initiating

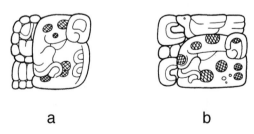

a   b

Fig. 10-28   Yaxchilán rulers: a) Itz'amná B'alam; b) Yaxun B'alam.

many sculptural programs and downtown building projects. A great warrior renowned for his conquests and captives, Itz'amná B'alam successfully consolidated his political power in this sector of the Usumacinta Valley, outstripping his neighbors downriver at Piedras Negras and probably controlling much of the trade in this area.

Yaxun B'alam (ruled A.D. 752–768): Yaxun B'alam, called Bird Jaguar IV, inherited his father's kingdom after some ten years of struggle, militarily dominating the region in order to claim his prize. A great builder and patron of the arts like his father, Yaxun B'alam's seventeen-year reign left Yaxchilán among the most formidable of cities ever built in the Maya world. Unfortunately short-lived, stability in the western Maya region gave way to increased conflict and political fragmentation, ending in the still unexplained collapse of Maya civilization within a century. Evidence suggests that the end came much more swiftly for the Usumacinta Valley, and within a generation or so dynasties at both Yaxchilán and Piedras Negras had completely stopped producing monuments.

Artists' Signatures and Titles

By the mid-1980s, David Stuart, an epigrapher of extraordinary acumen, had achieved one of the truly great discoveries of not only Maya inscriptions, but of world art in general. Examining hieroglyphic texts on pottery vessels, he found that one glyph changed entirely when the vessel happened to be carved. He quickly realized that the version used with painted vessels, in its most common form **AJ tz'i-b'(i)** or *aj tz'ib'*, yielded the Mayan word for "scribe," based on the root *tz'ib'* "to write." The other, he assumed, meant that the vessel was carved. In time, Stuart was able to identify such phrases as genuine artists' signatures.

Few civilizations in the world have acknowledged their artists, an occupation more commonly associated with manual labor than an exalted skill. Not until after the Renaissance did artists regularly sign their works, with the exception of potters' marks and Greek sculptors of the Classical Age.[2] Maya artists' signatures therefore occupy a very special place. Note that both men and women could serve as painter-scribes, although no confirmed female sculptors have yet been identified.

Painters and Sculptors: Artists' names generally appear in the Primary Standard Sequence on pottery vessels as part of an elaborate dedication

and name-tagging phrase. (See Chapter 14.) In contrast, genuine signatures occupy rather unpretentious, out-of-the-way places on monuments
and pottery vessels, often incised in the surface of the background. Up to
ten sculptors' signatures have been identified on certain monuments (for
example, El Peru Stela 34), indicating that especially large and impressive
pieces, but also some smaller ones, involved the collaborative effort of
master artists working in teams. The presence of signatures demonstrates
how monuments for smaller sites were sometimes created by sculptors
from the regional capital, and either produced at the secondary center or
transported there after the work was completed.

Artists' names and signatures generally begin with **U-tz'i-b'(a)** (*u
tz'ib'*) "his writing," or **yu-xu-l(u)** (*yuxul*) "his sculpture," followed by the
name of the artist himself. When used in sculptors' signatures on monuments, the **yu-xu-l(u)** sequence frequently becomes the title **AJ-u-xu-l(u)**
or *aj uxul* "He of the Sculpture," and is embedded in the artist's name
string, while on pottery **U tz'i-b'(a)** becomes **AJ tz'i-b'(a)** or *aj tz'ib'* "He of
the Writing" or simply "Scribe."

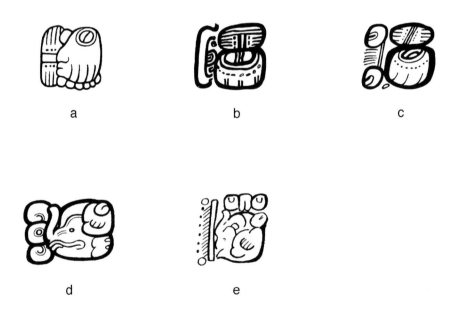

a   b   c

d   e

Fig. 10-29   Artists' titles: a) **tz'i-b'(a)** with head variant for **b'a**; b) **U tz'i-b'(a)**;
c) **AJ tz'i-b'(i)**; d) **yu-xu-[lu]**; e) **AJ u-xu-[lu]**.

Aj Naab': Very common in Late Classic texts, this important title reads "He of Water" (**AJ na-b'i**), although exactly to what it refers or its connection with artists has proven problematic. Epigraphers identify individuals who take this title as "artists" in a general sense, nonspecific in terms of "painter" or "sculptor," while certain kings of Palenque take names with similar-sounding compounds, as in Janab' Pakal "Flower-Shield." The term *naab'* "water" may relate in some way to the use of liquid paint.

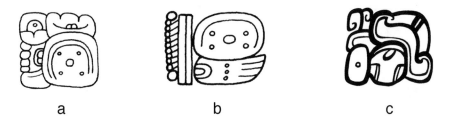

a   b   c

Fig. 10-30   Artists' titles: a) *aj naab'*; b) *aj b'ich'*; c) *sak chuwen*.

Aj B'ich': A more obscure artist's title, **AJ b'i-ch'(a)** or *aj b'ich'* occurs mostly if not exclusively among artists from Piedras Negras. Its translation remains uncertain.

Sak Chuwen: Meaning "resplendent artisan" or "pure artisan," the title relates to descriptions and images of scribes as monkeys, a concept that survives in the *Popol Vuh*. Somewhat rare, the compound most commonly takes the form of a "cap" partly surrounding the **CHUWEN** sign, prefixed with the logogram **SAK**, meaning "pure" and "resplendent" (and alternatively "white").

NOTES

1. My biographical description of Jasaw Chaan K'awil derives in part from remains found in his tomb, Burial 116, and various provenanced and unprovenanced hieroglyphic texts.
2. For example, Michelangelo signed only one work in his lifetime, the *Vatican Pietá*, and only then because he chanced to overhear some Lombards misattribute his work to their countryman. Thus angered, he chiseled his name along the strap running across Mary's breast, to guarantee that no one would ever again misidentify its creator.

CHAPTER 11

●
▬▬

Relationships

Of interest to Maya scribes were not only the names and titles of illustrious people but also their relationships with family members and lords of other cities. Direct subordination was noted alongside more oblique references to political ties, as an important ruler might have commanded the allegiance of a multitude of lesser sites, or may himself have owed allegiance elsewhere. From these records epigraphers have documented the changing hierarchies and shifting political fortunes of much of the ancient Maya world.

Parentage Statements

Perhaps the most important relationships to be documented, judging by the number of times these were mentioned, were ties between the *ch'ul ajaw* and his parents, especially if the latter were highly renowned. Scribes might mention a ruler's family for a variety of reasons, but particularly if any question arose over the son's succession. Thus Yaxun B'alam IV, the Late Classic ruler of Yaxchilán, stressed his descent from Itz'amná B'alam, going so far as to portray both parents in the upper register of such monuments as Stela 11.

Parentage statements tend to occupy the final clause of the subject's name phrase.

CHILD OF MOTHER

Chris Jones of the University Museum of Pennsylvania first correctly identified the sets of glyphs denoting "mother" and "father." Intrigued because
rulers often formally recognized the previous king, in conjunction with
additional names clearly denoting a female, Jones reasoned that the paired
male and female statements referred to the subject's parents.

a   b

Fig. 11-1   Generic "child of" glyphs: a) **U lo-t(i) CH'AM**;
b) **U B'A U CH'AM-li**.

In parentage statements, "father" and "mother" each take distinctive
"introductory glyphs," with the "mother" designation and name usually
written first. However, a nearly identical introductory phrase can charac-
terize both parentage statements on occasion, incorporating **CH'AM** "harvest," and approximately yielding **U CHIT CH'AM** and **U B'A CH'AM**,
which can be glossed as "his father's harvest" and "he goes as the harvest
of," respectively.

The more specific "child of mother," as epigraphers nickname the
female introductory statement, is most commonly depicted as an outstretched hand reaching left (similar to the glyph "to take"). The hand
either presents a "curl" sign (T578af), an upside-down **AJAW** (T534), or
the day sign **B'EN** (T584). When combined with the prefix T126 **ya**, the
glyph probably reads **YAL** or *yal* "her child." Another common version
spells **U JUN-TAN-(na)** "his or her cherished one." This introductory
statement is then immediately followed by glyphs that incorporate the
mother's personal titles and names. A final, rare form joins T126 **ya** with a
"scroll-mouthed" leaf-nosed bat, unreadable in Mayan but known to mean
simply "mother of." In this case, the name of the son follows.

Yaxchilán Stela 11 includes the formal names of Yaxun B'alam's mother
as part of his name string (G1–G3), beginning with the **YAL** form of "child
of mother" and followed by her main personal designation **IXIK IK'** (Lady
Wind; H1). Her personal titles include **CHAAN-na-l(i)** (*chaanal* "heavenly";

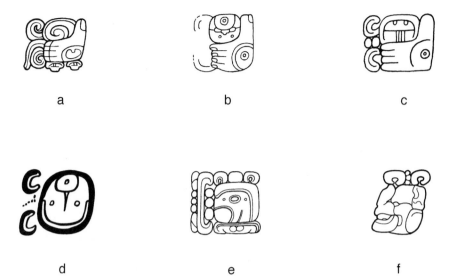

Fig. 11-2 "Child of mother": a) curl-in-hand; b) **AJAW**-in-hand; c) **B'EN**-in-hand; d) phonetic spelling of *yal*, **ya-la**; e) **U JUN TAN-(na)** "cherished one"; f) "mother of."

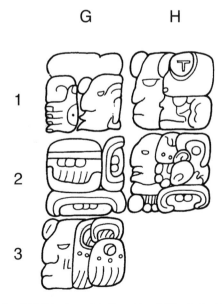

Fig. 11-3 "Child of mother" on Yaxchilán Stela 11, front, lower glyph panel, G1-G3.

G2), and the formal designation **IXIK AJ k'u-{JUN}-n(a)-li** (*ixik aj k'ujunil* "Lady of the Books"; H2). The name ends with **IXIK b'a-ka-b'(a)** or *ixik b'akab'* "Lady Standing-One."

CHILD OF FATHER

Like "child of mother," the "child of father" introductory glyph can include a "harvest" phrase—"his father's harvest" or something approximate, probably in reference to the "child" as "the blood of" the parent. More specific introductory "child of father" statements take the forms **U NIK** or *u nik* "the flower of" (and alternatively **U NIK-il**), and **yu-NEN** "the child of," with the final element of the latter depicted as a jaguar tail (*nen* means "tail" in Yucatec).

a   b   c

Fig. 11-4   "Child of father": a) *u nik*; b) *u nikil*; c) *yunen*.

Yaxchilán Stela 11 also incorporates the name of Yaxun B'alam's father as part of his extended name phrase (H3–I4). Beginning with **U B'A U CHIT**—a variant of the standard "child of father" introductory expression—the name continues with a titular sequence that includes what may be **B'A ch'a-jo-{ma}** (G4), followed by the standard "numbered *k'atun*" expression **JO K'ATUN AJAW** ("Five *K'atun* Lord") that provides the father's age. The name continues down column I with his personal designation, **ITZ'AMNÁ B'ALAM** (Shield Jaguar), his "captor expression" **U CHAAN AJ NIK-(ki)** ("Captor of Aj Nik"), followed by the double Yaxchilán Emblem Glyph and the by now familiar *b'akab'* title.

Fig. 11-5 "Child of father" on Yaxchilán Stela 11, front, lower glyph panel, H3-I4.

Wife

Found mainly in codices, the sequence **ya-TAN-(na)** or *yatan* "wife," accompanies scenes of the elderly male god Itz'amná having "lap sex" with the young goddess Ixchel—sex performed face-to-face with the female partner seated in the other's lap. So far only a few similar collocations have been found in Classic Period inscriptions, for example, on Piedras Negras Stela 8 in reference to the wife of Ruler 4, and on Naranjo Stela 23 in the name phrase of Ixik Wak Chaan Ajaw of Dos Pilas.

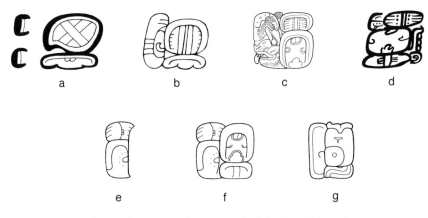

Fig. 11-6   Relationship terms: a) **ya-TAN-(na)** "wife of" (*yatan*);
b) **yi-tz'i-n(a)** "younger brother" (*itz'in*); c) **i-tz'i wi-WINIK-(ki)**
(*itz'in winik*); d) **i-tz'i wi-WINIK-(ki)** (*itz'in winik*); e) **su-ku**
(*sukun*); f) **su-ku WINIK-(ki)** (*sukun winik*); g) **yi-cha-n(i)** (*yichan*).

Siblings and Other Relatives

Other members of the ruler's family were sometimes mentioned, including brothers and uncles. To write "younger brother," the scribe employed variants of the word *itz'in*, spelling it phonetically **i-tz'i** and **yi-tz'i-n(a)**, "younger brother" and "his younger brother," respectively. Some examples add logographic **WINIK** with or without phonetic complements, yielding "younger brother person." "Older brother" and "older brother person" take the forms **su-ku** (*sukun*) and **su-ku WINIK** (*sukun winik*). Brothers can also be referred to as "companions." Very rare, the term *yichan* or **yi-cha-n(i)** denotes "mother's brother," for the subject's uncle on his mother's side.

Companions

Individuals named in inscriptions often performed the action of the text "in the presence of," "before," or "accompanied by" other individuals, including "all the gods" or a whole "host of gods." This companionship statement is made explicit in one of several ways. The most common form, probably meaning simply "companion," reads **yi-ta-ji** or more briefly **ta-ji** (*yitaj*). Originally identified as the general term for "sibling," few epigraphers currently regard it as such, preferring the broader concept "in the company of." Beginners should beware of misidentifying another, similar collocation—**ya-ti-ji**—that occurs only with the names of the "Paddler Gods" and that means "to bathe" (see Chapter 13: Gods and Supernaturals).

Another glyph with a more restricted meaning but conveying the same general idea takes the form **yi-ch(i)-NAL** or *yichnal*, usually interpreted as "in the company of," "with him," or "together with." More recently David Stuart suggested the gloss "before them," where the verbal statement describes the subject performing an action "in front of" or "before" someone else, often pairs or hosts of gods.

Fig. 11-7   "Companions": a) **yi-ta-ji**; b) **yi-ta-ji**; c) **yi-ch(i)-NAL**.

Political Relationships

Relationships helped form larger political aggregates of more than one city or town, "spheres of influence" that, by Late Classic times, seem to have divided into two major groups, those controlled by Tikal and those controlled by Calakmul. Over a period of several years rulers were successively installed at Caracol, Naranjo, Dos Pilas, Cancuen, and El Peru "under the authority of" rulers at Calakmul. The implications are that certain smaller centers of population "owed allegiance" to those of greater political influence.

U Kab', "Under the Authority of"

The most important glyph that denotes an "authority" relationship reads
u kab' or *u kab'i*, and has a checkered history in terms of how epigraphers
have translated it over the years. Originally glossed "in the land of," based
on the main sign's clear "earth" associations (it incorporates the day sign
KAB'AN, or T526), the collocation was later read "in the territory of." Nor
have scholars always agreed on the main sign's value, variously interpreting it as **KAB'** and **KAJ**. Today, most epigraphers accept the value
KAB' and interpret it as "by the doing of" or "under the authority of."

Regardless of how epigraphers eventually settle the issue, the sequences
U KAB', **U KAB'-ji**, and **U KAB'-ji-ya** clearly attribute an action undertaken
by an individual as being initiated by a second person in a position of higher
authority. On a panel from the Piedras Negras satellite center of El Cayo, the
local ruler is said to accede as *sajal*, or "underlord," **U KAB'-ji-ya** "under the
authority of" Sak Tzi Ajaw, the "lord of Sak Tzi."

a   b   c

Fig. 11-8   "Under the authority of/by the doing of": a) symbolic variant;
b) head variant; c) head variant.

Simon Martin and Nikolai Grube, two leading epigraphers of the current generation, have tracked the use of the *u kab'* compound and other
"relationship" glyphs to determine who did what and under whose
authority. In this way the two scholars established that the political organization of the Classic Maya was considerably more complex than once
believed. In general terms, Calakmul seems to have eclipsed Tikal by
drawing the latter's allies into its own political sphere, effectively surrounding Tikal with hostile dynasts. After recording its own victories
against Calakmul during the reign of Jasaw Chaan K'awil I, Tikal eventually regained power by wooing back or conquering its rebellious subordi-
nates and thus reestablishing political control over the central lowlands.

YAJAW

Like the *u kab'i* compound, the term *yajaw*—"lord of" or "his lord"—designates a close political relationship, stipulating that the one who is named preceding the glyph functions as the underlord or vassal of the individual named in the phrase that follows. In this way *yajaw* links two separate names in a hierarchical relationship.

Any title of rank and most nouns can take the third-person possessive pronoun to indicate possession, either in the form of the Set A ergative pronoun *u* or the prevocalic pronoun *y*. For example, *yajaw, yatan, yotot, yeb'al* and so forth all indicate that the thing, quality, or person in question *belongs* to someone or something else. Thus, on Piedras Negras Stela 13, a signature of one of the sculptors who carved the monument indicates that he is the **ya-ja-wa KALOMTE'** or "underlord" of the *kalomte'*, the Piedras Negras ruler.

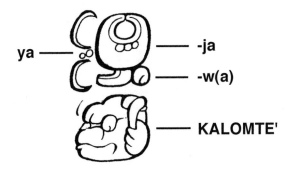

ya —— -ja

—— -w(a)

—— KALOMTE'

Fig. 11-9   Artist's signature, Piedras Negras Stela 13, F2-F3.

When used with the title *ajaw*, **ya** converts the word "lord" to "lord of" or "his lord," so that the one whom the text names *before* the title is said to be the "lord of"—that is, the *under*lord of—the one whose name follows. From these collocations the reader can easily grasp that certain rulers

ya- —— AJAW

Fig. 11-10   "Lord of."

claimed control over underlords, rulers, nobility, artisans, and others as the equivalent of their "vassals," illuminating the Classic political hierarchies beyond what can be gleaned from *u kab'i* glyphs.

YETE'

One final sequence sheds light on the hierarchical relationships of Classic Maya towns. Problematic in terms of the phonetic value of its components, the glyph takes the approximate form **ye-e-te'**, based around a "shell" sign that reads **e**. One meaning of *yet* in Ch'ol is "authority, office," with *yetel* glossed as "by," or "in the authority of." However, *yetel* may simply serve as another expression for "companion."

ye-   -te'

Fig. 11-11   "By" and "in the company of/under the authority of."

Summary

Our understanding of relationships and political offices helps to clarify who controlled what during the Classic Period, and offers one of the more exciting frontiers of hieroglyphic decipherment. We know that rulers traveled to participate in important social events. We also know exactly *where* many of the events "witnessed" or performed "under the authority of" more powerful lords took place. Through precise decipherments the inscriptions now give the names of the towns, regions, and geographical locations where rituals of Maya civilization were carried out. This is the subject of Chapter 12.

CHAPTER 12

● ●
━━━━

Locations and Objects

Decipherment of the Maya script was long divided between the "phonetic" approach of scholars like Knorosov, and the "calendrical-astronomical" position of Thompson. After Heinrich Berlin, an unassuming German history teacher living in Guatemala, identified the so-called Emblem Glyph, others like Proskouriakoff quickly recognized names and events. This led to an understanding and acceptance of the script's historical and phonetic features, and the possibility of advanced decipherment, which until then had been obstructed by the prevailing views of the script's limited purpose.

One of the most important results of this new spirit of scholarly achievement was the identification of not only events and personal names, but of a whole host of geographical locations, or toponyms, and seats of political power. Names of specific buildings within these "territories," important monuments, and a full range of objects have come under the scrutiny of epigraphers as well, enriching our knowledge of Maya culture far beyond what any scholar envisioned a few decades ago.

Directional and Color Glyphs

Central to the Maya worldview were the cardinal directions—east, west, north, and south—that were emphasized by the agricultural nature of Maya society and its dependence upon cycles of the sun and rain. In Maya inscriptions "east" or *lak'in* takes the form of a "sun bowl"—a ceramic vessel marked with the "sun" sign **K'IN** (T533) and resting atop another **K'IN** sign, with the latter taking its usual phonetic complement **-(ni)**. "West," traditionally read *chik'in*, has been identified as the **chi** "hand" sign with **K'IN** infix, that like *lak'in* is prefixed to the **K'IN-(ni)** collocation. Note that when the hand component grasps a blade or lancet it reads **OCH** "enter," as used in "death" expressions (see Chapter 9), rendering *och k'in* or roughly "enter the sun," in reference to sunset. The glyph for "south," or *nojol*, takes the logographic form T74.136:578.178 **NOJOL**. "North" is read as *xaman* and written symbolically **xa-MAN-(na)**, or portrayed in personified form as the head of a young lord with the prefix **NOJ**, meaning "great." Alternatively "north" may be spelled **na-NAL-la** or *nal*.

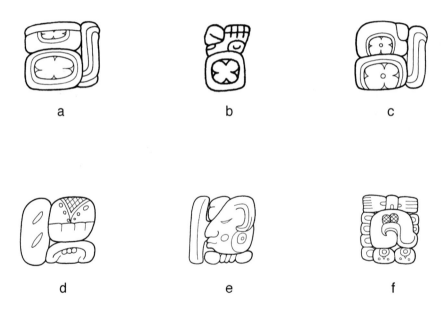

Fig. 12-1   Glyphs for the cardinal directions: a) *lak'in* "east"; b) *och k'in* "west"; c) *och k'in* "west"; d) *xaman* "north"; e) *nal* "north"; f) *nojol* "south."

"Color" glyphs, as epigraphers call them, often accompany directional signs, with the two elements forming a "color-direction" pair. **CHAK** "red" corresponds to "east," the color of the rising sun. **EK'** "black" corresponds to "west," the color of sunset and death. **SAK** "white" corresponds to "north" and the sun's daily zenith, and **K'AN** "yellow" corresponds to "south," equivalent to the sun's nadir. In addition, **YAX** "blue-green" signifies the color of the center of the world. Certain colors also have "extra" significance, so that *sak* "white" means "resplendent," *chak* "red" means "great," *k'an* "yellow" means "precious," and *yax* "blue-green" means "first."

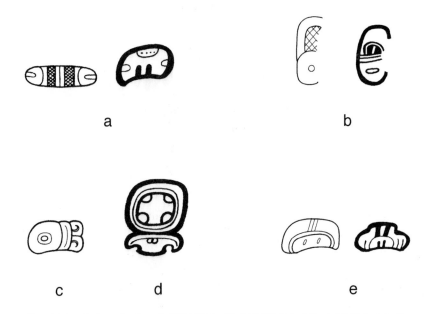

a   b

c   d   e

Fig. 12-2   Color glyphs: a) **CHAK** "red"; b) **EK'** "black"; c) **SAK** "white"; d) **K'AN** "yellow"; e) **YAX** "blue-green."

Emblem Glyphs

It was Heinrich Berlin who first noticed that certain collocations tended to end "personal" names, though Berlin took great care in applying neutral terms to any glyphs under his study. Consisting of several relatively constant affixes and a variable main sign, Emblem Glyphs suggested place names or the names of ruling lineages because they were generally associated with specific sites, with only a few easily explained exceptions. Although the meaning of Emblem Glyphs continued to elude scholars for years, their identification with specific sites has more recently made possible the reconstruction of a general idea of political territory and affiliations.

One of the two standard affixes found on Emblem Glyphs consists of a prefix drawn from the "water/blood group"—a series of signs with dotted elements originally mistaken as water droplets but now known to represent drops of blood from the rite of "scattering" and auto-sacrifice (T32–41). Usually read **K'UL** (Yucatec) or **CH'UL** (Ch'olan), and more recently **K'UJUL**, all of which mean "divine, holy," signs in this group often take "attachments" corresponding to the glyphs for **YAX**, God C, **K'AN**, and others, but without changing the value or meaning of the "blood group" sign.

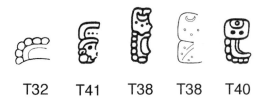

T32   T41   T38   T38   T40

Fig. 12-3   Examples of **CH'UL/K'UL/K'UJUL**.

The other standard affix used in Emblem Glyphs consists of the well-known title **AJAW**, usually in its T168 logographic form that signifies "lord." **AJAW** customarily surmounts the main sign, although sometimes it is detached and occupies an adjacent glyph block in personified form. In the former instance the sign can take the phonetic complement T130 **-(wa)** placed as a subfix to the main sign, so that logogram and phonetic complement "bracket" the main sign along the top and bottom.

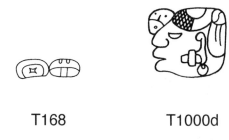

T168   T1000d

Fig. 12-4   T168 and **AJAW** head variant.

Variable main sign elements take many different forms, including multiple glyphic elements or "clusters." In any case, the reading order always begins with the prefix **CH'UL** or **K'UJUL**, followed by the main sign, then **AJAW**. As an example, the Tikal Emblem Glyph, whose main sign reads **MUT** or **MUTUL** "bird," forms **K'UJUL MUTUL AJAW**, or "Divine Mutul Lord."

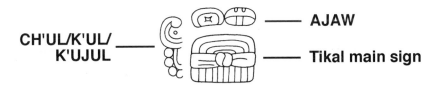

Fig. 12-5   The Tikal Emblem Glyph and its affixation.

Emblem Glyphs—well over three dozen of them—have been identified for virtually every major population center of ancient times, as well as many unknown sites. For example, epigraphers have known for years about the "Snake Head Emblem," at first thought to denote an unknown ruin that scholars designated for convenience "Site Q." Some years later a number of epigraphers identified this site as El Peru, a badly looted city off the Río San Pedro Martyr northwest of Tikal. Today we know that the Snake Head Emblem, read **K'UJUL CHAN AJAW** "Holy Snake Lord," is most likely the Emblem Glyph of the mega-metropolis Calakmul, located in southeastern Campeche just over the border from Tikal in modern Mexico.

Fig. 12-6   The Calakmul Emblem Glyph.

Other problems surround Emblem Glyphs apart from the identification of their corresponding sites. Certain glyph compounds behave syntactically like Emblems and incorporate Emblem Glyph affixes, but otherwise appear abnormal. These irregularities can include confusing multi-element main signs and odd prefix variants that lack usual **CH'UL** features or that turn the **CH'UL** element into what appears to be the main sign. The most famous nonstandard "Emblems" are those of Caracol and Chichén Itzá.

The presence of T168 **AJAW** and its variants indicate that Emblem Glyphs refer to *individuals*, and specifically to kings or rulers when preceded by the element **CH'UL**. Variable main signs, however, pose somewhat

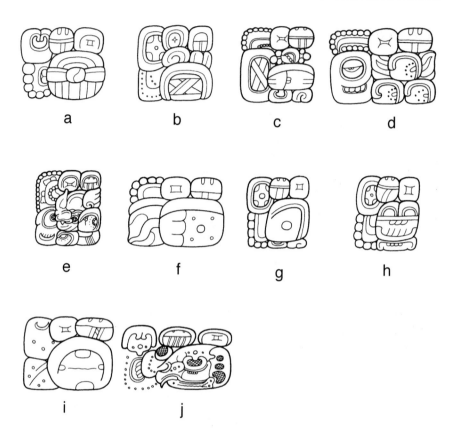

Fig. 12-7   Emblem Glyphs: a) Tikal; b) Naranjo; c) Machaquilá; d) Seibal;
e) Copán; f) Piedras Negras; g) Yaxchilán 1; h) Yaxchilán 2;
i) Palenque 1; j) Palenque 2.

of a difficulty. For example, Tikal's sign was used by Dos Pilas and certain
other sites in the Petexbatun region, and Yaxchilán and Palenque each
owned more than one Emblem, with Yaxchilán using both simultaneously.
In the case of Dos Pilas, historical connections link that site to Tikal, suggesting its founding in Middle Classic times by splinter groups who established a rival claim to the Tikal Emblem. Such evidence casts doubt on
whether the main sign serves as a toponym or site-specific indicator, as
opposed to a symbol of an individual social group, some form of political
organization, or some other largely intangible quality.

Titles of Origin

While the debate over Emblems and their significance continues, other more geographically specific glyphs connecting individuals to "places of origin" have been found. Prefixed with T12 **AJ** "he of" or one of its allographs, these designations function as titles linked to place names and other descriptive information. Hence the sequence **AJ-wa-k'a-[b'(i)]** or *aj wak'ab'* means "He of Wak'ab'" or "The Man from Wak'ab'," although to where or what Wak'ab refers remains unknown. Actual Emblem Glyphs can serve as the main element of the title, for instance "He of Naranjo," "Lady of Tikal," and *Aj K'an Witznal* ("He of Ucanal"). In other cases, what may be descriptive terms are used instead of an Emblem or place sign, resulting in phrases like *Aj K'echat* "He of Crooked Penis." In this example, such a title would suggest that the individual referred to possessed a very crooked member, but there may have been a town or geographical location called "Crooked Penis," as yet unidentified. Finally, certain titles specifying origin may refer to locations within an actual site, as in the **AJ CHAN wi-ti-k(i)** or *Aj Chan Witik* sequence from Copán, believed to name a specific location somewhere within the Copán city-state.

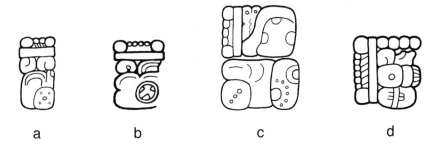

| a | b | c | d |

Fig. 12-8   Titles of origin: a) *Aj Wak'ab'*; b) *Aj K'an Witznal*; c) *Aj K'echat*; d) *Aj Chan Witik*.

Toponyms

True toponyms do exist in Maya inscriptions, for both physical and mythological locations. Toponyms typically follow a standard sequence that begins with a "secondary verbal statement" taking the form of the Anterior Date Indicator (ADI) described in Chapter 6 and reading *utiy,* meaning in this case "it happened at." The actual name of the place where "it happened" then follows. Hence on Naranjo Stela 23 after stating *u tok' pakal* "war," the text reads **u-ti SAK JA'** (*uti sak ja'*), "it happened at Sak Ja'" or at "White Water."

u   -ti SAK   JA'

Fig. 12-9   **u-ti SAK JA'**, "it happened at Sak Ja'."

One or more special "toponymic signs" often precede a location's proper name. These include the signs T606 **TAN**, the T563 "sky" sign read **CHAAN** or **KAAN**, and signs from the "impinged bone" set. Used also in the unrelated "child of mother" glyph, T606 **TAN**, usually with the phonetic complement T23 **-(na)**, signifies in this instance "the center of." **TAN** and **TAN-(na)** can interchange with, or supplement, the "impinged bone" glyph that depicts the end of a human long-bone (T571) and that overlies, in most but not all cases, a partially crosshatched field. Elements that replace the bone and that form a "substitution set" include the **K'IN** sign (T544), a disembodied eyeball (T598), or a fleshless jawbone (Tnn). At one time thought to read **PAN** (of unknown meaning), then later **KUN** "seat," the

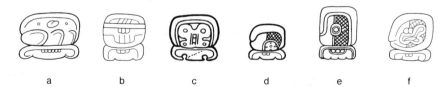

a   b   c   d   e   f

Fig. 12-10   Toponymic signs: a) T606:23 **TAN-(na)**; b) T563:23 **CHAAN-(na)**;
c) **CH'EN-(na)** impinged bone; d) **CH'EN-(na)** impinged **K'IN**;
e) **CH'EN-(na)** impinged eye; f) **CH'EN-(na)** impinged bone.

"impinged bone" and its allographs probably read **CH'EN** "cave," with the implication that locations so designated refer to actual caves. However, temples were thought of as "sky caves" or man-made caves, and therefore many of the locations mentioned in toponymic phrases may name architectural rather than natural features. Like **TAN** and **CHAAN**, signs that have the value **CH'EN** take the phonetic complement **-(na)**.

An example of a toponymic reference is the sequence **TAN CH'EN-(na) MUTUL** "Center of the Tikal Cave," that is doubtlessly a reference to one of Tikal's monumental pyramids and comes from one of the Tikal wooden lintels.

Fig. 12-11 **TAN CH'EN-(na) MUTUL** "in the center of the Tikal cave."

Finally, there are numerous references in Maya texts to mythological locations. Among the better known is the "black hole" or *cenote* place, spelled **EK' WAY NAL**, located at the point in the northern nighttime sky around which the stars pivot. Other examples relate to the Maya's concept of "paradise" as a location with multiple layers, incorporating references to *Jo Chaan* "Five Sky Place" and *Na Jo Chaan* "First Five Sky Place," among several other "numbered skies."

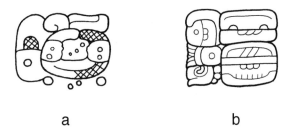

a   b

Fig. 12-12 Mythological locations: a) *ek' waynal* "Black Hole Place"; b) *utiy na jo chaan* "it happened at First Five Sky Place."

Names of Buildings

In addition to geographical features such as mountains, lakes, and caves, inscriptions name as locations the architectural plazas and buildings of specific towns, which were the settings for parades, religious ceremonies, and events of state. Although many location names follow the verb *utiy* "it happened at," others occur in more complex formulaic statements akin to the Primary Standard Sequence written on pottery vessels (see Chapter 14). Indeed, the vast majority of texts lead to or highlight dedication phrases honoring buildings, monuments, or other objects as the primary purpose of an inscription. Everything prior serves as background information to set the stage for the featured event. (See Chapter 15: Discourse and Structural Analysis.)

Dedication formulas open with either the God N-Step Set verb, that may read **TAB'** and signifies "was presented" or "was dedicated," or the **OCH K'AK'** verb "enter the fire," which refers to the dedicatory ritual cleansing of buildings by entering them with burning braziers of incense. The subsequent glyph gives the proper name of the object being dedicated, followed by the statement **U K'AB'A** "was its name." Sometimes **U K'AB'A** takes an inserted adjective like **K'UJUL** "divine" or another descriptive term, rendering the phrase **U K'UJUL K'AB'A** "was its holy name." Immediately following comes the *class of object* so named, whether **OTOT** "home," **NA** "house," or the glyphs for "altar" or "plaza" (both of uncertain phonetic value). **OTOT**, the most common class of buildings dedicated in inscriptions, graphically represents a Maya house in profile view, complete with substructure, back wall, and roof. **OTOT** "home" may imply ownership, since a home can only be considered such when lived in by someone. In contrast, **NA** "house" more generically represents the concept of "building."

When the building named by the dedication phrase precedes the name of the building's owner, the class of object generally takes a possessive pronoun—indicated in the case of **OTOT** by the phonetic sign **yo-**, yielding **y(o)-OTOT** or *yotot*. For example, on the edge of Yaxchilán Lintel 23 we find the dedication of **U pa-si-l(i) yo-OTOT-(ti)** (*u pasil yotot*) by "Lady Xok," or "the opening (doorway) of her house, Lady Xok."

Monuments and Other Objects

Different types of monuments each take a distinctive "class of object" name, based on the category to which they belong. Thus inscriptions refer to *lakam tun* "banner stone" to describe stelae or upright stone shafts, *k'an*

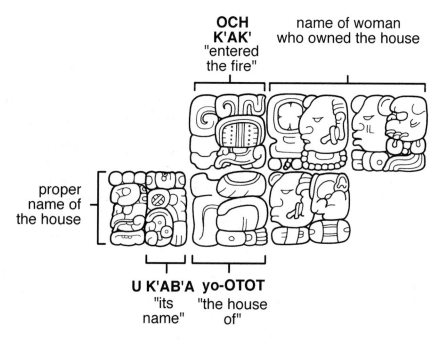

Fig. 12-13   Building dedication phrase from Yaxchilán Lintel 56, H1-H2.

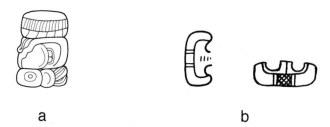

Fig. 12-14   a) **OTOT** "home"; b) **NA** "house."

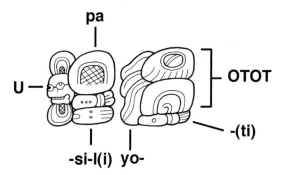

Fig. 12-15   Building dedication phrase from Yaxchilán Lintel 23, B2-C1.

tun "yellow/precious stone" for wall plaques such as Palenque's Tablet of the 96 Glyphs, and *pakab'* for door lintels. Another category consists of objects with flat sides, commonly represented with cross-shaped signs that have "leaves" in their corners. Used to refer to altars and stone slabs such as the Palenque sarcophagus lid, these signs may also refer to plazas and courtyards.

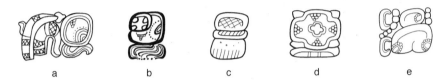

a   b   c   d   e

Fig. 12-16   Names of monuments: a) *lakam tun*; b) *k'an tun*; c) *pakab'*;
d) "altars, courtyards, plazas"; e) "altar."

Tribute

For years archaeologists and other scholars were unable to find much evidence to reconstruct Maya political and economic systems. Indeed, Maya towns were viewed as more or less autonomous city-states, with little to suggest trade between sites or regions on any significant scale. Cities were only loosely unified, with personal relationships the key mechanisms of exchange.

This view has begun to change in recent years. David Stuart, Stephen Houston, and others have been instrumental in identifying records of tribute payment, especially in connection with scenes depicting the presentation of dignitaries. Evidently nobility from subject towns regularly presented mantles, pottery vessels, foodstuffs, and other items as "payment" to rulers whom they served, whom in turn presumably remitted similar items to *their* overlord.

Glyphs for "tribute" include **pa-t(a)** and **pa-ta-n(a)** or *patan*, often prefixed by bar-dot numerals that indicate the "quantity" of tribute or "X-amount of tribute." In the same vein, the sequence **i-ka-tz(i)** on Piedras Negras Throne 1, and the sequence **ta-i-ki-tz(i)**, on a stela fragment from Jonuta, both mean "burden," "load," and by extension "tribute." Similarly, a few rare pottery vessels contain phrases where *ikatz* precedes **U to-jo-li** or *u tojol*, rendering "bundle . . . his payment." Lastly, the term *yub'te'*, found in the Cordemex dictionary with the meaning "tribute mantle," appears hieroglyphically as **yu-b'u-te'** followed a few glyphs later by the *u tojol* compound "his payment."

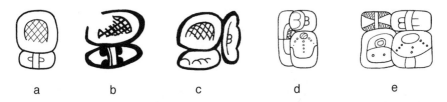

a   b   c   d   e

Fig. 12-17 Glyphs for "tribute" and related items: a) *pat*; b) *pat*; c) *patan*; d) *ikatz*; e) *ta ikatz*.

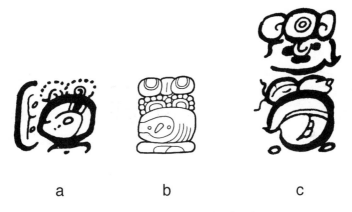

a   b   c

Fig. 12-18 Glyphs for "tribute" and related items: a) *u tojol*, calligraphic version; b) *u tojol*, monument version; c) *yub'te'*.

Summary

A multitude of different objects and "everyday things" were referred to in the Maya script—stones (*tun*), water (*ja'*), helmets (*kojaw*), stairways (*eb'*), stone braziers (*sak lak tun*), shells (*jub'*), thrones (*tzam?*), among many other useful and aesthetic objects. From headbands, books, houses, lintels, and doorways, to holes, earspools, bloodletting tools, and mock "sweat-baths," the inscriptions record a wide range of personal and public items often tagged in terms of what *kind* of thing they were and given proper names. In addition, numerous geographical, astronomical, and mythological locations were featured as indications of territorial and spiritual dominion. The items presented in this chapter represent only a selection, indicating the great range of inscriptional references. The beginner will find a quantity of items to examine, always with the chance of discovering something new.

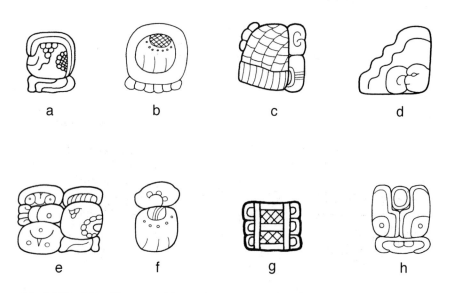

Fig. 12-19   Miscellaneous objects: a) *tun* "stone"; b) *ja'* "water";
c) *kojaw* "helmet"; d) *eb'* "stairway"; e) *sak lak tun* "brazier";
f) *jub'* "shell"; g) *tzam* "throne"; h) "ball court."

CHAPTER 13

●●●
——

Gods and Supernaturals

For the Maya of modern times all that is animate and inanimate carries within it the equivalent of *ch'ulel,* or "soul stuff" (although the term varies from one language group to another). The same was true in ancient times, so that each living creature, each stone, tree, or house possessed an animate spirit that made it a living, breathing entity. In this sense, virtually everything was "deified," endowed with abilities that were beyond what we, in our technological world, would call "natural."

Certain powerful entities also existed outside the tangible realm of "ordinary" sense perception, beings who possessed distinctive physical forms and costume attributes. These were the Maya gods and goddesses, the supernatural "unseen" forces that controlled the physical events of life as well as the inner psychological and emotional ones.

"The Heavenly God, the Earthly God, All the Gods"

As mentioned in earlier chapters, the glyph for "god" resembles a kind of "monkey" face known as God C and takes the phonetic value **k'u** (T1016). When combined with one of the "water/blood group" prefixes, the glyph becomes T41 **CH'UL** or **CH'UJUL** (Ch'olan) or **K'UL** or **K'UJUL** (Yucatec), meaning "divine" or "sacred," a designation especially common with

243

Emblem Glyphs and names of rulers or other high-placed nobles. Together with the female profile glyph **IXIK**, it reads *k'ul ixik* or "holy woman," and with the sequence **WINIK-(ki)**, "holy man." "Things," or objects, too can be designated "holy" simply by prefixing God C to the thing named.

Fig. 13-1   God C and God C with "water/blood group" prefix.

a   b

Fig. 13-2   "Holy People": a) *ch'ul ixik* "holy woman";
b) *ch'ul winik* "holy man."

The names of the gods themselves are expressed in Maya texts, but also present are general terms for specific groups of gods. For instance, by adding T41 to "sky" and "earth" we have **CH'UL CHAAN CH'UL KAB'**, "Holy Sky God, Holy Earth God." With T178 **-la** or T84–86 **-NAL** the same phrase reads *ch'ul chaanal ch'ul kab'al*, "the Heavenly God, the Earthly God." Clusters of gods sometimes take signs known from calendrical designations, as on Tikal Stela 31, where the "half-period"—**TAN-LAM-aj**—and the glyph for "one *b'aktun*," or **JUN PIK**, tell us that "eight thousand Sky and Earth gods are half diminished." The passage relates that all of

Fig. 13-3   "Holy Sky God, Holy Earth God."

these gods, as the personifications of the various *b'aktunob'* in one cycle, are "half over."

[TAN]
LAM-ja

CH'UL
CHAAN

JUN

PIK

CH'UL
KAB'

Fig. 13-4   "8,000 gods half diminished."

Another reference to multiple gods may invoke the concept of "all" or "the whole set." Written **o-la-si K'U** or *olis k'u*, meaning "all the gods" or "the whole set of gods," the phrase occurs on an unprovenanced panel from the lower Usumacinta River where it follows the verb *yichnal* "before them." Thus we have an event that takes place "before the whole set of gods."

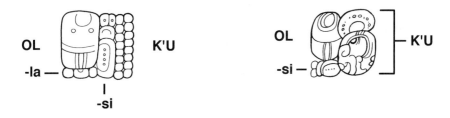

OL

-la

-si

K'U

OL

-si

K'U

Fig. 13-5   *Olis k'u* "all the gods."

Lineage Founders

In Chapter 10, Names and Titles, we discussed the "Successor" title that documents a king's order of succession within his town's dynastic sequence. The **TZ'AK** (T573) and **TAL** (T676) glyphs, together with numerical coefficients, count the ruler's succession since the legendary founding of the site or else since the founding of the royal dynasty. In most cases where the "count of kings" has been identified, the name of the founder follows the succession number. Founders generally date from the Early Classic Period or even mythological times, and appear half-deified when represented pictorially. Where the founder's name occurs, the count implies that the ruler acceded as the "sixteenth king," the "twenty-seventh king," or some other number *since* the reign of the founding ruler. For example, Tikal Stela 5 names Yik'in Chaan K'awil, who acceded in A.D. 734, and calls him **U WUK K'AL TZAK-b'u-il YAX EB' XOOK**, or "the twenty-seventh successor of Yax Eb' Xook." Here the founder's name refers to an individual who acceded hundreds of years before the contemporary ruler.

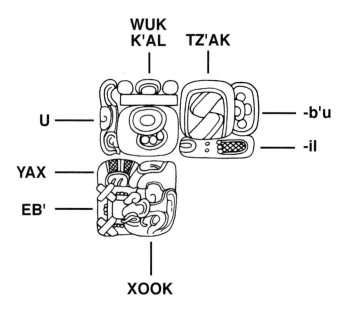

Fig. 13-6   Tikal Stela 5, A5-A6: *u wuk k'al tz'akb'uil Yax Eb' Xook* "the twenty-seventh successor of Yax Eb' Xook."

     Yaxchilán and Copán each record extensive successor counts, although in the case of Yaxchilán the count ends early in the Classic Period, despite the fact that numerous important rulers acceded for many years thereafter. Yaxchilán's founder takes the sign for "penis," or **AT** (T761), prefixed by T115 **yo-** and attached to the sign for "jaguar," or **B'ALAM**, yielding *Yoat B'alam*—"Penis Jaguar." In contrast, the successor count at Copán appears relatively complete, extending to the sixteenth ruler since the dynasty founder Yax K'uk' Mo' "First Quetzal Macaw." Archaeological evidence indicates that the Copán founder was neither myth nor legend, and that Yax K'uk' Mo' ruled the city from A.D. 426 to approximately 437, towards the end of the Early Classic Period.

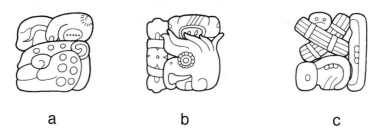

a   b   c

Fig. 13-7   Founders glyphs: a) Yaxchilán's Yoat B'alam;
b) Copán's Yax K'uk' Mo'; c) **CH'OK TE' NA**.

Naranjo and Quirigua each record one or two "successor statements," but their content leaves considerable doubt about their ultimate meaning. Naranjo, a relatively minor site compared with Tikal or Copán, provides a record of a "thirty-fifth" ruler, whereas Tikal had less than forty numbered rulers altogether and Copán only sixteen.

A generic but incompletely deciphered "founder glyph" also exists, consisting of crossed fasces-like bundles as the main sign with T542 and T4 **-na** meaning "house." The glyph seems to record literally the "founder's tree house," and possibly reads **CH'OK TE' NA**.

Vision Serpents

An important series of supernaturals found at different Classic Period sites are the Vision Serpents that appear in contexts of bloodletting as "hallucinations" brought on by blood-loss and pain. Especially common on lintels at Yaxchilán, which portray a variety of individuals actually undergoing self-mutilation, Vision Serpents appear from smoke-scrolls and vomit renowned ancestors and other deified creatures. Among the supernaturals disgorged by the Vision Serpents are personifications of "blood" and the "smoking axe" god known as K'awil.[1]

The most famous Vision Serpent takes the shape of a scaled deity of the type associated with central Mexico and the ancient city of Teotihuacan. Known as Waxaklajun U B'a, or euphemistically as "Eighteen Rabbit," the particular serpent designated by this glyph lent his name to the Copán ruler who was thirteenth in succession, the famous Waxaklajun U B'a K'awil who fell victim to Quirigua in A.D. 738. The Waxaklajun U B'a Vision Serpent bears an intimate relationship with warfare, with the scale-encrusted head sometimes serving as a Maya war helmet.

Another well-known Vision Serpent, who appears at Yaxchilán and elsewhere, goes by the simple name of Noj Chan, "Great Serpent."

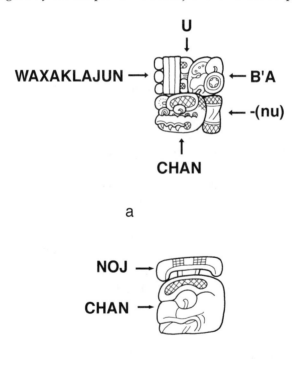

Fig. 13-8   Vision Serpents: a) Waxaklajun U B'a; b) Noj Chan.

Way, Wayob'

In the late 1960s a writer by the name of Carlos Castaneda popularized the "teachings of Don Juan," wherein shamanic powers allowed him to leave his body and roam the world in the form of his *nawal* or spirit counterpart. The term *nawal* comes from the Aztec language Nahuatl and relates to the word *nahuali*, meaning "sorcerer." The *nawal* represents the "co-essence" or *ch'ulel*, a manifestation of the spirit that can take different physical forms, including those of animals and supernatural creatures.

In Maya hieroglyphic inscriptions, the glyph for "co-essence"—the equivalent of the *nawal*—takes the form of an **AJAW** sign half covered with jaguar pelt. Read **WAY**, the sign identifies the spiritual co-essence of individual human beings. Thus the supernatural's proper name precedes **U WAY** "his co-essence," which is followed by the name of the person who possesses this spirit entity.

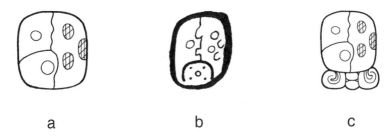

| a | b | c |

Fig. 13-9   Glyphs for "co-essence": a) **WAY**; b) **WAY-[b'i]**; c) **WAY-(ya)**.

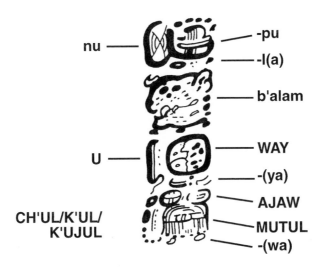

Fig. 13-10   *Nupul B'alam, u way k'ujul Mutul ajaw* "Nupul B'alam, co-essence of the holy Mutul (Tikal) lord."

Individual **WAY** or **WAYOB'** make appearances on countless polychrome ceramics and are often shown "floating" in a kind of anti-gravitational netherworld well above the ground. Others are shown dancing, as on the famous Altar Vase excavated at Altar de Sacrifícios, Guatemala. These *wayob'* possess names, allowing the tabulation of a "cast of characters" of the Underworld.

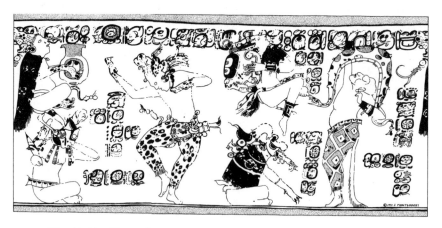

Fig. 13-11   The "Altar Vase," from Altar de Sacrificios, Guatemala.

The Pantheon of Major Gods

Near the turn of the twentieth century, Paul Schellhas, a German epigrapher working with the barkpaper codices of the Post Classic Period, and in particular the Dresden Codex, isolated as many gods as he could find and assigned them letter-designations as nicknames of convenience. Thus was born the sequence that, in the absence of decipherable names, scholars still refer to as God A, God B, God C, and so on. Since that time, many gods so designated have been identified in inscriptions on monuments and pottery vessels, along with many additional deities that were evidently exclusive to the Classic Period. The result is that epigraphers have steadily deciphered the hieroglyphic names of a wide range of gods. While the complete pantheon of Maya gods known by their hieroglyphic names is too extensive to be included here, a few key gods reappear with enough regularity, especially as titles or personal names of rulers, that a brief description is in order.

Itz'amná, God of Gods: Also known as God D, Itz'amná serves as a counterpart to the *Popol Vuh's* First Father, and is recognizable by his square eye and aged characteristics. The shield-like device with tassels that serves as his forehead element figures in the name of Itz'amná B'alam of Yaxchilán. Beginners should take care not to confuse the forehead element with the logogram that reads **NUUN**.

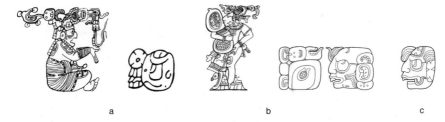

a b c

Fig. 13-12   Maya gods: a) Itz'amná, portrait and hieroglyph;
b) Jun Nal Ye, portrait and hieroglyph; c) K'inich Ajaw.

Jun Nal Ye, the Maize God: Also a sort of primordial First Father, Jun Nal Ye functions as the Classic Period Maize or Corn God and was the father of a later set of gods known as the Hero Twins. Nominal elements for Jun Nal Ye include the phonetic spelling **JUN-NAL** and the head of a human being that frequently has fish barbels along his face and an upside-down "T" or tau tooth, read **YE**. According to artistic sources, he was born from a lightning-split turtle carapace at the beginning of time when the world was first conceived.

K'inich Ajaw, the Sun God: Mentioned in Chapter 3, Introduction to the Calendars, K'inich Ajaw represents the number "four" in Maya mathematics and serves as the square-eyed Sun God. Apart from his distinctive eye, his diagnostic features include the four-petaled **K'IN** flower that represents the day.

The Hero Twins: In the creation story of the *Popol Vuh*, the Quiché Maya's Book of Council, two sets of twins embark upon fantastic journeys at the behest of the Death Gods, rulers of the Underworld. The first twins, one of whom was probably the Post Classic equivalent of Jun Nal Ye (but called Hun Hunapu in the *Popol Vuh*), lost their lives to the Underworld gods, but in a strange twist of mythological magic one of the dead twins impregnated an Underworld princess who journeyed onto the earth's surface and gave birth to the second twins, the so-called Hero Twins Hunapu and Xbalámque. In Classic Maya inscriptions, especially on painted pottery vessels, the counterparts of the Hero Twins take the names Jun Ajaw and Yax B'alam, and figure in countless narrative mythological scenes with very close counterparts in the *Popol Vuh*. (See Chapter 14: The Primary Standard Sequence.)

Fig. 13-13   The Hero Twins: 1) portrait and hieroglyph of Jun Ajaw;
b) portrait and hieroglyph of Yax B'alam.

The Palenque Triad: During the Classic Period certain Maya towns regularly extolled specific sets of gods, who were essentially local patron deities. One of the best-known sets is the Palenque Triad, so-called because of their special prominence at Palenque near the western fringe of Classic Maya settlement. The Palenque Triad are distinctive gods who were born not long after the Maya creation episode, in mythological time more than two thousand years before contemporary records at Palenque. Originally named GI, GII, and GIII (or God I, God II, and God III), the Palenque Triad possess personal attributes that render them unmistakable.

GI represents a tau-toothed god with fish barbel and shell earflare, probably representing Chaak (see below). GII takes the full-figure form of

GI   GII   GIII

Fig. 13-14   The Palenque Triad: a) GI; b) GII; c) GIII.

a reclining anthropomorph with long nose, a mirror in his forehead, smoke scrolls, and an umbilical cord. His full portrait depicts him reclining along his back with hand curled, indicating that the god represents an infant. GIII takes the **K'INICH** title, the personified **AJAW** within a cartouche, and a "checkerboard" sign with T130 **-wa** postfix.

GII clearly represents the god K'awil (see below), the patron of royal bloodlines and sometimes nicknamed by scholars Smoking Axe, Smoking Celt, or the Manikin Scepter.

GIII, sometimes called the Jaguar God of the Underworld (JGU), represents the sun in its nighttime aspect, and serves as the personified form of number "seven."

K'awil, God of Royal Bloodlines: Identified by his distinctive "smoking mirror" and forehead axe, K'awil functions as the formal emblem of royal bloodlines, a kind of metaphor for "generations." As such, he serves as the Manikin Scepter, the symbol of royal authority held by Maya kings, and certain sculptures depict him as infant-like, cradled in the arms of kings and queen mothers. Full portraits of K'awil depict one leg that transforms to become serpentine, with the serpent's head replacing the little god's foot. K'awil often emerges vomit-like from the maw of vision serpents, particularly double-headed ones held as serpent bars in the arms of rulers. K'awil undoubtedly represents the second member of the Palenque Triad (see above).

Fig. 13-15 K'awil, god of royal bloodlines, portrait and hieroglyph.

Chaak, the Rain God: The counterpart to the Central Mexican deity Tlaloc, Chaak bears intimate associations with rain, thunder, and lightning. Chaak is portrayed most often with an extra-long nose and wearing a shell diadem or earflare, as seen on the god Jun Nal Ye. In northern Yucatan, images of Chaak cover the friezes of architectural facades, their long-nosed masks stacked vertically along the buildings' corners like totem poles.

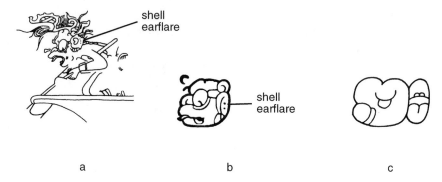

a   b   c

Fig. 13-16   Chaak, the Rain God: a) portrait; b) name glyph, head variant; c) name glyph, phonetic spelling.

Ik' K'u, the Wind God: Epigraphers and art historians have long identified the capital "T" sign as symbolic of the wind and the Wind God. Used as a shape for windows in palaces at Palenque and elsewhere, the capital "T" figures as the day sign **IK'**, itself intimately associated with "wind" and the "breath of life," hence its use in the verb for "death" where it indicates, "life extinguished." Only recently discovered, the glyph for "Wind God" takes the usual **IK'** sign prefixed with T23 **na**, though the **na** seems

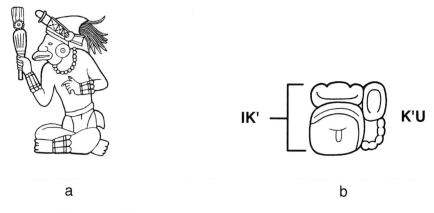

a   b

Fig. 13-17   Ik' K'u, the Wind God, portrait and hieroglyph.

to function as an integral component of the **IK'** logogram. The combination then takes a rare prefix version of one of the "water/blood group" affixes read **CH'UL**, **K'UJUL**, or **K'UL**, meaning "god." The compound reads *Ik' K'u.*

The Paddler Gods: Maya iconography—the delightfully executed scenes rendered on monuments, pottery, and other materials—regularly incorporates the image of two old gods with distinctive markings literally paddling canoes. The most famous scene, MT38a from the tomb of Tikal's Jasaw Chaan K'awil, depicts the ruler disguised as the young Maize God and accompanied by an iguana, a spider monkey, a parrot, and a shaggy dog, with the Paddler Gods mounted fore and aft and paddling the canoe with animation. As the patrons of bloodletting rituals, the Paddlers take name glyphs that depict the broad ends of their paddles and that are marked with **K'IN**—the sun sign—and **AKB'AL**—the symbol for darkness. Their personified versions depict one god with jaguar markings, the other with a stingray-spine bloodletting tool piercing the septum of his nose.

Stingray Spine Paddler   Maize God   Jaguar Paddler

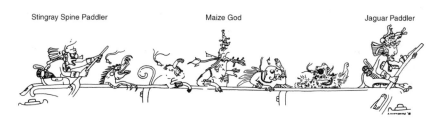

Fig. 13-18   Tikal MT38a.

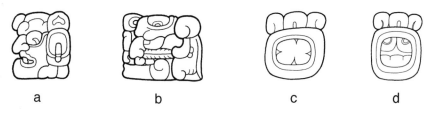

a   b   c   d

Fig. 13-19   Name glyphs of the Paddler Gods: a) head variant, Jaguar Paddler; b) head variant, Stingray Spine Paddler; c) symbolic variant, Jaguar Paddler, **K'IN**; d) symbolic variant, Stingray Spine Paddler, **AKB'AL**.

Among those glyphs that immediately precede the names of the Paddlers, the hand-grasping-fish verb known from bloodletting rites denotes "to conjure," or **TZAK**. Hence the Paddlers themselves were explicitly conjured through blood-loss. The canoe is thought to represent the bowl used to collect blood during these rites. Late Terminal Classic monuments from Ixlu, Jimbal, and Ucanal show the Paddlers literally bathing the scenes below them with the precious *itz'*, the sanguinary flow of cosmic spirit, or blood. Consequently one of the glyphs that regularly precede the Paddlers' names is **ya-ti-ji** "bathe." (See Chapter 9: The Major Events, "Bathe or Water.")

❊ ❊ ❊ ❊ ❊

Many individual towns had their own local patron deities who were conjured, invoked, performed "in front of," nourished and extolled by the people. As the divine inhabitants of the temples, statues, and other "houses of the holy," the gods of the Maya world were the *raison d'être* for the architectural grandeur of Maya cities.

NOTE

1. Recent epigraphy suggests that what appear to be serpents in many of these cases are in fact "centipedes," or chapat (singular, spelled **cha-pa-t(a)**).

CHAPTER 14

●●●●
▬▬▬

The Primary Standard Sequence

Among the most widely circulated works of art created by the Maya, small-scale portable pottery vessels offer scholars a unique window onto the everyday world of the royal elite. For the most part cylindrical vases and plates, Maya pottery vessels often carry symbolic and narrative images that were carved in low relief or incised, or that were painted in multiple or polychrome colors. Pottery served a variety of functions, from plainware vessels used for preparing and storing foodstuffs, to more elaborate forms that were exchanged among the elite as items of prestige and cherished as personal heirlooms. Fine polychrome vessels were interred along with the personal possessions of deceased kings or other members of the nobility, and were included in their tombs to hold foodstuffs for sustenance during the journey into the afterlife.

Despite being one of the largest, most important, and most spectacular sources of artistic motifs, as well as an exceptional source of hieroglyphic inscriptions, for years pottery vessels were ignored by scholars largely because the majority originated from illegal operations of tomb robbers. Not wishing to encourage theft and appalled at the rapid destruction of the myriad of unprotected sites that made easy targets for looters, scholars went so far as to declare all questionably obtained artifacts off-limits to research. More significant, the nature of pottery inscriptions—which incorporate a wide range of unusual glyphs and often "senseless" pseudo-glyphs that were never meant to be read—discouraged research even after the great breakthroughs of Berlin and Proskouriakoff.

Until relatively recently, few scholars questioned the prevailing logic that data from looted art should be disregarded. On the other hand, others have argued that all evidence ought to be examined, regardless of origin, so long as an object's authenticity can be established beyond reasonable doubt.

One of the first to champion the latter opinion was Michael D. Coe, who first brought pottery vessels and their inscriptions to general attention in 1973 when he published *The Maya Scribe and His World*. Coe argued that narrative pottery scenes related episodes similar to those from the *Popol Vuh*, the sacred "Book of Council" of the Quiché Maya, and specifically the adventures of the primordial pair called the Hero Twins.[1] He suggested that hieroglyphic pottery inscriptions were perhaps mortuary chants or ritual hymns analogous to the Egyptian Book of the Dead, meant to prepare the deceased for the journey into the Underworld. It was Coe who first noticed the repetitive nature of inscriptions that ran around the vessels' outer rims, dubbing them the Primary Standard Sequence (or PSS) because of their highly uniform nature.

Since that time, Coe's work has proven both right and wrong. Scenes on pottery do indeed relate episodes similar to the *Popol Vuh*. The PSS, however, has proven much less esoteric and much farther removed from sacred ritual than first supposed. Instead, the simple "name-tagging" of objects found on monuments, as first shown by Peter Mathews and elaborated upon by David Stuart, Nikolai Grube, Barbara MacLeod, and Stephen Houston, comprises the bulk of what the PSS tells us. In other words, rim inscriptions on pottery provide the name of the object's owner and additional related information such as who made the vessel and for what it was used. The Primary Standard Sequence, therefore, has proven to be remarkably mundane in its content.

The Basic Formula

In its most basic form, the PSS simply names who owned the vessel, or the one for whom the vessel was made. Other, more elaborate versions function as descriptive tags for the type of vessel it was, how it was used, and who made it.

The Primary Standard Sequence has three common versions. In its simplest expression, a possessed noun, corresponding to a type of vessel, precedes the personal name of an individual (discussed in Chapter 10), which corresponds to the name of the vessel's owner. For example, we have the sequence **yu-ch'a-b'i-l(i)** or *yuch'ab'il* "his/her drinking vessel," which is followed by the owner's name. *Yuch'ab'*, however, represents only one of several possible types of vessels.

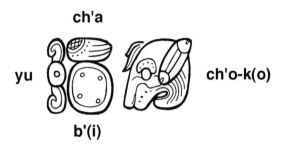

Fig. 14-1   PSS: possessed noun and name of vessel's owner.

A second, slightly more complex version adds a prepositional phrase between the possessed type of vessel and the owner's name. The intervening prepositional phrase specifies the vessel's contents, usually a kind of chocolate or maize beverage.

The third and most elaborate PSS takes the possessed noun, the prepositional phrase, and the name of the vessel's owner, but prefaces the usual components with an elaborate "dedication" phrase identical in many respects to house and object dedications in monumental inscriptions. These dedicatory phrases take an "introductory glyph," followed by a dedicatory verb generally of the God N-Step set variety (see Chapter 9: The Major Events, House, Monument, and Object Dedications), and a descriptive phrase that names the type of decorated surface as either carved or painted.

Other variations exist that are typically based on the addition of elements such as a Calendar Round and supplementary historical information.

Although quite simple due to its extremely limited content and structure, the Primary Standard Sequence incorporates numerous unusual and often rare variants of otherwise standard signs. These can appear confusing because of their fluid, energetic calligraphy, especially when dealing with the more complex and unusual head variants. Furthermore, textual styles vary considerably from region to region, as do painting styles in general, ranging from the relatively plain "Codex" vessels of the El Mirador/Nakbé region to the detail-filled "resist" style vessels from the area of Naranjo.

Because of the broad range of variant glyphs in the Primary Standard Sequence, the following discussion draws on the most common and

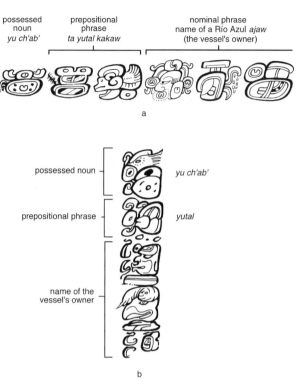

Fig. 14-2 PSS: possessed noun, prepositional phrase, plus name of vessel's owner; a) from K1446; b) from Robicsek and Hales 1981: Vessel 126.

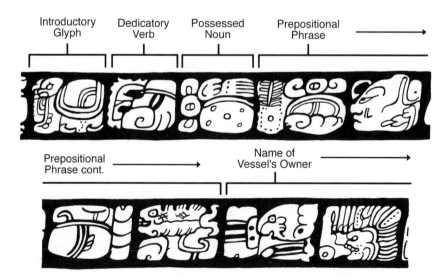

Fig. 14-3 Full PSS.

"standard" glyphs, sampling from an otherwise bewildering selection. In addition, while the PSS rarely incorporates more than twenty glyphs at any given time, the most elaborate versions can include upwards of thirty separate glyphs. Thus the beginner must take the following as no more than a general introduction.

The Introductory or Presentation Phrase

Usually comprising two glyphs—an introductory statement and a dedication verb—the "presentation" phrase opens the PSS and sets the stage for what follows. While the standard "mirror" glyph typically serves as the introductory sign, sometimes an initial Calendar Round precedes it, with the introductory glyph itself followed by one of three possible dedication verbs. Very rarely, all three versions of the dedication verb can occur together back-to-back in the same text.

Introductory Glyph: Based on the "mirror" sign (T24ms) and prefixed with T229 **aj** as phonetic complement, the PSS introductory glyph or "Initial Sign" includes the verbal suffix **ya** (T126) and reads something like *aj-ya* or *aya*. Although its precise transcription remains problematic, its meaning seems to be "came into being." An alternative interpretation of this compound reads **aj-li-ya** or *aliy* "to say" or "it is said."

Fig. 14-4   Variants of the PSS introductory glyph.

Dedication Glyph: Incorporating either the well-known God N verb (T1014a), the "step" verb (T32:834v), or the "flat hand" verb (main sign T713a), the dedication glyph follows the introductory collocation and signifies "was presented." Both the "step" and God N versions probably read **TAB'-yi** (*tab'iy*), although arguments for **JOY** and **JUY** have been offered. The "flat hand" also serves in clauses pertaining to the dedication of stelae and Period Ending rites, and likely reads **K'AL**.

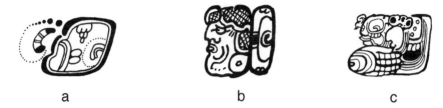

Fig. 14-5   PSS dedication verb: a) "step" variant;
b) God N; c) "flat hand" variant.

The complete introductory phrase can be transcribed as *aya tab'iy*, and paraphrased as "Came into being, was presented, was blessed."

Surface Treatment

It was the "surface treatment" portion of the PSS that led David Stuart to identify the now famous glyphs for artists and artists' signatures during the mid-1980s. Stuart observed that a phrase frequently employed in the Primary Standard Sequence varied depending on whether the surface was painted—the most common surface treatment—or carved. He argued that the glyphs of this clause alternated between the words for "writing" and "sculpture."

U Tz'ib': Incorporating any of the allographs from the substitution set for the third-person possessive pronoun **U** (typically T1), the *u tz'ib'* collocation also takes the main sign **b'i** (T585) and the well-attested prefix **tz'i** (T243), yielding **U tz'i-b'(i)** "his writing." *U tz'ib'* is the most common expression for surface treatment, and also occurs in rare instances with the prefix **AJ**, "he of"—in other words, "he of the writing" or "scribe."

Fig. 14-6   The PSS "surface treatment" phrase: a) **U tz'i-b'(a)**;
b) **AJ tz'i-b'(i)**; c) **yu-xu-l(u)**.

Yuxul: Prefixed by the glyph that incorporates the prevocalic third-person possessive pronoun for words beginning in a vowel, in this case **yu-** (T61 or 62), the *yuxul* glyph takes the head of a leaf-nosed bat for its main sign (T756a), generally but not always infixed with phonetic **lu** (T568). However, the **lu** frequently occurs either "out-of-order" before the bat head or as a separate glyph block, and rarely with the addition of the postfix **-li**. The collocation reads "his sculpture."

Yich: Optionally present either before or after the "writing" or "sculpture" statement, the sequence **yi-ch(i)** or **ji-ch(i)** reads *yich* (*jich*) "its surface."

Fig. 14-7   Variants of *yich*.

Najal: Although its precise function remains unknown, the sequence **na-ja-la** or *najal* may be a grammatical suffix for *u tz'ib'*.

Fig. 14-8   *Najal*.

When *yich* or *jich* is combined with either *u tz'ib'* or *yuxul*, the "surface treatment" portion of the PSS reads "the painting of its surface" or "its surface was painted," or alternatively "its surface was carved." What we now have of the PSS reads, "Came into being, was presented, the painting/carving of its surface." As Barbara MacLeod has observed, this is a "blessing" statement, one that makes the vessel "proper."

Vessel Type

Of particular interest, from the PSS we have the Maya's own names for the vessels they manufactured and used. The PSS names three different types of vessels, and possibly four, with each type "possessed" by the addition of a third-person pronoun.

Yuch'ab': Meaning "his drinking vessel" or "his drinking cup," the *yuch'ab'* glyph names a type of cylindrical vessel or vase common in Late Classic times and often painted with the most elaborate of the narrative poly-chrome scenes made during this period. The sequence occurs most frequently as **yu-ch'a-b'i**, a collocation easily confused with *u tz'ib'* but that carries a different meaning altogether. The *ch'ab'* or *k'ab'* type vessel is the most common ceramic mentioned in the PSS.

a   b   c   d

Fig. 14-9   Vessel type: variants of *yuch'ab'* "his/her drinking vessel."

U Lak: Found in the PSS on flat plates or platters, the *u lak* glyph clearly means "his plate." The sequence takes the phonetic form **U la-k(a)** or a variant main sign composed of a "death's head" (Tnn), and identifies the second most common type of vessel mentioned in the PSS.

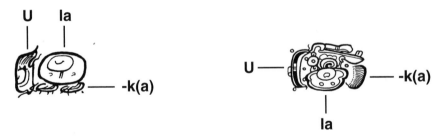

Fig. 14-10   Vessel type: *u lak* "his/her plate."

Jawte': Spelled **ja-wa-te'**, the *jawte'* glyph refers to a specific type of plate that has tripod feet, a rarer class of vessel than either of the two mentioned above.

a   b

Fig. 14-11   Vessel type: *jawte'* "his/her tripod basin": a) phonetic spelling with head variant; b) phonetic spelling with symbolic variant.

U Jay: An adjective occasionally precedes the vessel type *uch'ab'* and seems to specify "thin-walled," yielding *u jay yuch'ab'* "thin-walled his vessel." The name may refer to a "basin" type of ceramic.

Fig. 14-12   Vessel type: *u jay* "his/her thin-walled (drinking vessel)."

Up to now the PSS reads, "Came into being, was presented the painting/carving of the surface, his/her cup/plate."

Vessel Contents

What was contained inside of vessels—the "content" portion of the PSS—often proves the most interesting clause. The Primary Standard Sequence specifies three types of contents, all probably kinds of drink, although Maya narrative scenes on both pottery and monuments show vessels filled with other substances, especially *waj* or tamales.

Ta Yutal Kakaw: The most common type of substance specified by the PSS takes the form **ka-ka-w(a)** or *kakaw*, the original word for "cacao" or chocolate.[2] Often incorporating **TA-yu-ta-li** or **TA-yu-ta**, which is probably an adjectival qualification, the phrase may read "for fruited cacao," "for cacao food," or "for cacao seeds/beans." "Fruited" may refer to a flavoring or additive. References to *kakaw* were restricted to the tall cylindrical vessels called *uch'ab'*. Note that the prepositions **TA** and **TI** are interchangeable.

Fig. 14-13   Vessel contents: *kakaw* "cacao" **ka-ka-w(a)** and **ka-{ka-w(a)}**.

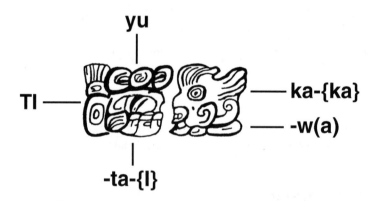

Fig. 14-14   Vessel contents: *ti yutal kakaw* "for cacao food."

Ti Ul: *Ul* or *atole*, not unlike watery cream of wheat, was made from cooked maize gruel and sometimes flavored with chile, honey, black beans, or certain flower blossoms. *Atole* was another favorite beverage of the Maya and other Mesoamericans, and is still consumed today in almost every Maya household. References to **TA-u-lu** and **TI u-l(u)** occur on vessels where diameter exceeds height.

Fig. 14-15   Vessel contents: *ti ul* "for corn gruel."

Ta Tzi Te'el Kakaw: Similar to *ta yutal kakaw*, the phrase *ta tzi te'el kakaw* incorporates an adjectival phrase preceded by the preposition *ta* and qualifying the nature of the *kakaw* beverage. *Tzi* means "fresh" and "new" in Ch'olan, while *te'* means "tree," giving the possible meaning "for tree-fresh cacao." The phrase may indicate that the beverage was made from the white pulp of the unripe cacao pod.

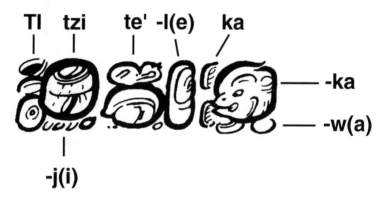

Fig. 14-16   Vessel contents: *ti tzi te'el kakaw* "for tree-fresh cacao."

Other qualifiers can precede *kakaw*, notably the **K'AN** cross (T281) with the possible meaning "ripe." The almost complete PSS now reads, "Came into being, was presented, the painting/carving of the surface, his/her cup/plate for fruited cacao/atole/tree-fresh cacao."

The Closure Phrase

Following the dedicatory and contents section, a "closure" statement adds the name of the one who owned the plate, vase, or bowl. This was often an

A.

AJ-ya/AJ-li-y(a)	-na-ja-[la]	yi-ch(i)/ji-ch(i)	U la-k(a)	K'UL cha-TAN WINIK
aya/aliy	-najal	yich/jich	u lak	k'ul chatan winik
"Came into being"/"It is said"	surface treatment	grammatical suffix "its surface"	"his plate"	"Holy Chatan Person"

B.

AJ-ya/AJ-li-y(a)	TAB'-yi	yu-ch'a-b'(i)	TA yu-ta-[l]	tzi	TE'-le	ka-[ka]-w(a)	CHAK ch'o-k(o)	KELEM
aya/aliy	tab'iy	yuch'ab'	ta yutal	tzi	te'el	kakaw	chak ch'ok	kelem
"Came into being"/"It is said"	"was presented"	"the drinking vessel"	"for fruited"	"fresh"	"tree"	"cacao"	"(of the) great lineage young person"	"youth"

Fig. 14-17 Examples of the PSS: a) *aya ? naja yich u lak ch'ul chatan winik* "came into being, was presented, its surface, his plate, the holy Chatan person"; b) *aya tab'iy yuch'ab' ta yutal tzi te'el kakaw chak ch'ok kelem* "came into being, was presented, the drinking vessel for fruited fresh tree cacao of the great lineage young person youth."

individual of elite status who may be recognizable from iconography or other inscriptions, or from identifiable Emblem and place-of-origin glyphs. Like names on monuments, those that close the PSS take the usual titles and epithets, both personal and general.

Summary

Instrumental in the decipherments of recent years, the Primary Standard Sequence occurs in various forms elsewhere in Maya inscriptions, such as in monument dedication statements. Snippets of the PSS occur in depictions of textile as well, most notably in the Bonampak murals (Room 1, Human Figures 5, 51, and 71) and on Calakmul Stela 9, where the formula seems to serve as a simple name-tagging device specifying the clothing's owner. Forms of the PSS also occur on portable objects other than vessels, including items of jewelry such as earflares. Perhaps no other decipherments have so illuminated the nature of the script, showing us that the overwhelming detail of Maya inscriptions masks an otherwise simple system.

a   b

Fig. 14-18   Elements of the PSS in the Bonampak murals:
a) introductory glyph and "step" dedication verb;
b) introductory glyph and God N dedication verb.

NOTES

1. Coe was anticipated in this by a brief remark published in 1950 by Franz Blom (Miller 1989).
2. The word "chocolate" derives from Aztec Nahuatl *chocolatl*, but the European term "cacao" derives from Mayan, as attested in hieroglyphic script by the form **ka-ka-w(a)** or *kakaw*, present from at least A.D. 700 onward. Most dictionaries omit the proper etymology owing to the glyph's relatively recent decipherment.

CHAPTER 15

≡

Discourse and Structural Analysis: Putting It All Together

Our journey through the world of the ancient Maya and their writing system has taken us piecemeal through the major hieroglyphs, while we occasionally stopped to explore how words fit together to form different types of phrases and longer clauses. But Maya inscriptions provide much more than just simple expressions, in many cases offering entire documents comprised of a variety of different sentences, for instance, epics consisting of hundreds of separate glyphs. The longest inscription—the great Copán hieroglyphic stairway of Structure 26—incorporates no less than 2,500 individual glyph blocks, arranged by sentences in a reading order that ascends from the bottom to top riser. The staircase inscription recounts the founding of the Copán dynasty and its succession of rulers, beginning early in Copán's history and covering a period of several hundred years.

To make long texts comprehensible, the Maya used basic patterns or "plot" structures (as do all storytellers). Thus reading a text requires not only identification of individual hieroglyphs, but also the ability to recognize discourse patterns and narrative structure.

In our last chapter we examined components of the Primary Standard Sequence, reading each glyph in order. Although made up of individual clauses, the PSS represents a single "sentence," one continuous "utterance" from beginning to end. Longer inscriptions combine a variety of sentences—often dozens of different sentences in one text, depending on the length and content of the glyphic material. The strategies used to highlight

271

key information and orient the reader are the concerns of "discourse structure," the way that sentences are combined for dramatic effect.

The Discourse Structure of Yaxchilán Stela 11

At first glance the text that we have been following since Chapter 2 seems "full" of many different hieroglyphic structures, and from our discussion we have learned that it contains several different clauses. The inscription begins by noting an Initial Series, itself comprised of individual phrases—the Introductory Glyph, the Long Count, the Supplementary Series, and the Calendar Round. Following the date, the text provides the verbal phrase "He acceded as Lord of the Lineage," followed by the names and titles of the subject. Thus we have an intransitive clause consisting of the verb and the subject; the sentence contains no object that the subject acts upon. The subject's name clause itself is divided into different phrases, including titular glyphs and both "child of mother" and "child of father" expressions. In actuality, this entire inscription, while incorporating multiple clauses, consists of one overall "sentence," in what is one of the most basic narrative structures employed by the Maya.

The Maya often abbreviated much of this information. For example, as noted in the chapters describing the calendars, the Long Count could be reduced to only the Calendar Round or Calendar Round and Period Ending. Name phrases might be limited to the individual's most important nominal glyphs, omitting parentage statements and compressing the titular sequence.

Multiple Episodes and Events

"Events," corresponding to sentences that contain a single verb or verbal phrase, could be organized into "episodes." To express an episode the scribe might employ several sentences, each of which relates a separate "event" or different information about the same event. Such use of multiple events within an episode tends to focus around a single date or an "implied" restatement of a previous date.

An easy example of an inscription with more than one episode (each of which has one event) is the "deity side" of Yaxchilán Stela 12 that opens on the Calendar Round 6 Ix 12 Yaxk'in (9.15.10.17.14) (A1–B2). The verb immediately follows at A2–B2—*u ch'ay u sak nik ik'il* "he died." Then come two

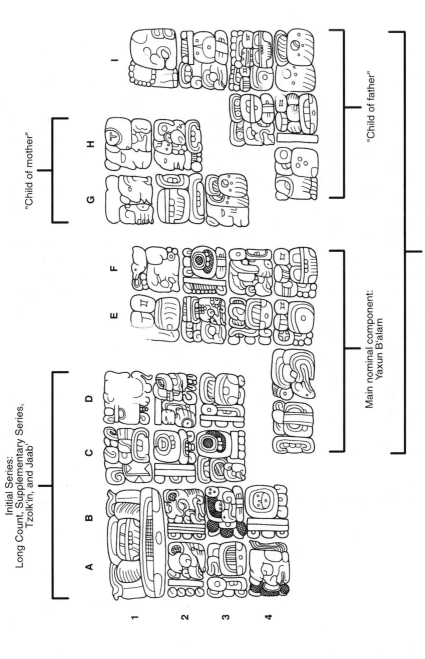

Fig. 15-1   Yaxchilán Stela 11, front, lower glyph panel.

titles, the *ch'ajom* "dripper" title (A3) and a "five *k'atun ajaw*" expression noting the individual's age—between eighty and a hundred years old (B3). Finally the text gives us the individual's personal name, Itz'amná B'alam (A4), with additional titles such as *u chaan Aj Nik* "Captor of Aj Nik."

While the death of Itz'amná B'alam, the first episode on Stela 12, appears to be the main action, in fact it merely represents "background" information, a setting of the stage for the next episode. Itz'amná B'alam's demise suggests that the remainder of the text should deal with an entirely different subject. This proves the case, as shown by the following clause.

B5 informs us *u tz'akaj* "was put in order," marked as a passive construction by T181 **-ja**. Since passives occur only with intransitive verbs, we should expect subsequent clauses to introduce a single subject without an accompanying object. On continuing, we find this to be true also. *U tz'akaj*, functioning in this case as the Distance Number Introducing Glyph, precedes the only DN in the text, 10.0.6 (A6), where the *winal* has been **deleted** since it stands at zero. *I-ut* "then it happened," links the Calendar Round that opened the text with the next Calendar Round at C1–D1 and tells us to *count forward* to reach the date 11 Ajaw 8 Sek, the *tun* ending 9.16.1.0.0. Immediately following the date is the verb (C2–D2), the well-known "seating" glyph (C2), spelled with positional verbal inflection and reading *chumwan* "was seated."

As one of the standard accession verbs, we know that the "seating" glyph precedes the office which the individual "accedes to" (B2), in this case *ti ajawlel* "in rulership." As in the previous episode, two titles follow (C3–D3), while a third names the individual who acceded as "Captor of Aj Uk" (C4). Finally, we learn who did the acceding, spelled out phonetically in D4–C5 as **ya-xu-n(i) B'ALAM**, the famous Late Classic ruler of Yaxchilán, Bird Jaguar IV. To close the text, the inscription provides Yaxchilán's double Emblem Glyph, or "Divine Yaxchilán Lord" (D5–C6), and ends on the ubiquitous title *b'akab'* "Standing One."

If we combine the texts from both Yaxchilán Stelae 11 and 12, we see at once that the latter relates the death of an individual who was not only an earlier ruler of Yaxchilán—Stela 11 calls him "*ch'ul* Yaxchilán *ajaw*," leaving little doubt—but who was also the father of Yaxun B'alam, the ruler on Stela 12 who accedes to "lordship." Thus, Stela 12 relates the death of the father and subsequent accession of the son in two separate episodes each connected to separate dates. (Notice that ten years and six days—the length of the Distance Number at A6—separated the two events, an unusual length of time for an interregnum. Fortunately we know from other inscriptions that Yaxun B'alam, the son, had to fight to

Fig. 15-2 Yaxchilán Stela 12, "deity side."

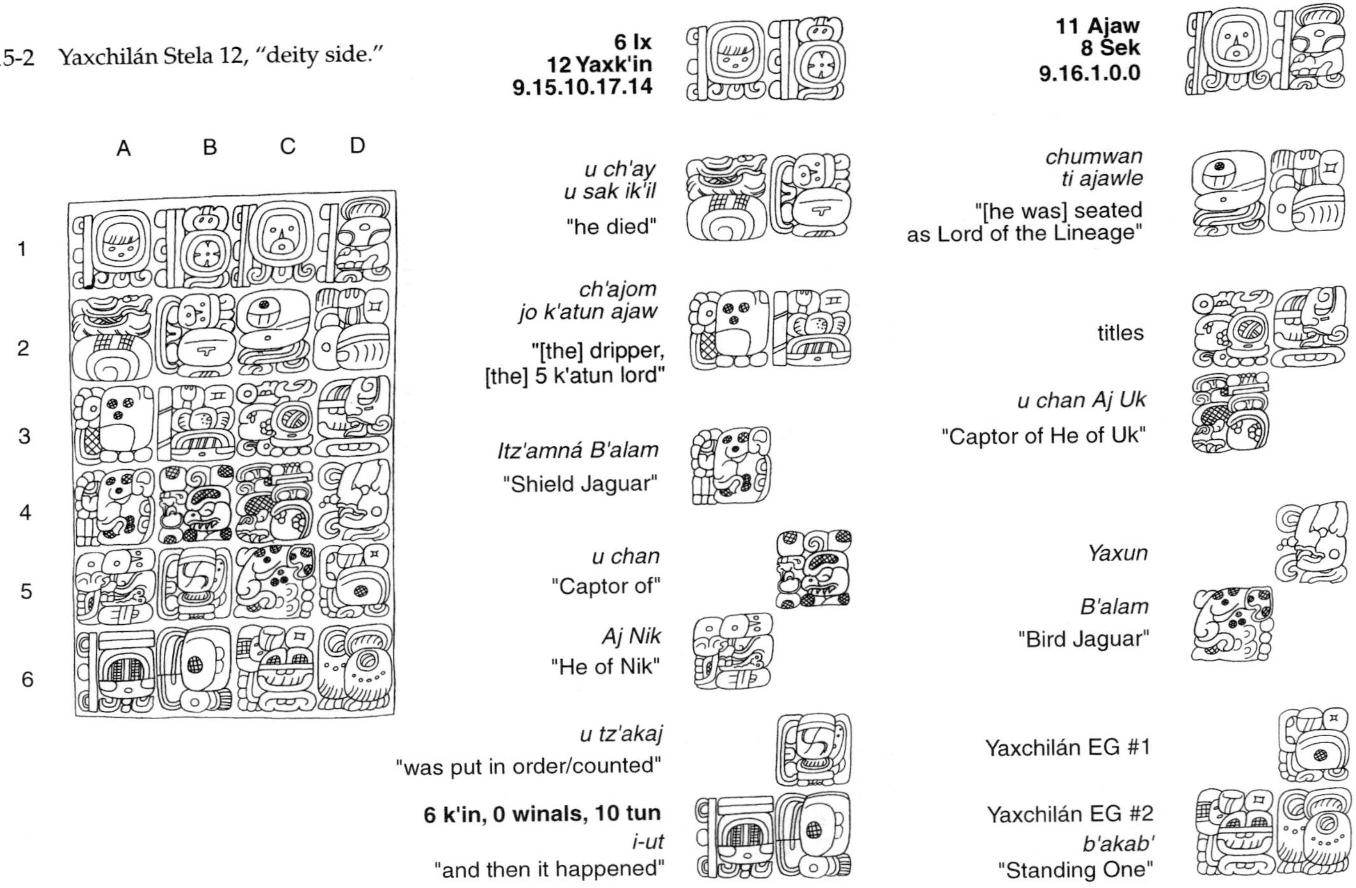
A
B
C
D
1
2
3
4
5
6
6 Ix
12 Yaxk'in
9.15.10.17.14
u ch'ay
u sak ik'il
"he died"
ch'ajom
jo k'atun ajaw
"[the] dripper,
[the] 5 k'atun lord"
Itz'amná B'alam
"Shield Jaguar"
u chan
"Captor of"
Aj Nik
"He of Nik"
u tz'akaj
"was put in order/counted"
6 k'in, 0 winals, 10 tun
i-ut
"and then it happened"
11 Ajaw
8 Sek
9.16.1.0.0
chumwan
ti ajawle
"[he was] seated
as Lord of the Lineage"
titles
u chan Aj Uk
"Captor of He of Uk"
Yaxun
B'alam
"Bird Jaguar"
Yaxchilán EG #1
Yaxchilán EG #2
b'akab'
"Standing One"

claim the right to his father's throne, suggesting why he failed to accede immediately.)

From the foregoing, several interesting features of scribal strategy help us to understand Maya discourse or "story structure." As previously noted, we can divide Stela 12 into two episodes. The first focuses around Itz'amná B'alam's death—the death of the father—and the other around Yaxun B'alam's attainment of the highest position in the land, his accession to "lordship." The two episodes are linked by a Distance Number, which provides the date of the second event and therefore moves the story forward to this new date and episode. The accession of the son stands out as the narrative climax, culminating the text and providing the inscription's *rationale*. Here the scribe is proclaiming the ruler's accession, while associating the new ruler with the previous one presumably as a means of reinforcing the new king's legitimacy. Of particular note, the one pivotal glyph (B6) is the Posterior Date Indicator *i-ut* that stands between the DN and second Calendar Round. Here the PDI serves as a **focus marker**, cluing the reader that what follows is the most important event of the story.

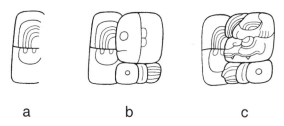

a   b   c

Fig. 15-3   The "focus marker" and Posterior Date Indicator (PDI):
a) *I*; b) *i-ut* symbolic variant; c) *i-ut* head variant.

Establishing an Event Line

In our analysis of Yaxchilán Stela 12 we followed a sequence of two episodes, each with its own date and event. The two dates occurred sequentially from the earliest to the latest event.

Not all texts lay out events in chronological order. If we examine a more complex inscription, we find that its "event line"—the chronological sequence of the various episodes—can sometimes stop, back up, go forward, back up again, and so on, establishing often complex temporal patterns. By working out each date and determining how the chronology works from episode to episode, we can establish the pattern of discourse or "story line" for the text as a whole. In addition, once identified, the *i-ut* **focus markers** can tell us which events were the most important ones. In long texts more than one event can take these markers.

By establishing these episodes or "chunks of text," as Kathryn Josserand, the principal investigator of Maya discourse calls them, we can find which episodes occur "on the **event line**" and which ones serve as "**background**." An **event line** functions as the story's "time line," the chronological series of events that move the action forward and that culminate in a **peak event**—the story's climax. In contrast, **background events** are the story's less prominent events and often function simply as "recaps" of previous information.

Foreground events—those events that occur on the event line—take either the **I** element (*I*) of the Posterior Date Indicator (PDI) or the complete PDI **I-u-ti** (*i-ut*), meaning "and then" or "and then it happened." **Background** events take the Anterior Date Indicator *utiy*, meaning "since" (although the reader should remember that the same glyph functions in toponymic phrases as "it happened at"). Completive intransitive suffixes act as markers similar to the ADI (most commonly **ji** and **ya**, which also regularly occur with *utiy*). When attached to Distance Numbers, **ji** and **ya** indicate that the count moves backward, and signal whether the discourse occurs in the completive or incompletive.

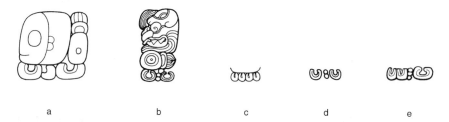

| a | b | c | d | e |

Fig. 15-4   The Anterior Date Indicator (ADI) and "background" markers:
a) *ut-i* symbolic variant; b) *ut-i* head variant; c) **-ji**; d) **-ya**; e) **-ji-ya**.

Discourse Structure on Piedras Negras Panel 3

Panel 3 from the Guatemalan site of Piedras Negras is an intriguing example that demonstrates many of the discourse strategies available to scribes. The work of two sculptors, both named in an embedded caption text, and one of the Maya's finest sculpted monuments, Panel 3 offers a kind of x-ray view of an assembly of *ajawob* and *sajalob'* that takes place inside and outside the "throne room" of the Piedras Negras ruler. The sculptors depicted the palace's two lateral walls along with an overhead swag curtain to represent the interior of the room, and around these features they arranged the main inscription, a fairly long text that runs down the left, then across the top, then down the right. Within this window-like frame—very unusual in Maya art—the enthroned ruler sits slightly off-center, bracketed by two groups of standing figures that include, on the right, two children and their teachers, and on the left three foreign dignitaries, each with their personal name captions. Just outside the room on the palace terrace, seven lords, including *sajalob'* and artists, are seated around a cylindrical tripod vessel and conduct an animated conversation, while inset texts relate additional information (to the left of the throne) and provide the names of the two sculptors who carved the panel (just to the throne's right).

The main inscription on Panel 3 (A1–V12) can be divided into three episodes. Episodes 1 and 2 each describe two events, while Episode 3 incorporates only one. In addition, Episodes 1 and 3 both have one event that has two parts, while Event 2 of Episode 1 has a more complicated three-part structure. In this way, an interesting, couplet-like structure emerges, setting up a pleasing rhythm. Each episode is dated and occurs in chronological order, with the three combined episodes covering a time span of approximately thirty-three years.

EPISODE 1, EVENT 1, PART 1

Episode 1 opens with an Initial Series that gives the Long Count position corresponding to A.D. 749 (A1–B7). Although a portion of the Long Count was badly damaged, all four components of the Calendar Round survive, as well as much of the Supplementary Series, allowing a secure reconstruction: A7 gives the Tzolk'in 5 B'en, E2 the Ja'ab' position 16 Ch'en. Since A2–B2 clearly includes nine *b'aktuns*, and A3–B3 fifteen *k'atuns* (note the *tun*-sign headdress representing "five" and the barest trace of the back of the lower jawbone, or "ten," for a combination of "fifteen"), the most likely position would be 9.15.18.3.13 5 B'en 16 Ch'en, which subsequent Distance Numbers confirm. On this date the first Lord of the Night (B7) "tied on his headband" (*u ch'a jun*) (C1). The current lunation was twenty-nine days (D1), and it was the "first lunation" (out of six) (C2). E1 tells us

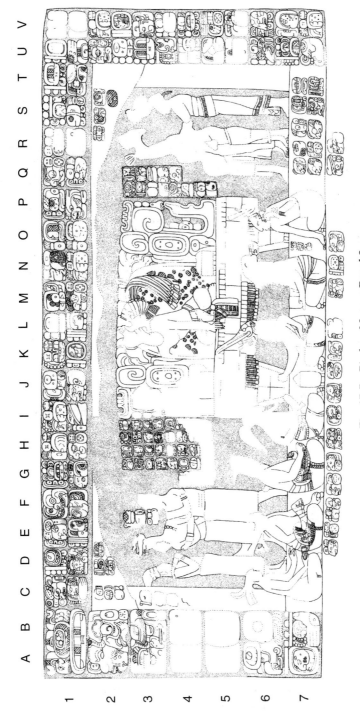

Fig. 15-5 Piedras Negras Panel 3.

u k'ab'a ch'ok—the lunation's "youthful name" was that given at D2, which remains undeciphered—while the expected length of the current lunar month was thirty days (F1).

A   B

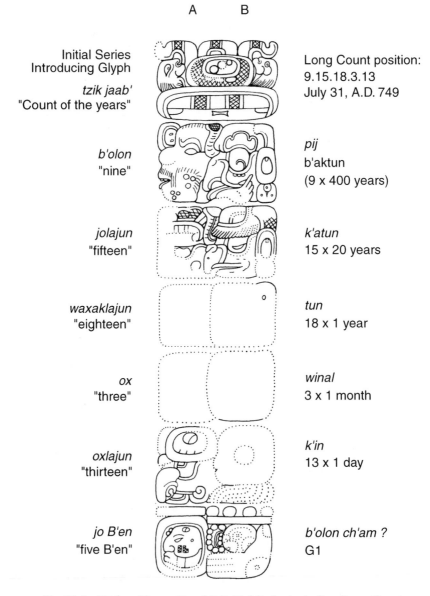

Initial Series
Introducing Glyph

tzik jaab'
"Count of the years"

Long Count position:
9.15.18.3.13
July 31, A.D. 749

b'olon
"nine"

pij
b'aktun
(9 x 400 years)

jolajun
"fifteen"

k'atun
15 x 20 years

waxaklajun
"eighteen"

tun
18 x 1 year

ox
"three"

winal
3 x 1 month

oxlajun
"thirteen"

k'in
13 x 1 day

jo B'en
"five B'en"

b'olon ch'am ?
G1

Fig. 15-6   Piedras Negras Panel 3, Initial Series including Long Count,
Tzolk'in, and Lord of the Night (A1-B7).

C	D	E	F
u ch'a junil	*b'olon k'al-jiy*	*u k'ab'a ch'ok*	*k'al lajun*
"tied on his headband"	"29 days, the current lunation"	"its youthful name"	"30 days" (length of the current moon)

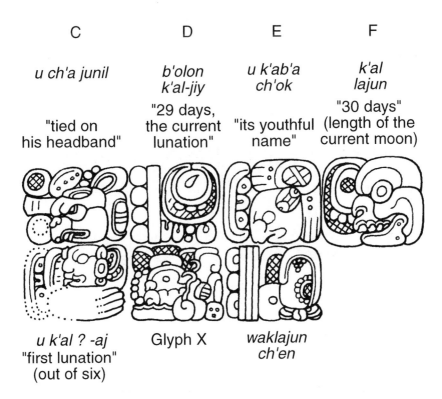

| *u k'al ? -aj* "first lunation" (out of six) | Glyph X | *waklajun ch'en* |

Fig. 15-7 Piedras Negras Panel 3, Supplementary Series and Ja'ab' (C1-E2).

This initial "temporal statement" is a fairly complete version of the several calendrical permutations around which the chronology of the remainder of the text will revolve. The Initial Series has provided the jumping-off point for the "story" that follows. In addition, the calendrical information given up to now serves as the anchor date of Episode 1.

We know from the way the Maya structured their language that what follows must include the episode's event or verbal phrase (F2–H1), telling us what action occurred. This reads **tzu-tzu-ja** "it was ended." The **tzu** is doubled because of the "doubler dots" prefixed to the sign's upper left corner. (**-ja** in this case transforms the verb into a passive construction.) The next sign tells us *u jun k'atun-lat* "his first *k'atun*" (G1), with the verbal phrase ending at H1 with *ti ajawlel* (remember the doubler dots on the sign for **le**). Thus the predicate reads, "It was finished/ended, his first *k'atun* in rulership."

F   G   H   I

u jun
k'atun-lat   *ti ajawlel*   Ch'ul Yokib'
Ajaw

"his first
k'atun"   "in office"   "Holy Canyon (?)
Lord"

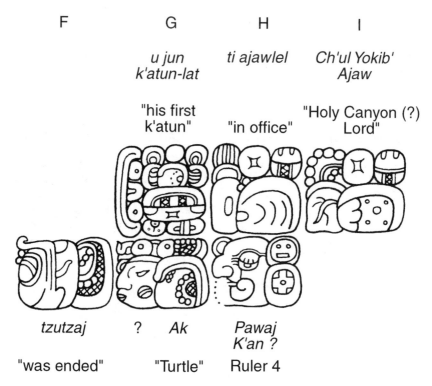

tzutzaj   ?   *Ak*   *Pawaj*
K'an ?

"was ended"   "Turtle"   Ruler 4

Fig. 15-8   Piedras Negras Panel 3, Episode 1, Event 1, Part 1,
verb plus nominal phrase (F2-I1).

The "one *k'atun*" statement of the predicate relates an "anniversary," the commemoration or "jubilee" of the completion of the ruler's first *k'atun* in office. From the same statement we can infer that the ruler acceded as lord of Piedras Negras on 9.14.18.3.13 7 Men 18 K'ank'in (November 13, A.D. 729), or one *k'atun* previous to our opening date, an assumption confirmed by the ruler's clear accession statement on Piedras Negras Altar 2, Support 2 (see Appendix I).

We now learn who the ruler was who celebrated this jubilee (G2–I1). Only partially legible, his name takes the designation **aj-ku** or *Ak* "turtle" (G2b), with the head of an elderly individual resembling God N of the God N-Step set (H1), though in this case having distinctive earflares and possibly reading **PAWAJ K'AN**.[1] His Emblem, however, leaves no doubt over which site he ruled (I1). Along with the standard **CH'UL** or **K'UJUL** "divine" prefix, it takes as its main sign the conflation of **ki** and **b'i** and the prefix **yo-**, or *Yokib'*, probably in reference to an enormous sinkhole located near the town. This yields *Ch'ul Yokib' Ajaw*—"Divine Piedras Negras Lord." This is the titular sequence of Ruler 4 who ruled the town for slightly more than twenty-eight years.[2]

What we have now is equivalent to "On 9.15.18.3.13 it ended, his first *k'atun* as ruler, Lord Pawaj K'an, the Divine Yokib' Ajaw."

EPISODE 1, EVENT 1, PART 2

Everything encountered up to this point represents a single "sentence" that ends with the Piedras Negras Emblem Glyph (I1). However, the sculptors of Panel 3 decided to introduce a second part to Event 1 (J1–K1), offering additional information about what happened on the same date. J1 states that "He witnessed it" (**yi-la-ji** or *yilaj*), a transitive completive construction that, because Part 1 concerned Ruler 4, must involve another person.

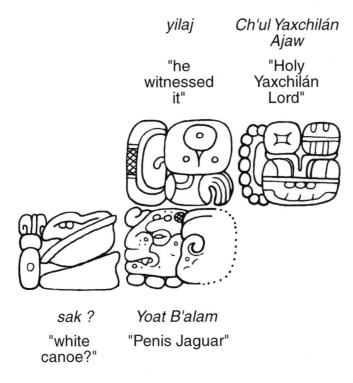

yilaj Ch'ul Yaxchilán
Ajaw

"he
witnessed
it"

"Holy
Yaxchilán
Lord"

sak ? Yoat B'alam

"white
canoe?"

"Penis Jaguar"

Fig. 15-9 Piedras Negras Panel 3, Episode 1,
Event 1, Part 2 (J1-K1).

I2 incorporates the sign for "white," or **SAK**, prefixed to a bloodletting bowl (Tnn), although some epigraphers identify the sign as a "white canoe." The head and upraised paw of a jaguar follow, a combination known to substitute for the name Yoat B'alam (J2). This in turn precedes another Emblem Glyph (K1), in this instance the "split-sky" sign denoting the town of Yaxchilán. Part 2 therefore names the Yaxchilán founder known from "successor statements" at that site, whom we are told "witnessed" the jubilee of Ruler 4. We can be fairly sure that someone who was considered a "Holy Yaxchilán Lord" and who held the same name as the founder "witnessed" the ruler's *k'atun* jubilee, since the founder himself had died long ago. Panel 3 announces that Ruler 4 celebrated his twenty-year anniversary along with someone of exceptionally high status from Yaxchilán.

EPISODE 1, EVENT 2, PART 1

Two days later (L1) on 7 Men 18 Ch'en (K2–L2), but still within the same episode or series of linked events, another event took place that introduces additional information about the *k'atun* jubilee. On this new date *ak'otaj ti em-mo'* "was danced the Descending Makaw" (M1–N1), and "Ruler 4, the Divine Yokib' Ajaw" did it (M2–N2).

EPISODE 1, EVENT 2, PART 2

Our scribes go on to relate the "fine details" of this continuing celebration that has so far involved Ruler 4 and his "guest" from Yaxchilán, with the ruler himself dancing on this momentous occasion. At O1–P2 we learn that "on this night" *u ch'ab'-in*—"he drank"—and that it was *ti kal*, "he drank to get drunk," with the intoxicating substance named as *kakaw*, the chocolate beverage of the fermented kind. Specifically Q1–R1 identifies "who got drunk" as Ruler 4.

EPISODE 1, EVENT 2, PART 3

In the final statement of Episode 1, we learn where the celebration that involved dancing and drinking actually took place (*utiy*—"it happened at") (Q2). The text gives a specifically named location (R2), the glyph for which unfortunately has been destroyed. Either the actual building would

K	L	M	N
	cha-lat	*ak'otaj*	*ti Em Mo'*
	"two days (later)"	"was danced"	"the Descending Macaw"

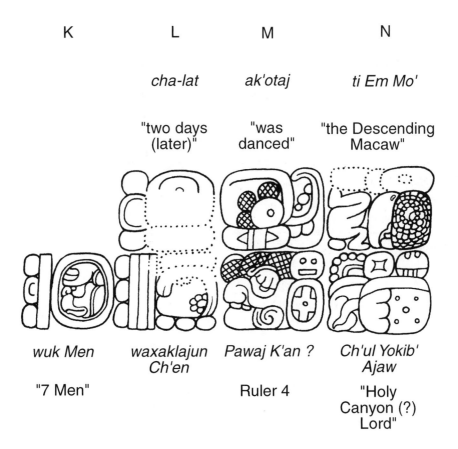

K	L	M	N
wuk Men	*waxaklajun Ch'en*	*Pawaj K'an ?*	*Ch'ul Yokib' Ajaw*
"7 Men"		Ruler 4	"Holy Canyon (?) Lord"

Fig. 15-10   Piedras Negras Panel 3, Episode 1, Event 2, Part 1 (L1-N2).

O	P	Q	R

ti ? k'in   *u ch'ab-in*   *Pawaj K'an (?)*   *K'in Ajaw*

"on this night"   "he drank"   Ruler 4   "Sun Lord"

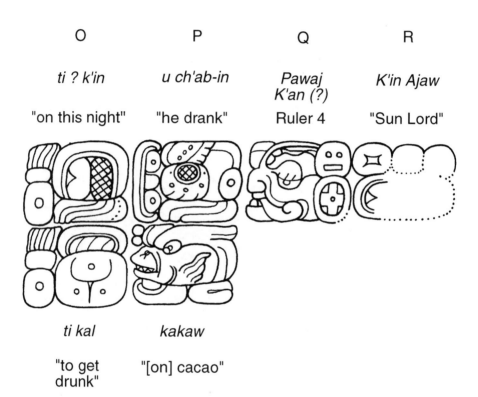

ti kal   *kakaw*

"to get drunk"   "[on] cacao"

Fig. 15-11 Piedras Negras Panel 3, Episode 1, Event 2, Part 2 (O1-R1).

have been named, or the general area of the extensive royal acropolis that crowns the northwest extremity of Piedras Negras.

Q   R

ut-i ?

"it happened   name of
at"   where it
                      happened

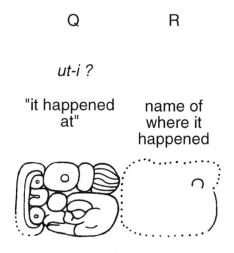

Fig. 15-12   Piedras Negras Panel 3, Episode 1, Event 2, Part 3 (Q2-R2).

✳ ✳ ✳ ✳ ✳

In the several parts of Episode 1, Event 2, we have a series of explicit statements relating what celebrations took place for the ruler's jubilee. These celebrations unfolded over a period of three days, the final events taking place at night (O1). The climax to what must have been a citywide affair involved Ruler 4's performance of the "Descending Makaw Dance," after which he (and presumably everyone else) got "drunk on fermented *kakaw.*"

From what we have read so far, it is obvious that the sculptured scene portrayed below the text depicts Ruler 4's *k'atun* celebration. Indeed, close examination of the original monument indicates that one of the individuals standing to the left of the enthroned ruler bears the Yaxchilán Emblem Glyph, and could conceivably portray Yoat B'alam, the individual who bears the namesake of the Yaxchilán founder. Also, among the seven lords seated along the palace terrace, two appear in animated conversation over a cylindrical tripod that likely holds *kakaw*. Another holds in his hand the *uch'ab'* or *uk'ab'* type of drinking vessel generally used for the consumption of chocolate. (The one at extreme right has an incised "dialogue text" in front of him that reads *'a winak-en* "I am your servant," and seems to be addressing Ruler 4 seated on his throne.)

EPISODE 2, EVENT 1

Here the text shifts dramatically, moving forward more than eight years from the time of the jubilee (S1–T1). This is indicated by a Distance Number of 8.8.2—the first full-scale DN encountered up to now. The text has taken a giant leap forward to what seem to be totally unrelated events. However, an inscription from upriver may help fill the gap; on 9.16.6.11.0 Yaxun B'alam, the actual ruler of Yaxchilán, defeated an enemy portrayed in submission on that site's Lintel 12, where Yaxun B'alam passes judgment on his prisoners in the company of Piedras Negras Ruler 4. Of great interest to readers is that the date of the battle falls only seventeen days before the date reached by the Panel 3 Distance Number, given at U1–V1. Although mostly obliterated, the Panel 3 position can be reconstructed as 7 Kab'an 0 Pax 9.16.6.11.17, because of the following Distance Number and Calendar Round (V4–U5). At U2–V2, the verbal phrase (only the left portion of which survives) gives the well-known statement *ch'ay u sak nik ik'il*—"it diminished, his flowery soul"—followed by the name of Ruler 4 (U3) and the Piedras Negras Emblem Glyph (V3). In other words, this is Ruler 4's death date.

Therefore the date on which the text states that Ruler 4 died was seventeen days after the joint war between Yaxchilán and Piedras Negras. The conclusion that many epigraphers have reached is that Ruler 4 may have been mortally wounded in the battle commemorated at Yaxchilán, although Panel 3 fails to mention that fact, if true. Whatever the case may be, Ruler 4's life ended on the opening date of Episode 2, at the age of fifty-six years old.[3]

EPISODE 2, EVENT 2

In addition to describing Ruler 4's demise, the Panel 3 scribes explain that something further happened "three days later" (U4), on 10 Ajaw 3 Pax 9.16.6.12.0. From this first clear, fully legible date, all other dates recorded on Panel 3 can easily be reconstructed. As none of the DNs have been damaged, we can use them to trace back to the damaged or missing elements of each CR one by one until we reach the Long Count position of the Initial Series.

The scribes soon tell us what happened on 9.16.6.12.0. Given as **mu-ka-ja**, the verb reads, "was buried" (V5). Further, we learn the probable name of the burial place—Jo Janaab' Witz, or Five Flower Mountain

	S	T	U	V
	cha k'in, *waxak winal-iy*	*waxak tun-i*	*wuk Kab'an*	*chum Pax*
	"2 days, 8 months"	"8 years"	"7 Kab'an"	"seating of Pax"

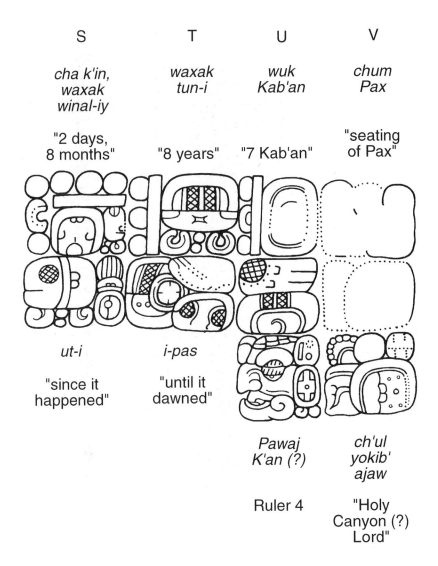

	S	T	U	V
	ut-i	*i-pas*		
	"since it happened"	"until it dawned"		
			Pawaj K'an (?)	*ch'ul yokib' ajaw*
			Ruler 4	"Holy Canyon (?) Lord"

Fig. 15-13 Piedras Negras Panel 3, Episode 2, Event 1 (S1-V3).

U   V

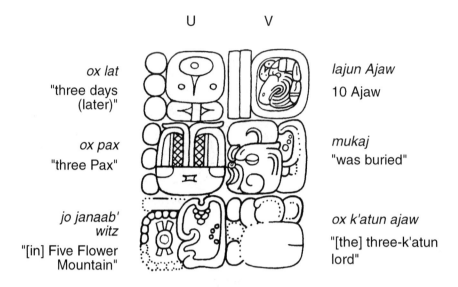

ox lat
"three days
(later)"

lajun Ajaw
10 Ajaw

ox pax
"three Pax"

mukaj
"was buried"

*jo janaab'
witz*
"[in] Five Flower
Mountain"

ox k'atun ajaw
"[the] three-k'atun
lord"

Fig. 15-14   Piedras Negras Panel 3, Episode 2, Event 2 (U4-V6).

(U6)—which may refer to one of the many impressive pyramids built at Piedras Negras. The person buried simply takes an epithet, Ruler 4's "numbered *k'atun*" title, telling us his approximate age at death. Ruler 4 was a "Three K'atun Ajaw"—between forty and sixty years of age, in accordance with his birth and death dates. Thus Episode 2 informs us of the death of Ruler 4, twenty-eight years, eight months, and four days after acceding as *k'ujul ajaw*. His burial took place three days later at Jo Janaab' Witz.

EPISODE 3, PART 1

Panel 3 introduces one more event that serves as the basis for everything so far related. In Part 1 of the panel's final episode, after a DN (U7–V7) that moves the narrative forward twenty-four years to 12 Imix 19 Sip 9.17.11.6.1, this climactic event takes place. While the verb itself has been lost (U9–V9), it involved the "Three K'atun Ajaw" (U10), which was an epithet for Ruler 4. Either a dedication occurred, or another event memorializing Ruler 4 that invoked his past celebration and the glory of his reign. Considering the scene portrayed and the glyphic story, it seems that Panel 3 was just one more of the several monuments commissioned for the glory of Ruler 4.

U   V

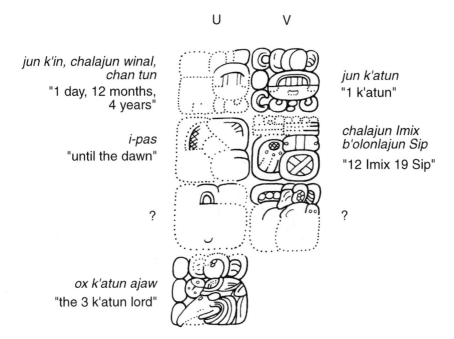

jun k'in, chalajun winal, chan tun
"1 day, 12 months, 4 years"

i-pas
"until the dawn"

?

ox k'atun ajaw
"the 3 k'atun lord"

jun k'atun
"1 k'atun"

chalajun Imix b'olonlajun Sip
"12 Imix 19 Sip"

?

Fig. 15-15   Piedras Negras Panel 3, Episode 3, Part 1 (U7–U10).

EPISODE 3, PART 2

One final surprise lies in store, however. In the last phrase of the inscription, it is told that someone else dedicated Panel 3. V10 explains how the dedication, the memorial in honor of Ruler 4, happened *u kab'iy*, "under the authority of" an individual named in the rather lengthy passage at U11–V12, all of which relates royal titles ending with the Piedras Negras Emblem Glyph. This names Ruler 7, who was probably the last Piedras Negras king and among the greatest known from that town. Therefore the entire panel leads through a series of background events to the "remembrance" of Ruler 4 by Ruler 7, who commissioned the panel (confirmed by the signatures of Ruler 7's two sculptors named just to the right of the throne). Rather modestly, as Peter Mathews has pointed out, Ruler 7 sought to glorify his predecessor, rather than himself.

Panel 3 can be paraphrased in the following manner. On the date 9.15.18.3.13 Ruler 4 celebrated his first *k'atun* anniversary, which was

U   V

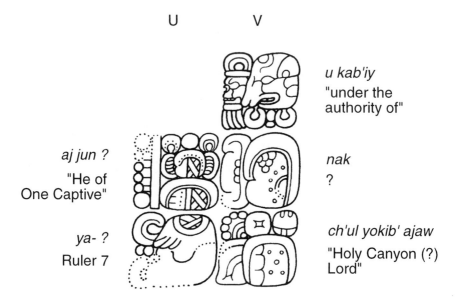

u kab'iy
"under the authority of"

aj jun ?
"He of One Captive"

nak
?

ya- ?
Ruler 7

ch'ul yokib' ajaw
"Holy Canyon (?) Lord"

Fig. 15-16   Piedras Negras Panel 3, Episode 3, Part 2 (V10-V12).

witnessed by an individual from Yaxchilán. Two days later Ruler 4 danced, and that night got drunk on *kakaw* in a continuance of the celebration. The text moves forward more than eight years to give us the date when Ruler 4 died (which may have been the result of wounds acquired in battle), and tells us that three days after his death Ruler 4 was buried in a place called Five Flower Mountain. Twenty-four years later Ruler 7 memorialized this earlier ruler by dedicating Panel 3 in his name.

Summary of Episodes and Events On Piedras Negras Panel 3

Episode 1:

Event 1:

Part 1:   First *k'atun* anniversary of Ruler 4   9.15.18.3.13
5 B'en 16 Ch'en
July 31, A.D. 749

Part 2:   He witnessed, Yoat B'alam   same date
of Yaxchilán

Event 2:

Part 1:   2 days later, he danced the   9.15.18.3.15
"Descending Makaw," Ruler 4   7 Men 18 Ch'en
August 2, A.D. 749

Part 2:   On that night, he drank to get   same date
drunk on *kakaw*, Ruler 4

Part 3:   It happened at (name of place lost)   same date

Episode 2:

Event 1:   8 years, 8 months, and 2 days since   9.16.6.11.17
that time, then he died, Ruler 4   7 Kab'an 0 Pax
November 30, A.D. 759

Event 2:   3 days later he was buried in Five   9.16.6.12.0
Flower Mountain, the 3 K'atun   10 Ajaw 3 Pax
Lord (Ruler 4)   December 3, A.D. 759

Episode 3:

Part 1:   1 *k'atun*, 4 years, 12 months, and   9.17.11.6.1
1 day since that time, he was   12 Imix 19 Sip
remembered, the 3 K'atun Lord   March 28, A.D. 782
(Ruler 4)

Part 2:   Under the authority of Ruler 7   same date

Chronology of Piedras Negras Panel 3

Main Text

Date A:

A1–E2	9.15.18. 3.13	5 B'en	16 Ch'en	IS

DN 1:

L1	2			Forward

Date B:

K2–L2	(9.15.18. 3.15)	7 Men	18 Ch'en	CR

DN 2:

S1–T1	8. 8. 2			Forward

Date C:

U1–V1	(9.16. 6.11.17)	7 Kab'an	0 Pax	CR

DN 3:

U4	3			Forward

Date D:

V4–U5	(9.16. 6.12. 0)	10 Ajaw	3 Pax	CR

DN 4:

U7–V7	1. 4.12. 1			Forward

Date E:

V8	(9.17.11. 6. 1)	12 Imix	19 Sip	CR

Incised Text

Date F:

X6–Y6	(9.16. 6.10.19)	2 Kawak	2 Muwan	CR

DN 5:

Z1	1. 3			Back

Date G:

A'4–Z5	(9.16. 6. 9.16)	5 Kib'	19 Mak	CR

NOTES

1. As suggested by Marc Zender (1999).
2. Precisely 1.8.8.4 (1 *k'atun*, 8 *tuns*, 8 *winals*, and 4 *k'ins*).
3. Reconstructable on the basis of his birth date given elsewhere at Piedras Negras and his death date given on Panel 3.

CHAPTER 16

●
═══
═══

Advanced Decipherment

The beginner should now be able to understand many short texts written by the Maya, and certainly any of those that convey basic events like birth, death, capture, or PSS and other dedicatory phrases. Many other texts, especially very long ones like those of the Temple of the Inscriptions or other Palenque "epics," may require an advanced knowledge of subject matter and more sophisticated analytical techniques. While these lie outside the scope of the present book, this chapter attempts to direct the way toward learning the Maya script in greater depth.

Techniques of Structural and Comparative Analysis

Instructors in today's workshops and conferences traditionally teach beginners who work with the more complicated texts to shade all of the dates, verbs, and name phrases with different colored pencils or highlighter pens. Theoretically, by coloring each component of each sentence the beginner can more easily discern "chunks of text" and identify the structural elements. More formally, epigraphers accomplish essentially the same thing by cutting up photocopies of texts and laying out each hieroglyphic sentence on graph paper in linear fashion, thereby reorganizing texts so that each date, each verb, and each name phrase align in vertical columns.

295

Techniques like these help to facilitate "structural" and "comparative" analysis. In the first case, by highlighting textual components either with colored pencils or by laying out each sentence linearly, the reader can better understand the various hieroglyphic parts and how they relate to the overall structure or discourse of the text. For purposes of comparison, linear structural analysis allows the reader to "stack" each type of grammatical component one above the other, in order to more easily search for those features which the various sentences may share, as well as how each component differs. Therefore astute readers will often be able to identify damaged glyphs that may be preserved elsewhere on the same monument or in other texts. The reader can simply scan the features of each column to check for similarities and differences between the names of each subject, for example, or between the inflectional patterns of each verb.

Decipherers employ almost as many methods of structural analysis as there are hieroglyphs. While the size of the squares of the graph paper hardly matters, some epigraphers prefer the smaller-sized squares and refuse to use anything else. Similarly, the materials used to hold down glyphs and affix them to the graph paper vary almost as widely as scholarly opinion does, with some epigraphers preferring removable Scotch tape that can be easily lifted off the paper and replaced. Others prefer post-it notes. Some even use blobs of clay which they stick to the back of the glyph then press against the graph paper![1]

I think the most convenient method is to use strips of ¾ inch Scotch Removable Magic Tape (Scotch 811, the kind in the blue box) and attach them to the top of each hieroglyph, positioning the majority of the surface of the tape above the glyph and taping the glyph's top edge along one of the **BOLD** lines of the graph paper. In this way, while securely taping the hieroglyph, you can write notes on the tape's surface just above the glyph, and then move tape and glyph to another location if you decide to re-position the text. As your analysis progresses, it may happen that you change your mind about how the scribes organized what they wrote, and you will want to rearrange your analysis. You also might find that you need more space, and may have to tape together several sheets of graph paper, again forcing you to realign your sentences. By affixing strips of tape to the *top* of the glyphs, you can easily move *both glyphs* and *notes*.

For starters, try organizing your linear arrangement by isolating individual components such as verbs, and so on. As a rule, it helps to isolate all dates along the left, leaving the right half of the graph paper for verbs, subjects, and objects. Once organized, you can proceed glyph by glyph with comparison of similar phrases, determining structural equivalencies and substitution sets. For example, you may find instances where two oth- erwise identical sentences vary only in the form of the verb, while sharing the same context. Structural and comparative analysis can help you to decide whether what appear to be separate verbs are really only variations of the same action. Structural analysis may also assist you in identifying couplet constructions or other discourse techniques. At the very least, you can use this type of analysis to establish an event line, as discussed in Chapter 15.

Advanced Analysis: Calculations Into the Extreme Past

Armed with information learned in this book, together with calendrical computer programs (see Appendices, Maya Calendar Programs) and any other available resources, the initiate can begin an exploration of some of the more challenging texts. The following offers a brief guide to the more "cosmic" narratives composed by the Maya.

CREATION EVENTS

According to the Judeo-Christian view, God created the universe in seven days. Modern scientific belief holds that all matter in existence was formed in a "quantum" fireball called the Big Bang, only ten billion years ago.

Both conceptions appear rather puny in comparison with the infinite scale of time conceived by the Maya during the Classic Period. The Maya believed that gods, who represented numbers, literally carried time in their arms or on their backs, in a constant relay that seems to have had no beginning or end. The Maya were convinced that the gods had relayed the *b'aktuns*, the *k'atuns*, and so on—and would *keep* relaying these periods— for as long as the gods existed. Consequently, when the cycles reach the node where the *b'aktun* cycle ends and reverts back to zero, the calendars start another sequence in the continuous larger cycles of epochs and eons that comprise the Long Count.

Towards the end of Chapter 3 we saw how the Long Count normally reaches as high as the *b'aktun*, the cycle of 400 years. Nevertheless, the cal- endar incorporates much larger orders, for most of which epigraphers still lack names. These larger periods include the **PIKTUN**, or 8,000 *tuns* (8,000 years of 360 days), the **KALAB'TUN** (160,000 years), the **K'INCHILTUN**

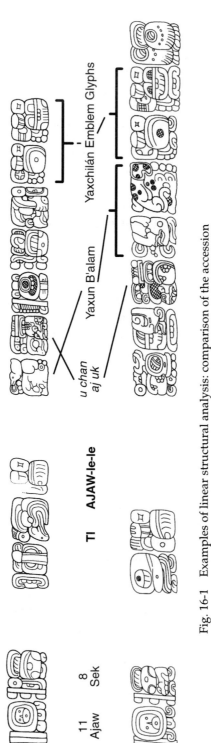

Fig. 16-1 Examples of linear structural analysis: comparison of the accession statements from Yaxchilán Stela 11, front, lower glyph panel, and Stela 12, "deity side."

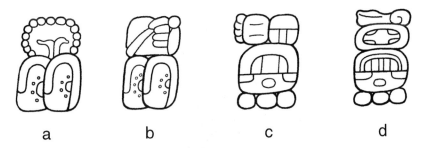

Fig. 16-2   Higher periods of time: a) *piktun*; b) *kalab'tun*;
c) *k'inchiltun*; d) *alawtun*.

(3,200,000 years), and the **ALAWTUN** (64 million years). Still larger periods of time exist as well, and since periods were multiplied by any numbers affixed to them, Maya scribes racked up extraordinary calculations, a few reaching so far into the past that even modern mathematicians have difficulty calculating them.

Cobá Stela 1

What is probably the longest single date ever recorded by the Maya occurs on the misnamed Cobá Stela 1,[2] from the great megacity of eastern Quintana Roo on the Yucatan Peninsula. Here, within the context of an Initial Series recording the "beginning" or "zero" date of the calendar, or 13.0.0.0.0 4 Ajaw 8 Kumk'u, the monument's scribes extended the number of periods to include nineteen positions above the *b'aktun*. Each position includes the number "thirteen," so that each period is to be multiplied that number of times. The result adds up to 41,943,040,000,000,000,000,000,000,000 years, an absolutely mind-boggling number more than 1,000 times greater than the "scientific" estimate of the age of the universe! This extraordinary number places the date 4 Ajaw 8 Kumk'u (13.0.0.0.0) within a context of larger epochs and eons.

Stela 1 records what happened on this "zero" date at A17, spelled **JAL-ja** "was made to appear," followed at B17 by **k'o-jo** or *k'oj* "the image." The text goes on to tell us that thirteen *b'aktuns* ended on this date (August 13, 3114 B.C.), an event overseen by the Paddler Gods.

Because Stela 1 provides so little information besides the date, to understand what took place on the eve of the current era—which technically began the *following* day—we have to turn to other creation texts, several of which survive.

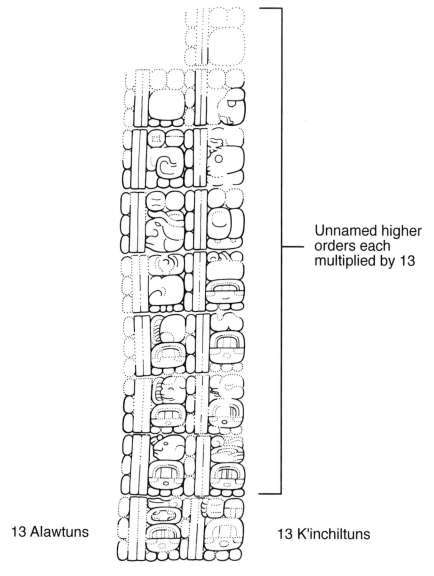

Unnamed higher
orders each
multiplied by 13

13 Alawtuns

13 K'inchiltuns

Fig. 16-3   Macanxoc Stela 1, extended Initial Series, part one.

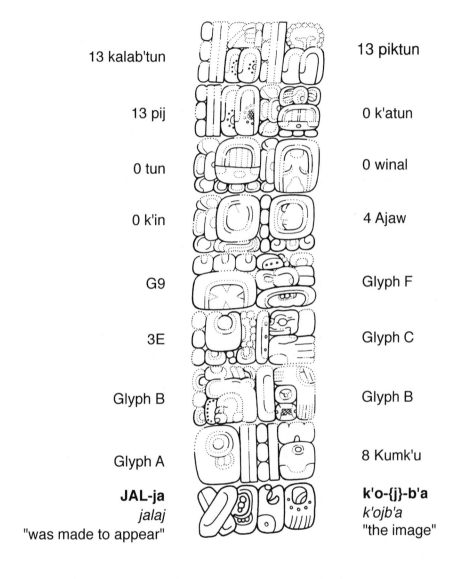

13 kalab'tun	13 piktun
13 pij	0 k'atun
0 tun	0 winal
0 k'in	4 Ajaw
G9	Glyph F
3E	Glyph C
Glyph B	Glyph B
Glyph A	8 Kumk'u
JAL-ja *jalaj* "was made to appear"	**k'o-{j}-b'a** *k'ojb'a* "the image"

Fig. 16-4 Macanxoc Stela 1, extended Initial Series, part two.

Quirigua Stela C

At Quirigua, too, the scribes narrated what happened at creation as *jalaj k'oj*—"the image appeared." Here, however, they tell how the Paddler Gods "planted" three stones (*ox kal tun*), not only giving us the name of each stone but identifying where these were erected—the Jaguar Throne Stone at First Five-Sky Place, the Serpent Throne Stone at "Earth" Place, and the Water Lily Throne Stone at Lying Down Sky Place. The setting of the three stones took place at Yax Ox Tunal—the "First Three-Stone Place." What we seem to have is the placing of the first hearthstones, the stones that traditionally make up the fireplace of the Maya house—which modern scholarship, especially the work of Linda Schele, has shown took place *in the sky*. The three hearthstones correspond to the three stars that comprise the belt in the constellation of Orion.

The Crack in the Turtle Shell

Maya creation texts disclose important astronomical phenomena, describing a series of primordial episodes or "celestial events" related to star-lore and conditions in the sky when the gods first made proper the world and all that it contains. To explore this aspect of creation, we turn to an important text, one from an unprovenanced panel looted from an unknown site and subsequently sold on the antiquities market. Equipped with the "creation date" 4 Ajaw 8 Kumk'u—the beginning of the Maya calendar—the surviving text tells us that the "first image was seen" (*yila-yi yax k'oj*) and that this image was an *ak*, or turtle. This was doubtlessly the turtle carapace out of which the Maize God was born, as shown on numerous painted ceramic vessels. The central act of creation, then, was the birth of the Corn God and, as Quirigua Stela C tells us, the placing of the three hearthstones— quite literally the stuff from which life was made.

Problems in Decipherment: Looking Forward

Other ramifications of the Maya's creation event have been investigated by Linda Schele and provide greater insight into Maya beliefs and culture. As a start, several extraordinary long-distance numbers worth exploring occur elsewhere at Quirigua (Stelae D and F), Yaxchilán (Hieroglyphic Stairway 2, Step VII), Palenque (the panels of the Temple of the Inscriptions and the

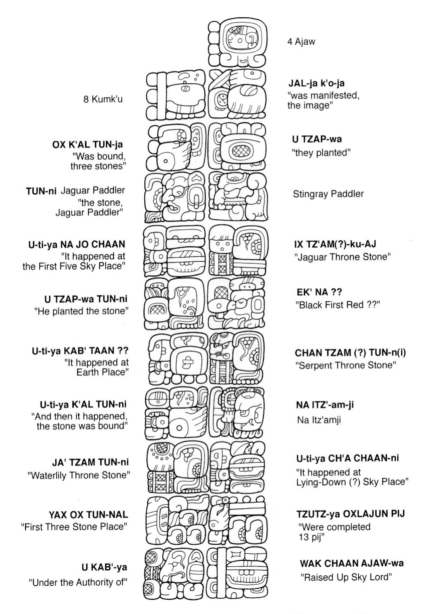

4 Ajaw

8 Kumk'u

JAL-ja k'o-ja
"was manifested,
the image"

OX K'AL TUN-ja
"Was bound,
three stones"

U TZAP-wa
"they planted"

TUN-ni Jaguar Paddler
"the stone,
Jaguar Paddler"

Stingray Paddler

U-ti-ya NA JO CHAAN
"It happened at
the First Five Sky Place"

IX TZ'AM(?)-ku-AJ
"Jaguar Throne Stone"

U TZAP-wa TUN-ni
"He planted the stone"

EK' NA ??
"Black First Red ??"

U-ti-ya KAB' TAAN ??
"It happened at
Earth Place"

CHAN TZAM (?) TUN-n(i)
"Serpent Throne Stone"

U-ti-ya K'AL TUN-ni
"And then it happened,
the stone was bound"

NA ITZ'-am-ji
Na Itz'amji

JA' TZAM TUN-ni
"Waterlily Throne Stone"

U-ti-ya CH'A CHAAN-ni
"It happened at
Lying-Down (?) Sky Place"

YAX OX TUN-NAL
"First Three Stone Place"

TZUTZ-ya OXLAJUN PIJ
"Were completed
13 pij"

U KAB'-ya
"Under the Authority of"

WAK CHAAN AJAW-wa
"Raised Up Sky Lord"

Fig. 16-5   Quirigua Stela C, the creation date and era expression.

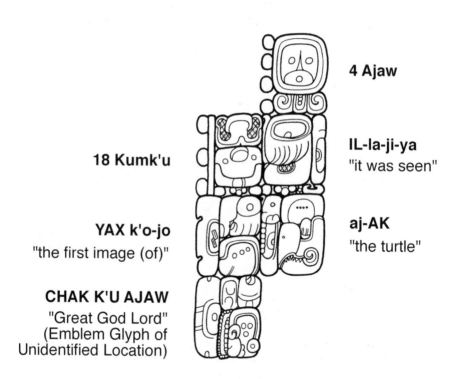

4 Ajaw

IL-la-ji-ya
"it was seen"

aj-AK
"the turtle"

18 Kumk'u

YAX k'o-jo
"the first image (of)"

CHAK K'U AJAW
"Great God Lord"
(Emblem Glyph of
Unidentified Location)

Fig. 16-6   Unprovenanced panel with creation date and era expression.

Fig. 16-7 Unprovenanced ceramic plate depicting the birth of the Maize God.

Group of the Cross), Copán (Stela C), Tikal (Stela 10), and Piedras Negras (Altar 1), reflecting the magnitude of the Maya's conception of time.

Yet extraordinary calculations hardly present the greatest challenge to today's epigrapher. Decipherment remains in a rapid state of change, with new discoveries being made almost monthly. Some of the thorniest issues involve the reading order of terminal signs on verbs and the nature of verbal inflection, around which a hard-hitting debate currently exists. In Chapter 8 we discussed the most common forms of verbs, but as decipherment progresses epigraphers continuously revise these categories, adding newer, subtler ones that reflect much more accurately the Mayan languages. Barbara MacLeod, Robert Wald, David Stuart, and others have proceeded well beyond simple completive, incompletive, passive, and positional verbs to identify examples of anti-passive constructions, mediopassive forms, and clitics, as well as other forms. Although for now these findings lack consensus, this work will lead to a better understanding of the written word.

Despite enormous progress in epigraphy, as things currently stand even the correlation with our own Gregorian calendar remains in question, with several epigraphers still challenging the commonly held Goodman-Martínez-Thompson theory (known as the GMT and used throughout the present book). By and large, however, no serious challenges to how epigraphers interpret Maya inscriptions have come forward, and certainly none from any scholar actually literate in Maya glyphs. Those few objections raised over issues of historical accuracy and whether inscriptions can be relied upon to reconstruct Maya society have, for the greatest part, fallen by the wayside.

How to Teach Yourself in Greater Depth

Those who wish to explore Maya inscriptions more seriously have several options available. Beginners would do well to learn as many individual glyphs and phrases as possible. They should also familiarize themselves with as many texts from as many individual sites as time and resources will allow. Structural analysis of each text in chronological order will serve to teach the reader the many subtleties of Maya texts, beginning with the earliest inscriptions and working towards the latest.

More serious students should invest in dictionaries for as many different dialects of Mayan as they can find. A good epigraphic library should include the *Cordemex Dictionary* of Mayan, the *Great Tzotzil Dictionary* published by the Smithsonian Institute, Wisdom's Ch'orti dictionary, and dictionaries of Tzeltal, Ch'olti, and Ch'ol. Most of these remain available either in current publications, or as photocopies of colonial manuscripts.

Serious students should also plan on attending at least one Maya workshop each year, preferably the nearly two-week Maya Meetings at Texas conducted annually in March. (See Appendix II.) Short of attending classes given by well-known epigraphers, few of whom actually offer courses in epigraphy, or else hiring, bribing, or kidnapping your own epigraphic guru, the student must otherwise rely on personal initiative, which should certainly involve getting hold of and studying every article, workbook, and resource on Maya hieroglyphs available. Towards that end, the Appendices provide a selection of sample texts ranging from easy to difficult, as well as information about the most readily accessible resources in current distribution, such as Maya calendar programs on the Internet.

One final observation is that my own experience has repeatedly taught me that newcomers to the field, in many cases individuals with little more than unbridled enthusiasm, have made enormous impact on the professional study of Maya inscriptions. Such was the case when Simon Martin appeared on the scene, or even Linda Schele in the early days of the Palenque Mesa Redonda. I would therefore encourage every prospective *aficionado* to pursue their dream of reading Maya glyphs, and to delve into Maya inscriptions with all the passion of their individual inspiration. In this way, epigraphy will never lack for new generations of enthusiasts. And who knows? You may be the one to decipher that stubborn reading that has eluded epigraphers for so long.

NOTES

1. Which tends to stain the paper with oils.
2. Found in the suburbs of Cobá, the monument actually belongs to the site of Macanxoc.

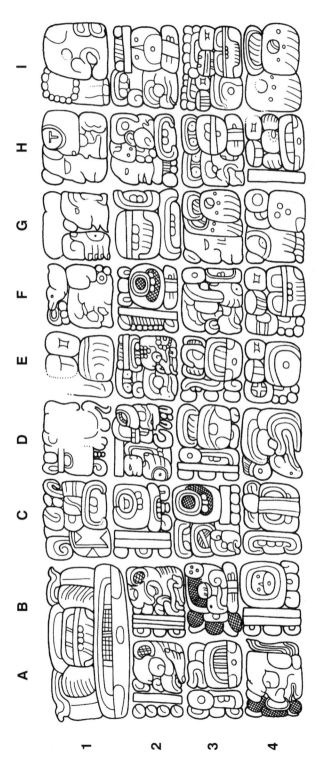

Fig. 2-2a   Yaxchilán Stela 11, Front, Lower Glyph Panel (*enlarged*).

APPENDIX I

Sample Texts and
Practice Inscriptions

Of course, any aspiring epigrapher needs an adequate supply of study material, an extensive body of inscriptions to analyze structurally or otherwise "read" in the more conventional sense. The following eleven examples, arranged according to their relative degree of difficulty, will help beginners start in that direction. Although not an extensive "corpus," they offer an interesting selection of different types of texts that concern a variety of subjects, ranging from artists' signatures and creation stories to an extensive narrative related to war.

Easy

El Peru, Stela 34, Column A: This example, together with the two short texts that follow, concern the same kind of subject. Hint: each text consists of an introductory glyph and name clause. The question concerns what *kind* of person they name.

Piedras Negras Throne 1, Columns A and F: Like the preceding example, these two short inscriptions name individuals engaged in a specific occupation and consist of an introductory glyph and name clause.

Yaxchilán, Lintel 3, Columns I and J: The tail end of a slightly longer inscription, Columns I and J provide the basic titles for Yaxun B'alam (Bird

Fig. 1A   El Peru, Stela 34, Column a.

Fig. 2A   Piedras Negras, Throne 1, Columns A and F.

Jaguar IV), named elsewhere in a portion of the text not given here. Hint: this sample contains a nice, equal mixture of logograms and phonetic spellings, with one personified numerical head variant.

Fig. 3A   Yaxchilán, Lintel 3, Columns I and J.

Piedras Negras, Stela 36: Consisting of two events, this brief inscription provides the most basic information about Piedras Negras Ruler 2 and can be easily deciphered in its entirety.

Piedras Negras, Altar 2: Somewhat more extensive than Stela 36, Altar 2 relates the same kind of basic information about Ruler 4 but continues further to provide information about two Period Endings. Altar 2 documents Ruler 4's reign as far as completion of the 16th *k'atun* of B'aktun 9.

El Peru, Stela 34, Columns C-J: The continuation of a text found on the sides of the monument, this brief two-part inscription refers to the ruler of Calakmul and a local noblewoman of great importance.

Tikal, Stela 22: The text on Stela 22 involves accession of the Kalomte'—Tikal's equivalent of a ruler—with some interesting titles and a parentage statement.

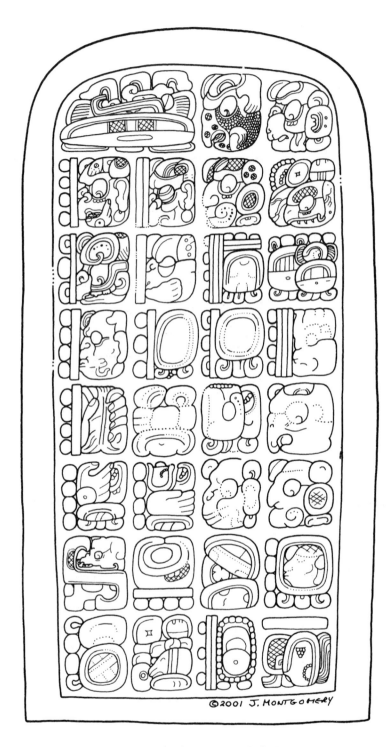

Fig. 4A Piedras Negras, Stela 36.

Fig. 5A   Piedras Negras, Altar 2.

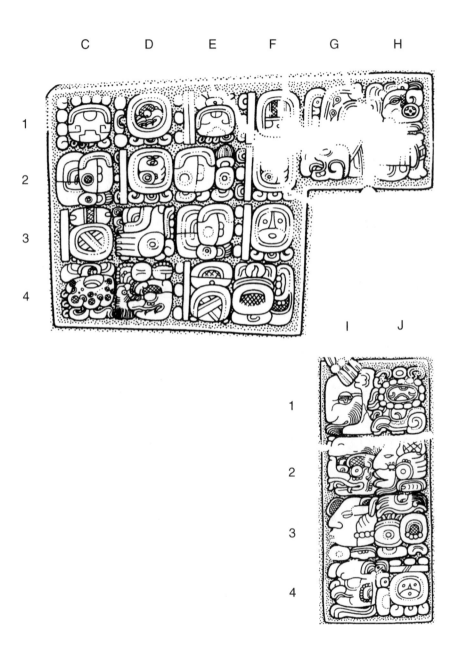

Fig. 6A   El Peru, Stela 34, Columns C-J.

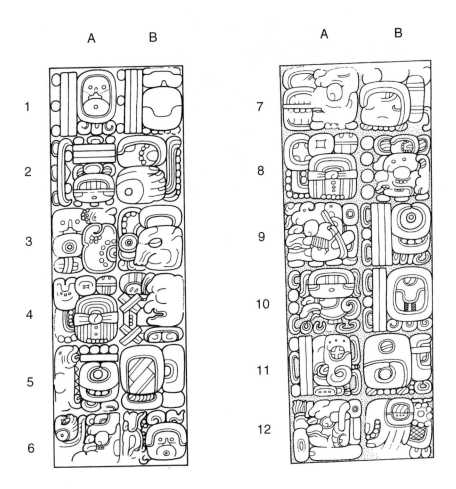

Fig. 7A   Tikal, Stela 22.

Kuná-Lacanhá, Panel 1: Concerned not with a local "king" but a subordinate to the lord of Bonampak, Panel 1 includes an interesting parentage statement and a number of specialized titles.

Difficult

Piedras Negras, Altar 1: One of the chief difficulties of Altar 1 is its bad state of preservation. Despite the challenge, much of the information can still be recovered. The text ranges over extremely long time periods, beginning well before the current era, which began on 4 Ajaw 8 Kumk'u, and possibly extending into the future. Once mastered, this makes a wonderful read. The structure of the text suggests that the inscription began on the now-destroyed top surface, which probably included an opening Long Count or Calendar Round corresponding to what survives of Date A (B1). The surviving inscription begins on the side of Fragment A at position A1, then continues along the sides of the altar on Fragments B, C, and D in that order. The supports were meant to be read last, beginning with Support 1.

Palenque, Tablet of the 96 Glyphs: Considered among the more elegant texts for its simplicity and narrative rhythm, the 96 Glyphs tablet presents a series of events that took place in a relatively short period of time, arranged in a kind of "couplet" structure. Most epigraphers consider this a good text for beginners to "cut their teeth" on. Have fun here, because long texts rarely yield so completely to decipherment. Drawing by Linda Schele, courtesy of the Foundation for the Advancement of Mesoamerican Studies, Inc.

Tikal, Temple IV, Lintel 2: Especially difficult in the sense that it includes numerous passages not entirely understood by professional epigraphers, this relatively long two-column text relates to war conducted by Tikal against Naranjo, a recalcitrant subject town only a few miles to the east.

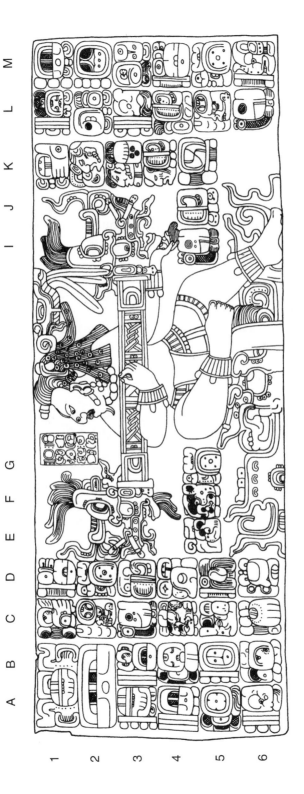

Fig. 8A Kuná-Lacanhá, Panel 1.

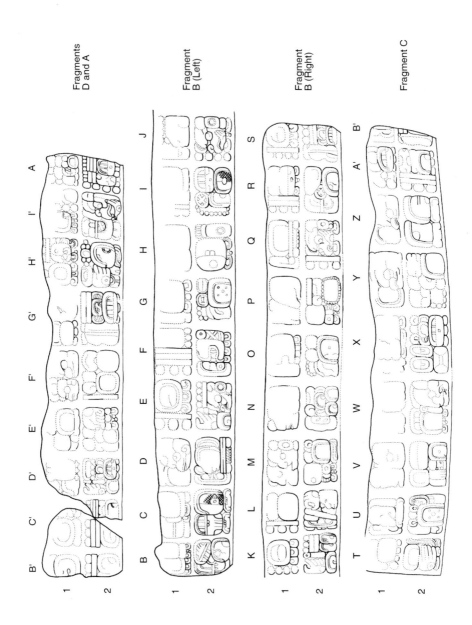

Fragments
D and A

Fragment
B (Left)

Fragment
B (Right)

Fragment C

Support 1

Support 2

Support 3

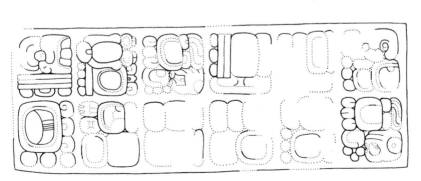

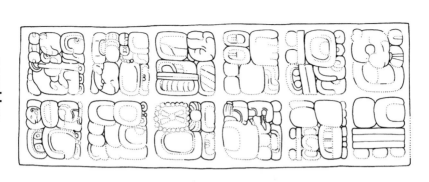

Fig. 9A   Piedras Negras, Altar 1.

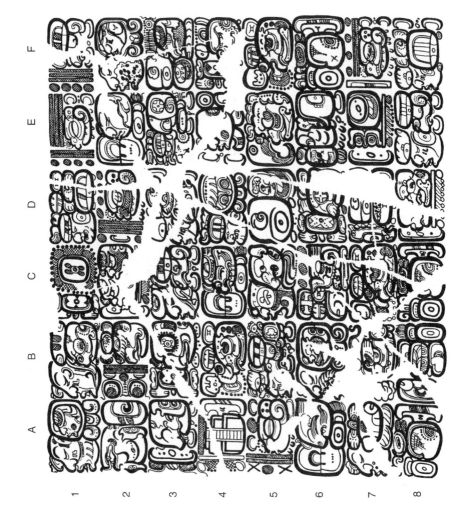

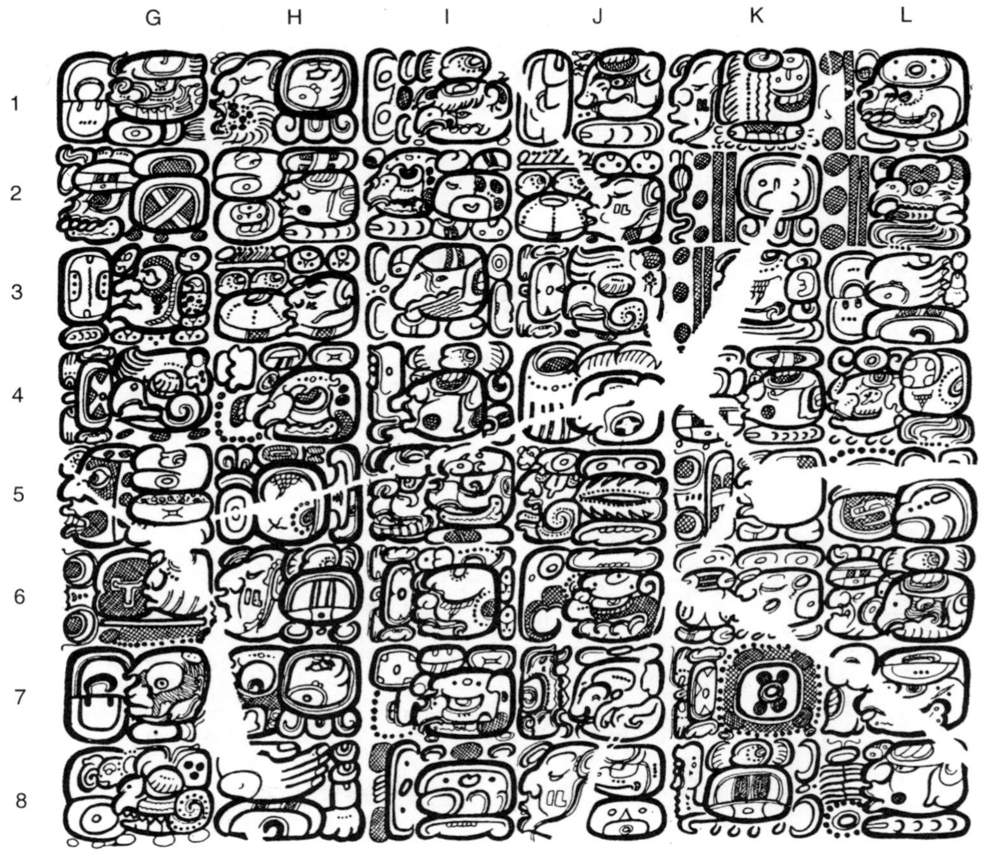

Fig. 10A   Palenque, Tablet of the 96 Glyphs.

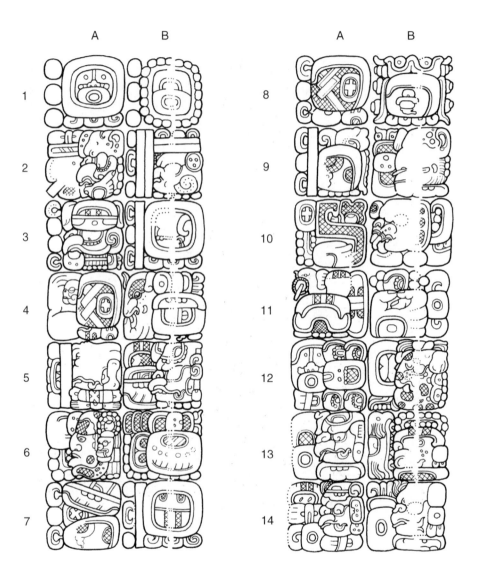

Fig. 11A   Tikal, Temple IV, Lintel 2.

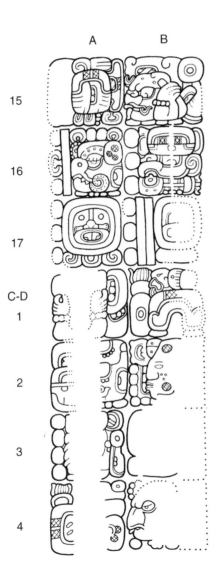

APPENDIX II

A Guide to Hieroglyphic Resources

Internet Resources

The Internet offers a wide variety of resources on Maya epigraphy, including numerous downloadable calendar programs of differing degrees of sophistication for both PC and MAC. Other sites offer extensive resources including hieroglyphic databases and programs that actually sound out individual signs, as well as online calculators for working out Maya dates.

MAYA CALENDAR PROGRAMS

Mesoamerica Archaeology WWW Page

This site has very nearly everything, including a variety of free calendar programs for PC, MAC, and UNIX. Programs have to be unzipped and decoded. Also offers downloadable hieroglyphic fonts and astronomical programs for determining glyph-related astronomical events.

http://copan.bioz.unibas.ch/meso.html

Maya Date

Offers a free downloadable Maya date calculator with a professional but complex interface. For Windows only.

http://www.mayadate.org

OTHER INTERNET RESOURCES

Rabbit in the Moon

Extensive information on Maya hieroglyphs, including an online date calculator that instantly converts any Gregorian date. Of special interest is its "Talking Syllabary" with .wav sound files, which provides the actual sound of individual glyphs. The site also teaches you to write your name in glyphs. This ranks among the best sites on the Internet.
     http://www.halfmoon.org

The Mayan Epigraphic Database Project

Includes an online glyph catalog with an extensive database that provides an image of each glyph and its pronunciation. Also offers the source of the pronunciation.
     http://jeffersonvillage.virginia.edu/med/home.html

Aztlan

A listserve with important discussions on a variety of Mesoamerican topics, including questions about hieroglyphic inscriptions, for both professionals and beginners. To subscribe, send a blank e-mail message to the listserver, together with the message text: subscribe Aztlan "Chris Doe" (substitute your name).
     listserv@listserv.louisville.edu

Notebook for the Kelowna Museum's Second Annual Maya Hieroglyphic Workshop Online

By Peter Mathews and Marc Zender. Offers an extensive introduction to the Maya writing system.
     http://www.acs.ucalgary.ca/~harriscj/mayaglyphs

Foundation for the Advancement of Mesoamerican Studies, Inc. (FAMSI)

268 South Suncoast Blvd., Crystal River, Florida. Contains several important archives of Maya inscriptions, including the Justin Kerr ceramic database,

and the Linda Schele and John Montgomery archives of technical illustrations, that can be downloaded at low resolution or acquired through FAMSI as 8½ × 11 hardcopy suitable for research.
http://www.famsi.org

Publication Series

Texas Notes

Commentaries and reports on Maya hieroglyphic writing. Published by the Center for the History and Art of Ancient American Culture (CHAAAC), Art Department, University of Texas. Available at University Kinko's, Austin, Texas.

Copán Notes

Commentaries and reports on the Copán Project. Published by the Copán Acropolis Project and the Instituto Hondureño de Antropología e Historia. Available at University Kinko's, Austin, Texas.

For a complete list of titles, prices and availability for both the *Texas* and *Copán Notes* contact Kinko's Copies, 2901 Medical Arts Street, Austin, Texas 78705. Telephone: 512-476-3242. Fax: 512-476-2371. University Kinko's also maintains files of numerous research reports, theses, dissertations, and other documents on Maya hieroglyphic writing.

Workbooks for the Maya Meetings at Texas 1986–2000

Contact Peter Keeler, Maya Meetings, P.O. Box 5645, Austin, Texas 78763. Telephone: 512-471-6292.

Transcriptions of the Workbooks for the Maya Meetings at Texas 1991–2000

Transcribed and edited by Phil Wanyerka. Contact Phil Wanyerka at 2293 Judy Drive, Parma, Ohio 44134. Other publications edited and transcribed by Phil Wanyerka include *The Proceedings of the Maya Hieroglyphic Weekend* for 1991 and 1992, presented by Peter Mathews at Cleveland State University.

U Mut Maya

Collections of reports from the Advanced Seminars, Maya Meetings at Texas. For information contact Tom and Carolyn Jones, P.O. Box 564, Bayside, California 95524.

Sources of Inscriptions

Corpus of Maya Hieroglyphic Inscriptions

Ian Graham, Project Director. Peabody Museum, Harvard University. This series includes about two dozen volumes offering inscriptions from a diverse range of sites. Order through the Peabody Museum.

Foundation for the Advancement of Mesoamerican Studies, Inc. (FAMSI)

268 South Suncoast Blvd., Crystal River, Florida.
http://www.famsi.org. See their listing under Internet Resources.

The Monuments and Inscriptions of Tikal: The Carved Monuments

Tikal Report 33, Part A. Museum Monograph 44. The University Museum, University of Pennsylvania, Philadelphia. Order through the University Museum.

The Monuments and Inscriptions of Caracol, Belize

University Museum Monograph 45. The University Museum, University of Pennsylvania, Philadelphia. Order through the University Museum.

The Pre-Columbian Art Research Institute

Offers an important selection of publications, especially concerning Palenque, with extensive drawings of inscriptions by Merle Greene-Robertson. Also produces a quarterly journal with articles on Maya epigraphy and archaeology. 1100 Sacramento Street, San Francisco, California 94108. Telephone: 925-284-8630. Fax: 925-284-8631.

Pictures of Record

Slide sets of archaeological sites, including photographs of individual hieroglyphs and complete texts. Produces ten separate sets on Maya sites, including all the major ones plus the Bonampak murals and Seibal, as well as seven sets covering Mexican sites and two "Mesoamerican surveys." 119 Kettle Creek Road, Weston, Connecticut 06883. Telephone: 203-227-3387. Fax: 203-222-9673. Products can be ordered online, where the company maintains an electronic database.

http://www.picturesofrecord.com

Annual Meetings

Maya Meetings at Texas

University of Texas, Austin. Contact Peter Keeler, Maya Meetings, P.O. Box 5645, Austin, Texas 78763. Telephone: 512-471-6292.

Maya Weekend

University Museum, University of Pennsylvania. 33rd and Spruce Streets, Philadelphia, Pennsylvania 19104-6324.

Maya Hieroglyphic Writing Weekend Workshops

Humboldt State University. Contact Tom and Carolyn Jones, P.O. Box 564, Bayside, California 95524. Fax: 707-822-0119.

Annual UCLA Maya Weekend

Institute of Archaeology, University of California, Los Angeles. MTM Destination and Convention Management, 204 Auburn Avenue, Sierra Madre, California 91024-1803. Telephone: 626-355-6402. Fax: 626-355-1080.

Bibliography

Adams, R.E.W.
1971   *The Ceramics of Altar de Sacrificios*. Peabody Museum Papers 63(1). Cambridge: Harvard University.

Berlin, Heinrich
1958   El glifo "emblema" en las inscripciones mayas. *Journal de la Société des Américanistes* 59 (n.s.) 47: 111–119. Paris.

1959   Glifos Nominales en el Sarcófago de Palenque. *Humanidades* 2(10): 1–8. Guatemala: Universidad de San Carlos.

1963   The Palenque Triad. *Journal de la Société des Américanistes* 52 (n.s.): 91–99. Paris.

1970a   The Tablet of the 96 Glyphs at Palenque, Chiapas, Mexico. *Archaeological Studies in Middle America*. Middle American Research Institute, Publication 26: 135–149. New Orleans: Tulane University.

1970b   Miscelánea Palencana. *Journal de la Société des Américanistes* [de Paris] 59 (new series): 107–128. Paris.

Blom, Frans
1950   A Polychrome Plate from Quintana Roo. *Notes on Middle American Archaeology and Ethnology:* 98.

Bowditch, Charles P.
1901   Notes on the Report of Teobert Maler. *Memoirs of the Peabody Museum* 2(1). Cambridge: Harvard University.

Bricker, Victoria R.
1986   *A Grammar of Maya Hieroglyphs*. Middle American Research Institute. New Orleans: Tulane University.

Chadwick, John
1958   *The Decipherment of Linear B.* Cambridge: Cambridge University Press.

Closs, Michael P.
1989   The Dynastic History of Naranjo: The Late Period. *Word and Image in Maya Culture.* W.F. Hanks and D.S. Rice, eds. Salt Lake City: University of Utah Press.

Coe, Michael D.
1973   *The Maya Scribe and His World.* New York: Grolier Club.

1992   *Breaking the Maya Code.* New York: Thames and Hudson.

Fox, James A., and John S. Justeson
1994   Appendix C. *Phoneticism in Mayan Hieroglyphic Writing:* 363–366. Albany: Institute for Mesoamerican Studies.

Grube, Nikolai, and Simon Martin
1998   *Notebook for the 22nd Maya Hieroglyphic Workshop at Texas.* Austin: University of Texas.

Harris, John F.
1994   *A Resource Bibliography for the Decipherment of Maya Hieroglyphs and New Maya Hieroglyph Readings.* Philadelphia: University Museum, University of Pennsylvania.

Harris, John F., and Stephen K. Stearns
1997   *Understanding Maya Inscriptions: A Hieroglyphic Handbook.* Second Revised Edition. Philadelphia: University Museum, University of Pennsylvania.

Home Life Productions
1999   *Edgewalker: A Conversation with Linda Schele.* Video film.

Hopkins, Nicholas A.
1988   Comments on David Stuart, 'Ten Phonetic Syllables'. In *Chol (Mayan) Dictionary Database, Final Performance Report,* Part I, by J. K. Josserand and N. A. Hopkins.

Houston, Stephen D.
1989   *Maya Glyphs*. Berkeley: University of California Press and the British Museum.

1997   The Shifting Now: Aspect, Deixis, and Narrative in Classic Maya Texts. *American Anthropologist* 99(2): 291–305.

Houston, Stephen, John Robertson, and David Stuart
2000   The Language of Classic Maya Inscriptions. *Current Anthropology* 41(3).

Houston, Stephen, David Stuart, and John Robertson
1997   Disharmony in Maya Hieroglyphic Writing: Linguistic Change and Continuity in Classic Society. Ms in author's archive.

Jones, Christopher
1984   *Deciphering Maya Hieroglyphs*. Philadelphia: University Museum, University of Pennsylvania.

Jones, Tom, and Carolyn Jones
1997   *Maya Hieroglyphic Workbook*. Prepared for the Weekend Workshops on Maya Hieroglyphic Writing held at Humboldt State University. Arcata.

Justeson, John, and Lyle Campbell
1984   *Phoneticism in Mayan Hieroglyphic Writing*. Albany: Institute for Mesoamerican Studies.

Kelley, David H.
1962   A History of the Decipherment of Maya Script. *Anthropological Linguistics* 4(8): 1–48.

Knorosov, Yuri V.
1952   Drevniaia pis'mennost' Tsentral'noi Ameriki. *Sovietskaya Etnografiya* 3(2): 100–118.

1954   *La antigua escritura de los pueblos de America Central*. Mexico, D.F.: Biblioteca Obrera.

1958   New Data on the Maya Written Language. *Proceedings of the 32nd International Congress of Americanists*, 1956, pp. 467–475. Copenhagen.

Kubler, George
1962   *The Art and Architecture of Ancient America*. New York: Penguin.

1969   Studies in Classic Maya Iconography. *Memoirs of the Connecticut Academy of Arts and Sciences*, Vol. XVIII.

Longyear, John
1952   *Copán Ceramics*. Carnegie Institution of Washington Publication 597. Washington, D.C.: Carnegie Institution.

Martin, Simon, and Nikolai Grube
1995   Maya Superstates. *Archaeology* 48(6): 42–46.

n.d.   Evidence for Macro-Political Organization Among Classic Maya Lowland States. Unpublished manuscript.

Mathews, Peter
1991–   *Notebooks for the Maya Hieroglyphic Weekend*. Edited and transcribed
1992   by Phil Wanyerka. Cleveland State University.

Miller, Mary Ellen
1989   The History of the Study of Maya Vase Painting. *The Maya Vase Book 1*: 128–145. New York: Kerr Associates.

Montgomery, John
1995   *Sculptors of the Realm: Classic Maya Artists' Signatures and Sculptural Style During the Reign of Piedras Negras Ruler 7*. M.A. thesis. Albuquerque: University of New Mexico.

Proskouriakoff, Tatiana
1960   Historical Implications of a Pattern of Dates at Piedras Negras, Guatemala. *American Antiquity*, 25(4): 454–475.

1961a   Portraits of Women in Maya Art. In *Essays in Pre-Columbian Art and Archaeology*, S.K. Lothrop et al., eds. 81–90. Cambridge: Harvard University Press.

1961b   The Lords of the Maya Realm. *Expedition* 4(1): 14–21.

1963   Historical Data in the Inscriptions of Yaxchilán, Part I. *Estudios de Cultura Maya*, 3: 149–167.

1964   Historical Data in the Inscriptions of Yaxchilán, Part II. *Estudios de Cultura Maya*, 4: 177–202.

Robicsek, Francis, and Donald M. Hales
1981   *The Maya Book of the Dead: The Ceramic Codex*. Norman: University of Oklahoma Press.

Ruz Lhuillier, Alberto
1954   Exploraciones Arqueologicas en Palenque, 1952. *Anales del Instituto Nacional de Antropologia e Historia*, ep. 6, 6(1): 79–110. Mexico.

Schele, Linda
1982   *Maya Glyphs: The Verbs*. Austin: University of Texas Press.

1987–   *Notebooks for the 11th, 12th, 13th, 14th, 15th, and 16th Maya Hieroglyphic*
1992   *Workshops at Texas*. Austin: University of Texas.

Schele, Linda, and Nikolai Grube
1994–   *Notebooks for the 18th and 19th Maya Hieroglyphic Workshops at Texas*.
1995   Austin: University of Texas.

1997   *Notebook for the 21st Maya Hieroglyphic Workshop at Texas*. Austin: University of Texas.

Schele, Linda, and Matthew Looper
1996   *Notebooks for the 20th Maya Hieroglyphic Workshop at Texas*. Austin: University of Texas.

Schele, Linda, and Peter Mathews
1974   Lords of Palenque: The Glyphic Evidence. *Primera Mesa Redonda de Palenque, Part 1*, pp. 63–71. M. Greene-Robertson, ed. Pebble Beach: Robert Louis Stevenson School.

1993   *Notebook for the 17th Maya Hieroglyphic Workshop at Texas*. Austin: University of Texas.

Schele, Linda, and Mary Ellen Miller
1986   *The Blood of Kings: Dynasty and Ritual in Maya Art.* Ft. Worth: Kimbell Art Museum.

Schellhas, Paul
1904   Representation of Deities of the Maya Manuscripts. *Papers of the Peabody Museum* 4(1). Cambridge: Harvard University.

Seler, Eduard
1904   The Vase of Chama. *U.S. Bureau of American Ethnology Bulletin 28:* 651–664.

Stephens, John Lloyd
1841   *Incidents of Travel in Central America, Chiapas, and Yucatan.* New York: Harper and Brothers. (Dover edition 1969.)

Stuart, David
1987   Ten Phonetic Syllables. In *Research Reports on Ancient Maya Writing* 14. Washington, D.C.

1988   Blood Symbolism in Maya Iconography. In *Maya Iconography.* Princeton: Princeton University Press.

1989a   *The Maya Artist: An Epigraphic and Iconographic Study.* Senior thesis, Princeton University.

1989b   Hieroglyphs on Maya Vessels. In *The Maya Vase Book* 1: 149–160. New York: Kerr Associates.

1995   *A Study of Maya Inscriptions.* Ph.D. Dissertation, Vanderbilt University.

Stuart, David, and Stephen D. Houston
1994   *Classic Maya Place Names.* Studies in Pre-Columbian Art and Archaeology No. 33. Washington: Dumbarton Oaks.

Stuart, David, Stephen D. Houston, and John Robertson
1999   *Notebook for the 23rd Maya Hieroglyphic Workshop at Texas.* Austin: University of Texas.

Stuart, George
1988   A Guide to the Style and Content of the Series *Research Reports on Ancient Maya Writing*, in *Research Reports* No. 15, Supplement, pp. 7–12. Washington, D.C.: Center For Maya Research.

1989   The Beginning of Maya Hieroglyphic Study: Contributions of Constantine S. Rafinesque and James H. McCulloh, Jr. *Research Reports* 29. Washington, D.C.: Center for Maya Research.

Thomas, Cyrus
1903   Central American Hieroglyphic Writing. *Annual Report of the Smithsonian Institution for 19033*: 705–721.

Thompson, J. Eric S.
1950   *Maya Hieroglyphic Writing: An Introduction*. Carnegie Institution of Washington. New edition: Norman: University of Oklahoma Press.

1962   *A Catalog of Maya Hieroglyphs*. Norman: University of Oklahoma Press.

Tozzer, Alfred M., ed.
1941   *Landa's Relación de las Cosas de Yucatán*. Papers of the Peabody Museum, Vol. XVIII. Cambridge: Harvard University.

von Hagen, Victor W.
1947   *Maya Explorer: John Lloyd Stephens and the Lost Cities of Central America and Yucatan*. Norman: University of Oklahoma Press. (Chronicle Books, San Francisco edition 1990.)

1973   *Search for the Maya: The Story of Stephens and Catherwood*. Westmead: Saxon House, D.C. Heath Ltd.

Wald, Robert F.
1994   *Transitive Verb Inflection in Classic Maya Hieroglyphic Texts: Its Implications for Decipherment and Historical Linguistics*. M.A. thesis. Austin: University of Texas.

Wanyerka, Phil, ed.
1999   *Proceedings of the Maya Hieroglyphic Workshop: Classic Mayan Language and Classic Maya Gods*. Parma, Ohio.

Whorf, Benjamin L.
1933   *The Phonetic Value of Certain Characters in Maya Writing*, Papers of
        the Peabody Museum of Archaeology and Ethnology, Vol. XIII,
        No. 2. Cambridge: Harvard University.

Zender, Marc
1998   *Ki Wech Kaminak'*: Death-Eye Iconography and Epigraphy in the Light
        of T15, T108, and T135 as Syllabic **cha**. Unpublished manuscript.

1999a   *Diacritical Marks and Underspelling in the Classic Maya Script: Impli-
        cations for Decipherment*. Masters thesis, Department of Archae-
        ology, University of Calgary, Alberta, Canada.

1999b   The Toponyms of El Cayo, Piedras Negras and La Mar. Austin:
        University Kinko's Supplemental File #27.

List of Illustrations

List of Plates

Index